FEARLESS FLYING

*The Complete Program
for Relaxed Air Travel*

FEARLESS FLYING

The Complete Program for Relaxed Air Travel

Albert G. Forgione, Ph.D.
and Frederic M. Bauer

BOSTON
HOUGHTON MIFFLIN COMPANY
1980

Library of Congress Cataloging in Publication Data
Forgione, Albert G
Fearless flying.
Bibliography: p.
1. Fear of flying.   I. Bauer, Frederic M., joint
author.   II. Title.
RC1090.F67   616.85′225   80-11155
ISBN 0-395-29123-2

Printed in the United States of America

S 10 9 8 7 6 5 4 3 2 1

Line drawings by Bette Hunt.

To Mae Forgione and Jane Bauer, who
keep our feet on the ground when
our heads are in the clouds.

Acknowledgments

We gratefully acknowledge the following people who have given their time so that others might learn the freedom of air travel.

Special thanks go to Carol Lutjens Borrows, whose concern for fearful fliers led her to seek my assistance in originating group programs at Logan Airport. Also, to the original Logan Airport crew from Pan Am: Flight Attendants Carol Lutjens Borrows, Jan Pope, and Carole Barlow; Captains "Mac" McIntyre and Bill Bender; First Officer Ed Olas; Flight Engineer Herb Bond, and Customer Services Coordinator Jay LaFrance.

We are greatly indebted to the personnel of Delta Airlines, who, since 1976, have so generously volunteered planes and personnel for our classes: Boston Station Manager Jerry Rousseau, Operations Supervisor Jim Dawson, Flight Attendant Jean Baglioni, In-Flight Services Supervisor Susan Cardinale, Senior Marketing Representative Ellie Cavaleri, Customer Service Representative Ed Ferrier, Cabin Service Supervisor Tony Ianachero.

We also thank the ground crews of TWA Boston for allowing students aboard planes on the ground for practice.

From United Airlines, Senior Flight Manager Ray A. Miller and Flight Attendant Sherri Barthelmess have been particularly helpful in the preparation of this book.

We are also indebted to Dr. Don Matthews and Dr. Robert Dean of the Boeing Company for their helpful contributions.

In addition, we thank Dr. Robert Heller, Dr. Simon Rosenberg, Air Traffic Controller Walter McConnell, Jim Pope, and Marrian Gleason for their help over the years; Ron Jones for his professional assistance; Bette Hunt for her care-full drawings; and LaDonna Blaich for skillfully typing a manuscript from two authors who rush pages back and forth like volleys on a tennis court.

Contents

FEARLESS FLYING

*The Complete Program
for Relaxed Air Travel*

Introduction

THIS BOOK was written to help you or someone you know deal with the nervousness, apprehension, and white-knuckled fear often associated with air travel. It is concerned with stress. Because of the interesting nature of stressors, agents that cause stress, however, this book also provides a bonus for people who already fly through the air with the greatest of ease.

A Personal Matter

What is a stressor? To understand, we must explore adaptation. Depending on our lifestyle, we are adapted to certain things. Without thinking, we get in our cars and drive to a destination. We are adapted to automotive transportation. An Australian aborigine, on the other hand, would be confused and frightened by a late-model sports car in action. He is not adapted to the experience. Therefore, he is stressed and the car is a stressor.

But stressors are not just the unfamiliar. Office noise is a long-term stressor. Although we may think we are adapted to it, this constant undercurrent exacts a price from us in stress.

When human beings are exposed to any change from a state to which they are adapted — for example, a fuel oil shortage requiring lower room temperatures — they become stressed.

Emotions also enter the picture, because stress involves a physiological burst of mobilization and an emotional response.

Emotionally and physically we're all different, so stressors affect each of us differently.

Ted, an avid boater, says he "doesn't like" to fly. This, as we'll learn later, is almost always another way of saying he's afraid to fly. Doris loves to fly but has a deep-seated fear of drowning. Naturally, Doris says she "doesn't like" to go sailing.

Stressors are a personal matter. Some people respond to stress as a challenge. When stressors enter their lives they feel little or no discomfort. They may even seek out stressful situations. (How many of us would *seek* the challenge of parachuting from 15,000 feet, scaling a 2000-foot vertical stone cliff, or diving to depths of 150 feet?) But in similar situations, the majority of us are subject to reactions that range from mild anxiety to panic. At the other end of the scale are people who live in a constant state of anxiety, attempting to avoid stressors of all types. This avoidance behavior, in its extreme form, is called agoraphobia, a condition that causes some individuals to remain locked in their houses for years.

Help for Everyone

The same technology that created modern jet travel and a world of other marvels to serve mankind also produced a spectrum of long-term or chronic stressors. From the abrasive noise of jackhammers, typewriters and chain saws to the queasy sight of a digital watch as it flashes out the minutes we're late for an important meeting, stressors assault all of our senses. A forest ranger, used to the clean fresh air at several thousand feet, will immediately be stressed by the polluted air of the cities. And so it goes.

For too many people, dealing with this constant undercurrent of stress simply means another drink of alcohol. Others seek oblivion in drugs.

Yet we are sitting under the greatest natural stress survival kit ever invented: the human brain. Properly supported, the brain can cope with the many stressors that confront us in daily living.

Several years ago, we began classes for fearful fliers at Logan

International Airport in Boston. The course lasted ten weeks. Around the third week of relaxation practice, we noticed something interesting. As people learned to understand their fear of flying, they began spontaneously to control their responses to other stressors in their daily lives — elevators, public transportation, enclosed spaces and even supermarkets.

Since the dynamics of all stress are pretty much the same, it's possible that dealing with one stressor — flying — can lead to a certain mastery over others. Once having learned the theory of electronics, for example, one can understand and often repair both high fidelity systems and television sets. The human mind learns patterns or soon generates patterns from isolated, learned events.

So it is our hope that this book will benefit more than just fearful fliers. Learning the techniques presented here can be helpful to anyone who experiences stress in daily living.

Where the Material Comes From

This is not one of those self-help books based solely on a new instant-gratification theory. What you'll find here is practical. It is drawn from my experience in helping fearful fliers over the years; from my work at Tufts University teaching dentists how to treat patients suffering from fear and other stress-produced dental problems; and from treating phobics in my private practice.

You'll learn to use techniques drawn from the disciplines of psychoanalysis, behavior therapy, psychophysiology, kinesiology, and nutrition. We have marshaled scientific data, clinical experience, and theories, both old and new, for the purpose of helping you overcome your fear of air travel.

Some of the material presented in this book is new, some is an integration from several disciplines, and some is a restatement of common knowledge. It may ruffle established medical, dental, and psychological practitioners. If so, we should remember that the advance of knowledge is historically marked with controversy. The restructuring of knowledge is, itself, a stressor.

Where We'll Go

When you think about it, flying in an aircraft is a natural stressor. In the sky, we are as alien as a bird in a submarine. For man in flight, ground rules no longer apply. The body is subjected to unfamiliar forces. We live and breathe in a pressure less than that at the surface of the earth, hurtling through thin air with no sensation of speed.

To top it all, we're generally far from home — both horizontally *and* vertically!

We'll sit together with this book and quietly examine your apprehension, anxiety, or fear. We'll do it in the comfort of your ground-level world (for those who choose not to read this on a plane). You'll learn that fear isn't limited to the mind, as most people think. You'll discover that we fear with our whole body, and consequently you'll learn how to treat fear holistically — with a stress-resistant diet, more comfortable breathing, relaxation exercises, reposturing of a few body parts, if need be, and positive mental pictures.

If you have opened this book, you probably belong to one of the following groups:

You've Never Flown

You're in the majority, but low air fares are bringing the eventuality of flight closer. You may see air travel as a complex mystery — an unknown adventure filled with strange whining sounds, roaring noises, and vapor trails across the sky. What you see may challenge your sense of order: a huge, heavy, metal object containing scores of people lifting off the earth.

Unless you purposely search out information, you usually hear the most vocal complainers, who misinform by exaggeration. Generally, these are people who have been stressed during flight.

This book provides information and coping techniques that will prepare you for your first flight.

You've Flown, Uncomfortably

You belong to another large group of people who travel by air with varying degrees of anxiety. Your discomfort may range from a nonspecific catch in the stomach as the flight attendant closes the door to a cold sweat and clenched fists. These natural reactions to stress are like loaded springs.

Even though you probably have a certain control over anxiety feelings, chances are you're hair-triggered and primed. You may be closer to losing control than you think. When other stressors accumulate, your tension may mushroom into a major panic. You are particularly susceptible if you are living through a period of "passage" in your life. From my experience, fear of flying erupts most commonly between the ages of twenty-five and thirty-five, when one is passing from young to middle adulthood and has probably been flying with apparent ease.

A woman I know controlled her anxiety through the stress of a long air trip but went into a panic on a much shorter flight — the flight to her father's funeral. She developed a phobia and did not fly for five and a half years. The added stress of bereavement had pushed her over the brink.

You're a Flight Phobic

You're not alone. More than 25 million Americans are like you: just plain afraid of flying.* Some have never flown and say they never will. Others have been flying for years and suddenly become seized with an uncontrollable fear. You are among a group of individuals whose careers are stymied by the inability to travel by air; grandfathers who have never seen their distant grandchildren; wives whose husbands have left them behind out of frustration. One of our fear-of-flying students was a travel agent who couldn't stand the sight of planes. He had

* Although many sources have indicated that because of fear 14 to 18 percent of the population avoids flying, a more recent study, by the Boeing Company (Dean and Whitaker, 1980), reveals that the scope of the problem is even greater. First it must be understood that the unpleasantness of flying in a state of anxiety does not seem to reduce the number of flights taken by those within

never flown and even avoided taking his clients to the airport. Yet he pined for the exotic places on the travel folders that surrounded him every day. Today, he flies through the air with ease.

Being afraid of flying can lead to a life controlled by avoidance — avoidance of flying, even avoidance of the *thought* of flying, which causes anxiety and apprehension.

Additionally, air-travel fear may become the basis for a complex network of avoidance. To justify your behavior, you may dwell on faults and accidents, in order to rationalize your avoidance of airplanes. The result is a life limited in scope and experience.

You're a Happy Flier

You enjoy the anticipation of flying. In a plane, you relax or sleep. It's no surprise to you that you are safer than you would

---

the air-travel population, but it may render the anxious flier susceptible to phobia, should acute stress occur during a flight. Socioeconomically, the 14-to-18-percent figure applies to those with incomes between $10,000 and $35,000 per year. Of those with incomes of less than $5,000, 30 percent report fear; and of those earning more than $35,000 per year only 9 percent report fear.

The airlines will soon have to confront the fact that approximately 21.3 million trips per year are lost because of fear of air travel. Fear of flying is associated with other fears, such as the fear of travel by ship, the fear of heights, the fear of deep water, the fear of crowds, and the fear of confined spaces.

In a country where 70 percent of the adult population has flown one or more times (data do not indicate what proportion of this percentage will ever fly again), 16 percent have never flown and are not likely to fly.

With reference to the stress associated with the transition from young to middle adulthood, it is interesting that the average age at which the onset of flying phobia occurs is 27 years. In addition, 46 percent of flying phobics have clinically important phobias (33 percent of that number have agoraphobia and 25 percent have claustrophobia). Generally, 69 percent of the population reports no anxiety or fear, 18 percent is afraid, and 13 percent is anxious. Of the 70 percent of the population that flies, 76 percent report no fear or anxiety, 14 percent are anxious, and 10 percent are afraid. Of those who have never flown, 54 percent report no fear, 10 percent are anxious, and 36 percent are afraid. The figures are quite impressive, then: twenty-four percent, or one out of four fliers, are either anxious or afraid, and 47 percent of those who have never flown are either anxious or afraid. In summary, approximately 30 percent of the general population has either anxiety or fear of air travel (in other words, approximately 44.6 million people). Of all people who fly, 25 percent are either anxious or afraid.

be at home in your bathtub. (It is a statistical fact that more people are injured in their bathtubs than in jet planes.) You may have difficulty understanding why some of your friends are afraid of flying, why anyone fears such an enjoyable experience.

This book has been written to liberate you regardless of the group to which you belong.

Reading it and practicing Active Stress Coping will help the first-time flier prepare himself for every new flying experience, from ticket-buying to baggage claim.

Anxious fliers, with a bit more practice, will learn how to measure their fear. They'll discover relaxation techniques that ensure more comfortable flights and will learn to apply psychological first aid if it's needed.

For flight phobics this book offers a proven ten-week program that has given jet-age mobility to hundreds of students both in private clinical practice and in our classes at Logan International Airport. The techniques described are now being used more and more all over the country. For this group, reward will follow practice and a more extended program than that required of first-time or anxious flyers.

Happy fliers will find here an original gift for less fortunate friends, which will eventually enable them to share the joy of flight.

In addition, this book may assist the professional therapist in treating the flight phobic or starting a group. The most rewarding experience in my career has been sharing the feelings of phobics, as they shed their fears and master their emotions during a "graduation flight." Flight phobics are generally bright, pleasant people, eager to expand life's experience.

To the countless flight personnel who serve the public day to day, this book offers systematic techniques for assisting those passengers who need help in overcoming flight anxiety.

Like the Lilliputian ropes that held Gulliver to the ground, each one an easily broken thread, a tiny network of stressors may be woven into a strong fabric that keeps us bound to earth. In the first chapter, we will begin to cut these ties, one by one.

With a little effort, you can learn to fly through the air with the greatest of ease.

ALBERT G. FORGIONE

1

Let's Sit Down, Relax, and Look at Your Fear

I HOPE YOU HAVE a comfortable place to sit and read this book, because much of what we are going to do together depends on a relaxed attitude. More than once, we're going to use your favorite chair during a quiet time of day.

Naturally, what each reader expects to accomplish will be different, but in general you can learn to relax, desensitize your fears, and become a fearless flier. Hundreds of fearful fliers have used the method I'm going to describe. Ten weeks from their first moment in our class, they completed a "graduation flight" and were welcomed into the ranks of relaxed fliers. Within approximately the same amount of time (twenty hours) most private clients learn techniques that allow them to fly with ease. The principles and techniques we use in class and in private therapy are explained in this book. Each step unfolds in the sequence you would experience if you joined one of our groups or became an individual client. Using this program over a ten-week period, you can actually treat yourself for air-travel fear.

Many graduates return to speak at the opening session of each new class. The initiates, most of whom feel alone in their flight apprehension, enjoy hearing these "veteran" air travelers relate their experiences.

"I used to get physically sick — just from thinking about the flight I'd have to make," says a bearded, bright-eyed young engineer. "Now, I can relax on takeoffs and landings, even sleep during the flight."

A former flight-phobic homemaker in her early forties tells about the trip *after* her graduation. "My husband and I flew to Bermuda — to the hotel where we spent our honeymoon twenty years ago. It was beautiful."

"I didn't care what anybody thought," says a college student. "I'd pull a sweater completely over my head when the plane took off. Now, flying doesn't bother me any more."

Each of these people had a reason for wanting to fly. Each took the first and most important step: recognizing and affirming that he or she had a fear of flying. Each made a decision to do something about it. They made a commitment to practice; they set a goal and achieved it.

Their first lesson involved taking a calm, relaxed look at fear. Let's examine what fear is and how we learn and unlearn it.

Happy Birthday from Mother Nature

The day we are born, we are given a gift called fear. We need never be ashamed of fear. It is as natural as breathing, an emotion we share with all creatures, from lions to llamas to rabbits. When appropriately focused, fear can help us avoid injury or save our lives.

Let's take a trip backward in time. This will allow us to apply the knowledge of modern science to one of our early predecessors, Oog, the Neanderthal man. He'll show us how fear prepares your body for survival.

We discover Oog walking through the forest one bright sunny morning. Oog is calm. His muscles are relaxed. His brain is receiving friendly, familiar signals. His heart is beating normally, perhaps seventy-five to eighty times a minute.

What he doesn't know is that a cave lion, intent on making Oog his breakfast, is lurking just a few bushes away. A twig snaps. In a flash — a few thousandths of a second — electric signals streak from the ear to a special alarm system in Oog's brain. Fear prepares our Neanderthal for a threat. His brain sends impulses to glands that release chemicals. Among them is epinephrine (adrenalin), whose mission is to tone or prepare the entire body for flight or a fight. These chemicals carry messages to the tissues of various organs:

"Okay, let's get that blood out of the stomach and into the larger muscles of the arms and legs where it can do some good."

"Come on, heart — start pumping. Better increase your rate to around 120 beats a minute."

"Let's have more sugar out of the liver and into the muscles; this is going to take a lot of energy."

The huge lion breaks out into the open. Now the brain, that incredibly complex three-pound survival kit, begins to function with all twenty-five watts of its electrical power.

Oog starts to run for his life. Thorns scratch and tear the flesh of his legs and face, but the brain has arranged to ignore feelings of pain during the present crisis. Neither does Oog bleed profusely, since fear has temporarily constricted the blood vessels in his face and limbs. Only later does he notice his wounds. Oog's senses are almost completely shut down to incoming stimulation. His whole being adopts a single purpose: run like hell.

His bowels and bladder empty, relieving the body of an excess burden and making it more able to move swiftly. In fact, his whole digestive tract has shut down (leaving him with what we, centuries later, call "butterflies" in the stomach). Since Oog has little or no saliva left, his mouth is dry; but he sweats profusely. The palms of his hands, his feet, and his armpits are all moist, lubricated for grasping a club and moving easily.

Reaching the mouth of his cave, our ancestor leaps inside, pulling a huge boulder across the opening. Fear and a body prepared by hormones from the brain have endowed him with superhuman strength.

Long after Oog's bones become fossils in an obscure rock, mankind marvels at acts made possible by the same chemicals: mothers lifting overturned cars from their children and exhausted shipwreck survivors hauling near-drowned companions into lifeboats.

Whether Oog had decided to stand and fight, or flee, as he did, the body functions would have been the same. Our Neanderthal man is long gone and most of the threats to his survival are extinct. The important thing to remember is that you and I share his fight-or-flight response to fear. It is a basic part of our being.

The Brain: Selecting the Best of Both Worlds

You can be sure that every time Oog thought of the sound of a snapping twig, he "saw" an instant replay of the cave lion in his mind's eye. Now this is important: whether his life was actually threatened or not, the brain sent out an alarm and his whole body geared for fight or flight.

All messages to the brain come from two worlds: the interoceptive world, made up of dull, vague signals from within; and the exteroceptive world, consisting of sharp images from outside the body, which are filtered through very refined sense receptors. We can be specific about things that come from the outside, because our bodies have been designed to pick up refined differences. But nature did not provide us with equal perception of the signals coming from inside the body.

This explains why anxiety can take the form of vague feelings. Because of its amorphous and ambiguous nature, anxiety can even stem from innocent events, foods, or mild stressors. It's difficult for us to define these sources, because the feelings resulting from them are vague and general.

Anxiety makes a certain demand on our consciousness. Its effect is like that of an alarm going off in the brain. A vague interoceptive alarm is probably at the root of your air-travel anxiety. Soon, you will learn how to discover and silence it.

If the conscious mind ever tried to become aware of all the interoceptive and exteroceptive impulses it receives at one time, it would quickly become overloaded. Every tiny movement, down to the brushing of a hair on an arm, is reported. Since our consciousnesses can pay full attention to only one thing at a time, while scanning up to six others, most reports are ignored. We never "think" about them. However, when the scanning and planning center associates an incoming signal with danger or creates an alarm of its own, that signal gets priority.

The catch is that our consciousness gives equal priority to nonspecific interoceptive alarms and sharply defined exteroceptive ones. An alarm is an alarm, so fight or flee. Many times an interoceptive alarm takes priority even if no exteroceptive threat exists.

Below the level of consciousness, a hubbub of traffic is going on. A constant flow of impulses keeps the tone of each muscle in the body. Other impulses go out by the thousands to counteract the effects of gravity, keep body balance, and maintain internal body pressures; tiny blood vessels constrict and relax according to preset sequences, to maintain life.

If one of these systems misfunctions, a priority alarm signals our consciousness: something is wrong. A stress has occurred.

Fear is a two-way street — both interoceptive and exteroceptive. If you think of a dentist's drill, associating its sound with the picture of a dental office, your body may react as if you were actually there, down to tense muscles and sweating. Many times, the fight-or-flight reaction gives us impulses to act in a way that's inappropriate for a given situation.

Thus the memory function of the brain can simulate a situation and actually create the sensory signals associated with it, triggering the physical and emotional reaction we call fear. The reverse may also be true. Without conscious awareness, feelings of fear in the body may evoke images of a threatening situation or make a relatively harmless situation *appear* dangerous.

Over and over again, we will refer to the effects of fear on the *whole* body. Fear does not reside in the brain alone. It is a series of interactions between the autonomic nervous system (which controls automatic body functions like breathing and heartbeat), the somatic-motor system (the nerves which connect to muscles that move), and the central nervous system (brain and spinal cord).

Fear is complex. It does not respond to the direct approach. Telling yourself that your fear of planes is groundless, for example, is a self-criticism — a compounding stressor. It actually makes you more defensive and more anxious. Similarly, gritting your teeth and trying to *think* your way through air travel won't work. In fact, you'll learn why gritting your teeth is probably the worst thing you can do. You'll also learn that thought and logic dissolve in the face of fear. You must be able to deal

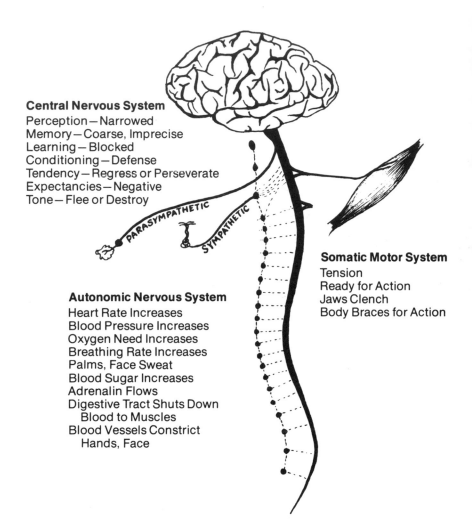

Central Nervous System
Perception – Narrowed
Memory – Coarse, Imprecise
Learning – Blocked
Conditioning – Defense
Tendency – Regress or Perseverate
Expectancies – Negative
Tone – Flee or Destroy

Somatic Motor System
Tension
Ready for Action
Jaws Clench
Body Braces for Action

Autonomic Nervous System
Heart Rate Increases
Blood Pressure Increases
Oxygen Need Increases
Breathing Rate Increases
Palms, Face Sweat
Blood Sugar Increases
Adrenalin Flows
Digestive Tract Shuts Down
   Blood to Muscles
Blood Vessels Constrict
   Hands, Face

How Fear Affects the Whole Body

with your breathing, your muscles, and your mental pictures. In order to control fear so that you can fly relaxed, you'll learn a few simple techniques that will help you coordinate the autonomic, somatic, and central nervous systems.

Do you enjoy bicycle riding, ice skating, skiing, or swimming? Think back to the first time you were on a bike, skiis, or skates. You wobbled, you were unsure. Learning took practice, but you improved. At first it was hard to notice the improvement. Then, as you felt more sure of yourself, you began to enjoy what you were doing.

Learning to cope with stress and fear is a new skill. Scientists have proved that it can be done, but like riding a bicycle it takes practice.

How We Learn Fear

You probably don't remember the first time you fell, or whether it was down a flight of stairs or up a step, but the example set up by the reaction of your parents may well have served as your primer in fear. One of the ways we learn to fear is by example. When a parent shows an intense reaction to a slight injury, a child feels that something very serious has happened. In fact, it's likely that the child will be more affected by the sudden reaction of the parent than by the actual pain of the fall.

Your first day of school was a potential smorgasbord of fear experiences. To begin with, the distance between yourself and your family suddenly grew astoundingly. You found yourself in a strange environment, separated from your normal supports. If, on top of all this, your doting parents gave you the impression that you were going through a serious and threatening situation, you may have acquired a sense of fear by example. Inadvertent cautions founded more on parental anxieties than on real dangers may have led you to the lasting impression that the world away from home is a precarious one indeed: "*Don't* cross the street. Stay *right with* the teacher. *Don't* talk to strangers. Keep *away* from animals."

You can also learn fear by what psychologists call modeling. If a parent displays anxiety before a flight, talking about the possibility of a crash, a child will learn that this behavior is appropriate for air travel. As a child, you were alert to the most subtle signals. Your parents' mood of travel anticipation had a lasting impact on you. When one parent started acting jittery, displayed irregular behavior, suddenly rushed packing, and had an argument with the other parent, your security was threatened. The emotional climate changed and you didn't know why. The established pattern will persist after you have grown up, even if the learning process has been veiled by the passage of time.

Parents aren't always to blame. You can also learn fear by what psychologists call conditioning. Let's consider Roy, a sales manager in his early thirties.

The day before Roy's flight from New York to San Francisco, his work is more frantic than usual. Last-minute pressures are at a fever pitch. Fighting traffic and stimulating himself with stressful thoughts about the possibility of losing a big order, Roy takes his business worries home with him. All night he tosses and turns, churning conversations over and over in his brain and fretting about how lousy he's going to feel in the morning if he doesn't get some sleep.

Roy has begun a classic chain of seemingly harmless acts that will lead to a serious anxiety attack. If asked about fear, Roy is one of the millions who would describe it in terms of the brain alone, ignoring the importance of his muscles, circulative system, and breathing apparatus. Without realizing it, Roy has weakened his psychological defenses with fatigue. It will become increasingly difficult for him to keep his feelings in check.

Now he inadvertently lowers the sugar level in his blood by skipping breakfast. He has some black coffee, with two teaspoons of sugar, and a cigarette. Nicotine, caffeine, and sucrose are drugs that stimulate the brain to release adrenalin, one of the chemicals involved in the fight-or-flight response. Adverse body chemistry is now at work. Going directly into his blood, the refined sugar triggers a heavy output of insulin, which removes the sugar from Roy's system so quickly that the residue of insulin lowers his existing blood sugar to a dangerous level. Roy thinks he's picked up and ready to go, but his body is already on overdrive, and there's a dangerous curve ahead.

Not only is Roy in a tense state but his thought processes are not going to function well. With each drop of adrenalin, the worries he brought home from the office intensify, until they seem to engulf him. He does not know it, but the sugar has actually weakened his muscles. To compensate, his body strains more, and the subtle feeling of being overwhelmed is reinforced.

Neither Roy's mind nor his body are ready for the stress that always occurs on takeoff. The acceleration of the plane, coupled with the cabin pressurization, creates physical changes. Normally, these effects are minimal on a healthy body. Today, however, Roy's anxiety-tuned system is not in the best condition to cope with them.

Once in the air, it's time for more coffee with sugar and a sweet roll. Roy's further intake of refined white sugar immediately weakens every muscle, but he doesn't know it. By the time this additional sucrose delivers a burst of energy, it will be useless to him in his weakened condition. Energy plus muscle weakness equals a greater feeling of anxiety. This chain reaction leads to a need for oxygen and also to increased stress on the already taxed chest muscles used in breathing. Had he eaten a piece of fruit or taken honey, the story would have been different. In the human body, refined white sugar, anxiety, and hypoglycemia (low blood sugar) are old friends.

Up to this point, Roy's actions have been more or less typical of any busy executive who flies. Unwittingly, he's set himself up to become a conditioned fearful flier.

Passing from one weather front to another, Roy's plane goes through some light turbulence. Trays rattle in the galley, and the seat-belt sign goes on. Sights and sounds become priority danger signals to his brain. He tightens the large muscles in his arms and legs. His chest muscles lock, making it more difficult to breathe, since these tense muscles demand more oxygen for their added work. Unconsciously Roy clamps his teeth together, further weakening his muscles while confirming and sending more danger signals back to his brain. He feels weak, panicked, and powerless.

His heart begins to race. Butterflies in his stomach. Hands sweat. Now he's trying to breathe against the tightened muscles of his upper body, which have become a taut strap across his chest. He needs even more oxygen. Breathing becomes shallow and rapid, and he exhales large quantities of carbon dioxide. A condition called alkalosis takes over Roy's blood. It heightens the sensations of tingling and detachment and makes him feel that he's about to die. This is hyperventilation.

Something else is happening. Roy's subconscious is relating this feeling of being overwhelmed to similar moments in his life. Like the night before a round of tough midterm exams in school, the first time his parents had a serious quarrel within earshot, or the final seconds before impact in an automobile accident. Electrical impulses are zapping around his head like flies — and none of them are good.

It's important to remember that everything happening to our unfortunate sales manager is reversible. He could have stopped this panic reaction before it started. Roy, and anyone else in a similar air-travel situation, is far from being physically overwhelmed. If he knew what you're soon going to know, he would be flying comfortably.

Meanwhile, Roy is out of control, and he's added another burden to his struggle. No grown man wants another person — not to mention a plane load of assorted strangers — to know he's in a state of anxiety or panic. At this point, he feels that every eye on the plane is watching him. He wrestles against his taut muscles, his breathless gasping for more oxygen, and his racing mind.

"Would you like something to drink?" asks the flight attendant charmingly.

His dulled senses had blocked out the sight and sound of the beverage tray rattling down the aisle. Seat-belt signs have long since been extinguished, and the plane is gliding smoothly over Illinois as Roy makes his next mistake.

"Y-yes, thank you. Vodka and tonic," he replies.

At 30,000 feet pressurized to the 5000-foot level, Roy is drinking the equivalent of one and a half vodka and tonics at ground level. That's the effect of the reduced oxygen pressure.

Alcohol is unique. It is absorbed directly from the mucous membranes of the mouth and stomach into the blood stream. It races through body tissues and enters the brain rapidly.

In Roy's case, the carbonation in the tonic increases the speed of alcohol flow from his stomach. Not only that, but cabin pressurization makes the carbonated drink more bubbly, releasing a heavy cloud of pure carbon dioxide surrounding poor Roy's already oxygen-starved head.

Roy took the drink under the mistaken impression that it would help him calm down. Instead, the altitude-potent drink slammed into the front part of his brain, deadening the very part he needed — the center of self-control, judgment, and inhibition.

Roy is overwhelmed by waves of weakness, his hands are trembling, and the magazine he's trying to read is beginning to blur; let's leave him and his conditioned fear, for the time being.

Appropriate and Inappropriate Fear

Here's the catch: While fear is a gift that can save your life, it can also make life miserable. The fear of about fifty percent of all anxious fliers is caused by specific "traumatic" incidents like the one I've just described. At any given moment, thousands of children and adults are learning, by example, modeling, or conditioning, to fear air travel. Unlike the Neanderthal man's fear, the fear they're learning is an overreaction that serves no useful purpose. Instead, it leads to further avoidance behavior and missed opportunities, not to mention physical and psychological discomfort.

We learn to associate heat with burning, and electric light sockets with shock. As our finger approaches a heated stove, we react to the real danger of being burned. Fear makes us retract the finger, sometimes quickly. We respond in the same way to an electrical fixture, because we fear a shock. These reactions are positive and protective. They're examples of *appropriate* fear.

But fear, being an emotion, is blind. Consciousness can be

tricked into gearing the system for a nonexistent threat. The body often generates cues associated with danger in situations where ease, calm, and even enjoyment should prevail. There's a spectrum of such fears, ranging from the fear of small animals and elevators to the fear of large social gatherings and the number 13. We used to tack an impressive Greek name to each new phobia as it appeared. Finally, the list became so long that psychologists now tend to refer to them all as "phobic reactions."

These fears, and the people who experience them, are frequently the subject of cruel and thoughtless abuse. In treating hundreds of phobics, I have first had to overcome the harmful effects of ill-advised humor and ridicule.

My generation grew up reading the comic strip "Casper Milquetoast." Casper was a gangling, henpecked character who feared his own existence. Fear seems funny. We want to laugh to cover our own fear and embarrassment. But every day, this seemingly innocent humor deepens the misery of phobics by compounding their fear. Time after time, people must be taught not to heighten their phobic reactions with fear of social rejection or ridicule.

There is a popular misconception that the presence of a single fear indicates a weakness in the entire personality. This is not true. Far from being weak, phobics are among the most intelligent and imaginative people you will ever meet. As one of our students, a 200-pounder, put it to a friend who was teasing him, "Just because I'm afraid of flying doesn't mean I can't knock you flat on your ass."

Step One: Don't Criticize Yourself

The first thing you can do — right now — to begin to overcome your fear of flying is resolve *not to criticize yourself*. Remember, the people who laugh at your fear are probably only covering up their own. More important, success in mastering your fear of flying depends first of all on learning not to worry about what other people think. In therapy, I tell my patients that one of their major tasks in life is to find out who their friends are and who their enemies are. Friends are people who are sensitive to you, respect you, and try to meet your needs. Enemies are insensitive and often ridicule you. Enemies can't be distinguished from friends by dress or appearance. Only by risk-taking behavior can you find out which are which. When you criticize yourself, you are acting more like an enemy than a friend. In a very real sense, you create an enemy within yourself. You need all the friends you can get. *So stop criticizing yourself.*

Physiological arousal (excitement) in an airplane is a natural human reaction. Air travel is clearly a stressful situation, when analyzed in terms of human experience. There you are, disoriented from the moment you walk down that narrow, slanting alleyway. You're strapped into a seat and sealed in a metal container that proceeds to emit high-pitched sounds and behave in an unbelievable manner. It weighs tons and yet rises into the air (contrary to your conditioned understanding of the laws of gravity). Its speed is another contradiction to your sensory system. Though it seems almost motionless, the container hurtles you through the air at six or seven hundred miles an hour.

I've already mentioned some of the stresses on the body caused by acceleration and pressurization. Now, add to all of this the fact that you are undeniably under the control of another person, an authority figure, distant and unknown — the pilot — and are the subject of close social scrutiny by other passengers, all of them strangers.

First-time fliers experience a natural form of anxiety called novelty anxiety — the tension caused by *any* new experience, from the first visit to a dentist's office to meeting strangers at a cocktail party.

All fliers feel the separation anxiety caused by distance from their normal emotional supports of home and family. (To some, this separation may be a relief; but for others it is threatening.)

Don't feel ashamed of your fear. And don't back away from admitting it because you fear what someone might say. Stand up and be counted, fearful flier! You are in the company of at least 30 million others! By facing your feelings and deciding to do something about them, you have joined an elite group: you are issuing your personal declaration of independence from unwarranted fear. You are refusing to join fear as a conspirator against yourself. You have decided not to foster feelings of guilt for being yourself.

Steppingstones to Fear

So far, we've discussed fear in terms of its universality among animals. But there are important differences between fear in lower and higher orders of life. The most dramatic of these differences is in the way fear is acquired — the steppingstones that lead to fear. Lower animals depend on muscle feedback and body posture to tell them when to be afraid. Humans are verbal and imaginative animals. We have the ability to generate fear-producing words and ideas with no outside stimulus involved. We create fear by association.

Put rats in a white cage that has an entrance leading to a black cage. Give them repeated shocks in the white cage, none in the black. They will soon learn to associate the painful stimulus (shock) with a formerly neutral stimulus (white cage) and will run into the black cage. There they will connect feedback (no shock) with a relaxed body posture. If placed again in the white cage, they will immediately seek to reenter the black. If placed in the black cage, they will assume a relaxed body posture.

We humans learn fear by association in the same manner, *with one significant difference.* Rats cannot communicate or imagine. Rat A will not say to rat B, "Look out for the white cage, it gives shocks," any more than rat B can imagine the feeling of pain associated with the work *shock.* So rat B will have to go through the same feedback/body-posture conditioning before he learns to fear the white cage. We can, and do, pass along the fear we learn by association. Further, we form fear internally, by means of our imagination.

Fear and Symbolic Behavior:
The Great Image Race

The proof that imagination is involved in learning fear has its roots in a famous laboratory experiment of the 1920s. A kind of race was conducted to compare the mental activity of various species, including five-year-old children. But this was a most unusual race. The contestants were timed, and the one taking the longest time was considered the winner.

Psychologists placed participants in a maze and gave them a choice of three paths to follow. The left path was a blind passage to nowhere. Down the middle path was a light bulb. The right-hand path was another blind alley.

All participants were taught that they would receive food by choosing the passage with the light. The light became a signal that set the occasion for a reward, provided one behaved in a certain way. Psychologists call this a *discriminative stimulus*.

What the experimenters wanted to know was whether various species differed in their ability to bridge a gap of time between actually seeing the light and being given the opportunity to step out of a cage, toward the reward of food. So they devised a way to hold the subject in a cage while the light was turned on and then off. After waiting for a given length of time, the animal was released. That time — between the extinguishing of the light and the release of the animal — was measured, and the psychologists watched to see if the animal would go after the food *without the light*.

The greater the length of time, they reasoned, the greater the possibility that some kind of internal message (other than body posture) was retained by the animal. In this case, the "message" would be something like an image of the burning light, associated with the center passage of the maze and the reward of food — a cognitive map, in other words.

During shorter delays, the animal faced the light when it went on and simply stayed in the same position. The longer the delay, the more difficult it became to hold the same pose.

You've probably guessed who had the longest time record

and won the "race." It was not the rats, who went in the correct direction only if released within ten seconds after the light went out, and only if they remained headed in the direction of the light. It was not the dogs, who achieved a maximum performance time of three minutes. It was the five-year-old children, who invariably went to the reward passage after up to twenty minutes delay.

Obviously, the children retained something more durable. We can safely assume this was a mental image. Many psychologists would use the term *symbol*; and these "symbols" in your mind may lead to the fear of air travel.

The body experiences more movement in a car traveling on a bumpy road at thirty-five miles per hour than it does in most turbulence a plane goes through. Somehow, sudden movement of the plane is considered terrible; while in a car the same movement is considered acceptable. The movement has become "misfiled" in the brain because the emotion of fear inhibits our powers of discrimination. We are likely to *generalize* that "every strange movement of a plane means terrible things will happen."

Generalization was one phenomenon explained experimentally by Pavlov. His classic work with dogs demonstrated how symbols form, and how they may become confused to such a degree that they affect behavior. Like many scientists, Pavlov set out to study one thing and wound up making a discovery in a different field. He was originally interested in measuring the volume of saliva emitted by dogs. He constructed an elaborate apparatus for performing this experiment.

Pavlov sounded a 500-cycle tone and followed it by feeding the dogs. After several training sessions, he obtained twenty drops of saliva with a sound of that exact frequency. But how would the dogs be affected by sounds that were similar in character but slightly different in frequency? He and his colleagues tried tones higher and lower. They learned that the dogs generalized: there was a salivation, but less than that produced at the conditioned tone of 500 cycles. The more they increased or decreased the pitch of the tone, the less saliva they elicited. Using tones of differing frequency, psychologists plotted a generalization curve. In other words, the greatest response accompanied the conditioned sound, but similar sounds got similar responses of a lesser degree.

So not only are we humans able to generate symbols with our imaginations, we are also capable of drawing similarities from a range of differing symbols — similarities that result in similar responses. Generalization, this ability to collect and respond to feelings or events that are similar to an original occurrence, is the most important quality of symbolic behavior.

We humans are much more complex than animals lower on the evolutionary scale. Our steppingstones to fear are many and varied. They lead in all directions. Symbolic behavior is the device by which we learn to associate images and situations with fear.

We paint pictures of an event in our minds, based not only on what we experience, read, and hear but also on other events that are similar. One picture leads to another, from which a third may emerge. Each image creates a feeling, and the feelings produced may even lead to images of their own. Thus we map a route to panic — or to pleasure. And the routes we establish are sometimes not clear to casual observation.

For example, getting on a plane can create the image of getting away on a vacation — escaping. But under the pressure of slight apprehension, this may be associated with the image of an unfinished job at the office, which suggests a failure to accept responsibility; this in turn can lead to a feeling of guilt.

In the Introduction, I mentioned a woman who had developed a severe flight phobia during a trip to her father's funeral. Her story illustrates the linkage of feelings, images, and symbols that produces strong fear.

At twenty-eight, Sally held a deep-seated anger toward her father, which stemmed from childhood perceptions of his alcoholic behavior — arguments with her mother and periods when he left home. His actions caused her to feel alone and abandoned.

Stepping aboard the plane to fly back for his funeral (death equaling another instance of abandonment), Sally still carried unexpressed feelings of anger deep inside. The defense and coping mechanisms that had kept her feelings in check for years were weakened by grief. At takeoff, the roar and power of the engines — like anger — triggered symbolic reactions. As the plane rose, these feelings surfaced and began to conflict with feelings of guilt. The stress of gravity, the roar of the engines, and the slight disorientation characteristic of flight found a vulnerable target. Sally panicked. She took a train home from the funeral and from that point on avoided planes, which became symbols of an unpleasant destination. Just thinking of flying triggered conflicting feelings. Her only way of coping with those feelings was to avoid flying.

Symbols are subtle but strong. Those who are under the control of a strong parent or spouse often react strongly to the control they relinquish by stepping aboard a plane. The confinement of the cabin and the control of the pilot become anxiety-provoking symbols of their own life situation, triggering an anxiety attack.

The classic example of extreme panic occurs when a demanding husband forces a fearful-flier wife to go on a flight with him. Her alternative is to have him abandon her and go on his own. Panic is unavoidable. Conflict and highly symbolic behavior join together, guaranteeing that the wife will cling symbolically to the husband during the flight. Being insensitive, he may try to reject her.

Fantasy: Our Friend, Our Foe

In the sense of creating mental pictures, everybody is an artist. Frequently, we reward ourselves and relieve tensions by stringing pictures together in fantasies — pictures in some ways realistic but in other ways magnified or distorted to satisfy our particular needs. We become not only artists but film editors, pulling and blending scenes from our experiences and producing the feelings associated with them. As we mix distortions and other images into the fantasy, new emotions appropriate to the course of our mental home movie erupt. The images lead to desired feelings, and the fantasy is complete. We're creating emotions that we could never achieve in real situations. This is a singularly human capability, and we will see that the construction of fantasies can represent both the beginning and the end of a phobia.

These little dramas played out in the mind's eye can lend great strength to both feelings and senses. For example, clinical hypnotists have found that elaborate sexual fantasies are helpful in the treatment of preorgasmic females — women who are unable to achieve a climax in sexual intercourse. Under hypnosis, the fantasy produces emotion that is strong enough to be perceived consciously. Once perceived, the emotion can be heightened to the point of physical release of the orgasmic pattern.

The reverse is also true, however. In a state of fear, people are prompted by their feelings to fantasize great distortions of reality. Here, emotion produces the fantasy. In a sense it can be said that fear hypnotizes us with our own creativity.

Fantasies can be so extreme that they make us afraid of things we've never experienced. We can construct images of the most natural human events and distort them to the point that they cause immobilizing fear. If you have never flown, the anticipation of air travel may be frightening you through a distorted fantasy. Similarly, if you have flown and are afraid of flying, distorted fantasies may be seeding your anxiety.

Logic has nothing to do with the fear produced by distorted fantasy. For example, when Earl became my patient he was twenty-eight years old and weighed eighty-eight pounds. He was suffering from *anorexia nervosa,* which means he regurgitated his food. Vomiting had become a way of controlling his body weight. One of the characteristics of this malady is avoidance of sexual behavior. Earl's fantasy was that if he ever had an erection and experienced ejaculation, his internal organs would become detached and gush out through his penis.

June, an attractive young woman of twenty-eight, had been told that masturbation leads to insanity. This folklore directed her into a fantasy that an orgasm causes unstoppable tremors and ultimately leads to insanity, complete with straitjacket. On airplanes, June experienced feelings far beyond her control, so she avoided them with a passion.

Barbara was a student in one of our Logan Airport classes. She attracted the favorable attention of several men in the class, yet at 135 pounds she had a negative body image: she fantasized that she was obese. She carried a mental image of standing up in the aisle of a plane, breaking through the floor, and plunging to the earth, miles below. On her first flight she sat constantly in one position, with her feet curled under her body.

An attorney named Larry fantasized that a plane bounded up and down like a yo-yo during turbulence. He believed that in fog no one knew how far the plane was from the ground, and consequently one dip would dash it to bits on the surface of the earth. As a result, he became a self-appointed alarm system. Sitting next to Larry, all you'd see was the back of his head, because he froze, nose pressed to the window, watching the distance of the plane from the earth. The sun could be blinding, but you'd better not ask him to lower the shade. And in a fog or cloud bank his panic was unbelievable.

Fear fantasies have great power. They not only stifle conscious perception of reality but also overturn and cancel out recent learning and serve as obstacles to the logical thought process. We see lurking animals that aren't there and hear the footsteps of nonexistent burglars. We're not able to decide what to pack because seeing the suitcase brings to mind a distorted fantasy reminiscent of a fearful flight.

That's what you might call the bad news. The good news is that we can take advantage of exactly the same processes to eliminate fear: we can use fantasy to evoke an emotion, by going through certain behaviors; and we can connect images, or employ symbolic behavior, and thereby form cognitive maps.

But images, symbols, and fantasies are highly individualistic. "Isn't that cigar you smoke symbolic of a phallus?" a student once asked Freud. He answered, "For *me* — it's a cigar." The word *flight* creates a pattern of freedom, relaxing images, new experiences, and relief in some people. To a flight phobic, it may sound the knell of a death wish that leads to a fright fantasy of disaster.

Many fears about the maintenance and function of an aircraft are actually projections of a flier's concern about himself and the possibility that he will not function well during the flight. Losing control of the plane is symbolic of losing control of oneself. In this frame of mind, people are sure they are all right: it's the plane that's all wrong!

Fantasy can cause a person who has never flown to develop rapid heartbeat and shallow breathing just from thinking about the closing of passenger compartment doors. To an apprehensive flier, the power and roar of engines at takeoff can symbolize feelings of anger long repressed within him. In turn, the unacceptable anger can trigger images of disaster, symbolic of guilt and further reprisal.

We don't necessarily think of these symbols consciously; we *feel* their effects. And the patterns of feeling are as individualistic as fingerprints. Indeed, *there is no one general fear of flying,* and there is no typical, fear-prone personality.

Air-travel anxiety is a general term that subsumes many fears, a few of which are:

- Fear of heights.
- Fear of being in an enclosed place.
- Fear of being restrained in a seat for long periods of time.
- Fear of entering a toilet on a plane.
- Fear of sudden and unexpected sounds that may indicate malfunction of the plane.
- Fear that if the motor stops, the airplane will plummet to the earth like a piece of lead (a fear unfortunately reinforced by careless use of language by the press).
- Fear that the pilot will have a heart attack and the plane will crash.
- Fear that a lightning bolt will hit the plane and consume it in fire.

These fears have companions — more complex fears that heighten the anxiety reaction:

- Deep-seated guilt feelings may cause individuals to relate the fear of crashing to punishment for things they feel they should not have done.

- Persons with distorted body images of excessive weight have expressed the fear of tipping the plane over by merely getting out of their seats.
- Some passengers have a strong fear of showing fear, of acting in a socially unacceptable way before other people.
- Fear of showing fear easily escalates into fear of social rejection.
- Many fears are related to the toilets in a plane. These vary from the fear of being flushed out of the plane by pressure to the fear of showing other passengers you have to use the toilet by getting up from your seat and heading toward it.
- Some people even experience fear based on a belief that in an airplane they are closer to God and hence to God's retribution.

Personalities of fearful fliers are also many and varied. Here are a few of them.

- *Dependent* — Tries to be pleasant to avoid rejection. Showing fear means acting in an unacceptable way; this will be followed by rejection.
- *Individualistic* — Aggressive and achievement-oriented, these people must always feel in control not only of the situation but of their feelings. They can't tolerate being placed in an airplane under the control of someone else.
- *Obsessive Moderate* — Afraid of excessive stimulation that may lead to wide swings in emotion. Needs to stay on an even keel. Emotionalism means losing control.
- *Worrier* — Identifies with worrying and caring for other people. Is the plane going to be all right? Will everyone on the plane be happy? These people feel that the only way they can keep control is by worrying.
- *Traumatic* — Someone like Roy, our sales manager, who set up his trauma with improper diet and other self-defeating behavior. These are not personality types but people who have learned to fear through real or imagined traumatic experiences.

In years of work with fearful fliers, I have seen hundreds of variations on these themes. Yet a thread appears to run through them all: a passenger is inescapably and undeniably under the control of another person, the pilot.

This sensitivity to external control is characteristic of two groups of people: those who are under the control of other people in their daily lives but deny it, and those who *must* be in control of the immediate situation. As air travelers, these people see themselves as powerless and unable to control their environment. This is a symbolic situation, reminiscent of times in their lives when they were helpless and under the control of others. It is, for them, intolerable.

Actually, the latter group must always be in control. While it is difficult for them to be passengers, many make excellent amateur pilots. They are often business executives, engineers, celebrities — highly controlling people, people whose lifestyle is based on their being in control.

For the other group, closed in by everyday controls, denial is easy. But in a plane roaring down a runway, denial is impossible. Symbols combine with and are reinforced by actual physical stress to provoke fear and fight-or-flight body reactions. These reactions are compounded when they come into conflict with the expected social behavior demanded by the restricted social environment in the passenger compartment. Anxiety, fear, and panic break into the open.

What We've Learned So Far

It should be clear now that fear is nature's gift. It's important that you recognize your fear as a pattern appearing not only in your brain but in your entire body, from head to toe.

We've seen that fear is a two-way street. Outside stimuli, such as the sight of a flight attendant closing a cabin door, can trigger it. Similarly, the brain can trigger fear reactions from within by its unique capacity for symbolic behavior; it has the capability to relive stressful situations, magnify scenes of past experience, and create impossible exaggerations of events.

We've discovered that feelings similar to fear can be unexpectedly precipitated by physical conditions such as fatigue, associated muscle tensions, caffeine, nicotine, low blood sugar, and alcohol. These conditions can set the occasion for acquisition of fear, escalate minor apprehensions into full-blown fear, or further reinforce an already existing fear.

We've learned about learning fear: we can acquire it by example, modeling, and conditioning.

Stress authority Dr. Hans Selye has said that "absolute freedom from stress is death." Just plain living involves stress adaptation. Problems arise when a positive stress (flying to a vacation spot, for example) is interpreted as a negative stress (such as air-travel anxiety).

Perhaps you've tried to reason yourself out of flight fear. Possibly you've attempted to insult yourself out of it. Maybe you've denied fear or tried to cure it by forcing yourself to fly. Later in this book I will explain why these efforts don't work, and outline the method used successfully by hundreds of formerly fearful and apprehensive fliers.

You are going to develop a new skill — that of clearing your mind of fear. Clearing fear is a game the whole family can play, and everybody wins. It's a game of skill that teaches comfortable breathing, muscle relaxation, concentration on and enjoyment of pleasant thoughts, and nutritional habits designed to maximize your stress-coping ability. It's a game that offers more prizes than a state lottery: a raise in pay, a second honeymoon, the sight of a new grandchild, the snow on the Alps, and the sun over Hawaii.

But remember, you don't go out on a tennis court for the first time and win a Davis Cup; you don't hit a home run the first time at the plate, or master contract bridge by reading a book. You accomplish these feats through practice, practice, and *more* practice. Many times you have practiced your fear response. Now, little by little, you will practice other responses that will clear your mind of fear. Reading this book is an intellectual process. To collect your reward in the form of freedom to fly fearlessly, you must practice your conditioning exercises.

So let's learn this new skill by taking one step at a time and practicing together. Ready?

2

Learning to Clear Fear

THE PUSH of a button is all that's needed to clear a pocket calculator or a million-dollar computer of information that has been recorded. The human mind is far more resistant to the erasure of its cumulated experience. Each event in life interlaces and interacts with memories of other events, behavior, emotion, and self-esteem, by way of symbolic processes. The major factor that keeps a behavioral pattern "on display," or up front, is the emotion associated with it.

At this time medical science knows of no instant remedy for inappropriate fear; but thanks to the efforts of Dr. Joseph Wolpe, we now know of a direct and proven way gradually to eliminate this unwanted emotion. By approaching the underlying emotion that maintains the unwanted behavior, we can "reprogram" ourselves. It is possible to change our behavioral response bit by bit — gradually and systematically. Dr. Wolpe's procedure of systematic desensitization provides the foundation for the method by which we can learn to remove unwanted fear from air travel. The basic idea of desensitization is that fear simply cannot coexist with relaxation. The more you relax the muscles, slow the breathing and heart rate, and present the mind with a peaceful scene, the more fear dissolves. It is a gradual, nonviolent dissolution. A person being desensitized for elevator anxiety starts learning to relax even before he thinks of pressing the call button. When that is accomplished, relaxation does not allow fear to occur at the thought of pressing the button. He proceeds gradually, step by step, until the thought of the doors closing triggers no fear. Floor by floor, patients gradually learn to ride to the heights of skyscrapers.

All of this stems from Wolpe's discovery, in 1958, that we can learn new, more comfortable reactions to sights, sounds, odors, ideas — any fear-provoking stimulus. By solving real human anxiety problems he demonstrated that emotional reactions are learned behaviors that can be changed by new learning.

Consider the psychology student who worked late one night in a college laboratory. Never noticing his presence, the janitor locked one of two doors connecting the lab to the hallway. When the student discovered this some hours later he began to rattle the door. It refused to budge. He shook it more violently. Finally, he kicked down the door to get out. Had he tried the second door, he would have found it unlocked.

High levels of anxiety produce two major psychological or behavioral reactions: perseveration (repeatedly shaking the door instead of looking around for another escape) and regression (reverting to an earlier and more helpless form of behavior, such as yelling or crying, or to more primitive alternatives, such as destruction of the barrier). Relaxation allows awareness, reality testing, and other intellectual processes to function.

What kind of relaxation is best for extinguishing fear? Wolpe focused on the work of another psychologist, Edmund Jacobson. In 1938, Jacobson published *Progressive Relaxation*, in which he described the value of progressive muscle relaxation. First used to help those suffering from insomnia, this technique gradually loosens the major muscle groups from the toes to the top of the head. It also teaches us that we can reduce chronic tension by voluntarily tensing and relaxing our muscles. A generation of college students trained in progressive relaxation is proof of its value as an aid for overcoming test anxiety, the fear of snakes and spiders, and other phobic reactions.

Active Stress Coping

The technique we have developed over the years since our first large group treatment of flight phobics blends diaphragmatic breathing methods with the work of Wolpe and Jacobson, causing the subject to relax the three major body systems: autonomic, somatic-motor, and central nervous.

It is called Active Stress Coping, because it uses *action* to counteract the stresses of flying as they occur. Diaphragmatic breathing calms the autonomic nervous system (dispelling the stomach butterflies and sweaty palms). A modified Jacobsonian relaxation exercise loosens muscles, and a guided image focuses the brain on tranquil thoughts and images. (See illustration on page 14.)

The Active Stress Coping method has three distinct parts, because we found early that different individuals respond to stress with different physical reactions. Some people respond by becoming obsessed with the stressor. Their reaction is highly mental. In other people, extreme muscle reactions predominate. These range from foot tapping and teeth grinding to actual aches and pains. Still other people may show more autonomic reactions, such as rapid heart rate, sweaty palms, and rapid breathing. And in many cases there may be equal reactions of all three systems.

The next chapter contains an evaluation exercise designed to show the relative activity of your autonomic nervous system, muscles, and brain. While you should learn and practice anti-stress breathing, relaxing, and imagery, this checklist tells you which aspect of Active Stress Coping will be most helpful to you in your program of stress reduction.

After all three parts of your body have settled into what Wolpe called a "response antagonistic to anxiety," we can bring on the "anxiety evoking stimuli." This is accomplished in a gradual and systematic way (hence the name of the method). One by one, we will separate and grade each piece of the air-travel experience, starting with an event as simple as looking at a picture of an airliner in flight. You will learn to relax while contemplating the events and stimuli that comprise preparation, boarding, in-flight experiences, and landing. If you fear air travel or have apprehension about flying, these little stressors are combining to form the complex web of Lilliputian bonds that tie you down. When you say to yourself, "I'm being silly; I'm just going to fly, and that's *it!*" you are straining against all of these threads at once. With this attitude, you criticize yourself (making yourself more anxious) and force yourself to become more powerless. You are as helpless as Gulliver. Collectively, the bonds are too strong. Failure is inevitable.

Instead, our strategy is to divide and conquer. If you are imaginative enough to feel anxiety in a normal air-travel environment, you are also able to confront graded air-travel images while your body is relaxed. Piece by piece, thread by thread, the bonds will break and fall away.

Remember that your ability to erase fear is just as strong as your ability to be afraid. By using the Active Stress Coping method, you will learn how to develop this ability and use it to your advantage. You will harness the very elements that created your fear and turn them into relaxation, comfort, and calm. With lower anxiety, you will, in turn, be able to learn new behaviors associated with flying.

Basically, air-travel anxiety is caused by the threat of powerlessness, of not being in control. Whether we feel trapped by the cabin enclosure; dependent on a metal mechanical contraption that's supposed to defy the law of gravity; at the mercy of the competence of the pilot; panicked by turbulence; or ashamed to show our fear in public, this feeling of powerlessness in the presence of a machine is unique to our technological society. Active Stress Coping teaches us that there is always something we can control when we find ourselves in a powerless situation: and that something is our emotions.

Instead of fighting our emotions (a contest that we generally lose), we calmly take charge by defusing them. One of our most fearful fliers recently did this through a takeoff, looked out of the window and exclaimed, "I never thought I'd see clouds from the top down until I became an angel!"

Instead of denying their fear, being afraid to show it, or even feeling guilty because of it, students of Active Stress Coping immediately know what they can *do* about it. They reduce its effect on their bodies, directing their minds to relaxing thoughts. This becomes a reflex action, automatic and immediate. The active stress coper takes charge right away so that his or her thoughts are not overcome by physical and mental anxiety signals.

Once anxiety is reduced, you can calmly test reality. This

means you have the ability to look out the window and watch the airplane wings flexing, while realizing that they were made to act that way (it's a natural shock-absorbing action). It means you can settle back with a magazine as the cabin door is closed. You have the freedom to breathe freely in a closed place, walk the aisles, and relax your grip on the arm of the seat. Once you test these realities with all three body systems relaxed and in harmony, you find out that things really are different from your expectations.

The Foundation: Eliminate the Enemy Within

A healthy body puts the odds for success in your favor. An inner enemy, such as motion sensitivity, temporomandibular joint syndrome, an anxiety-produced physical condition, or a faulty diet, can minimize or completely offset your active stress coping. An incorrect diet can interfere with any form of psycho-therapy for anxiety or fear. Active Stress Coping succeeds easily when it is built on a foundation of good health. So first we will discuss the elimination of internal stressors, in order to make you better able to deal with external stressors.

Ears and Fears

Think back to the last movie you saw in which there was an automobile "chase" scene — the kind with the camera looking over the driver's shoulder. How did you react to the sight of landscape swishing and darting back and forth through the windshield? If you had to close your eyes or look away because the picture made you nauseous and dizzy, you may have a vestibular problem — that is, a disturbance in the organ of balance in the inner ear that causes dizziness and disorientation. The symptoms of vestibular disorders usually result from an interaction between anxiety and an actual physical problem.

About fifteen percent of the students in our fear-of-flying classes at Logan Airport suffer from some vestibular problem. One student was especially baffling until I discovered that a vestibular condition was involved.

Mae easily mastered her relaxation exercises. She could let

the looseness flow through her body and reduce her anxiety — in the classroom. But aboard a plane, Mae's relaxation exercises didn't work at all. We couldn't figure out why. Finally, she confessed to other symptoms: dizziness when elevators stopped and a feeling at unexpected times that the room was spinning.

At my suggestion, Mae saw an ear, nose, and throat specialist, who tested her for motion sensitivity. During the course of this examination, he learned that a childhood mastoid operation had led to damage of the delicate organ of balance in her inner ear. He prescribed medication, which, in combination with relaxation exercises, allowed Mae not only to fly more comfortably but also to conquer nausea and eat a meal aboard a plane for the first time in her life. The exercises worked well, once the ear problem was solved. Mae, incidentally, is my wife.

Similar problems may arise from Meniere's disease, a disorder of the inner ear that results in dizziness and nausea. Head colds or any blockage of the ear tubes may also cause temporary dizziness. For this reason, we usually advise first-time fliers not to go aloft if they have upper respiratory infections.

Many vestibular symptoms disappear when the sufferer is in control of the situation. The person who can't stand the automobile chase on the screen, or the person who is an uncomfortable passenger, is usually perfectly content looking through the windshield while driving. The reason is that the subject's perceptions are centered on a specific task and he or she is unaware of body responses. A television producer I know suffered not only from vestibular problems but also from a fear of heights. Yet he perched on a sign atop the roof of one of Philadelphia's tallest buildings, directing a scene involving a circling helicopter. It was his concentration on the work to be done that momentarily blocked both the fear and the physical symptoms.

TMJ and Fear

Some parts of your body are more vulnerable to stress than others. Because of their complexity and the need for intricate patterns of movement, the jaw muscles and the joint where the jaw joins the skull (the temporomandibular joint) are often affected by stress. The effect this area has on other muscles in the body can be demonstrated, but why this happens is still not completely understood. What we do know is that misalignment of the upper and lower teeth can lead to severe symptoms, such as sharp pain or clicking that occurs when opening the mouth; jaw locking; temporal headaches; ringing in the ears; sensitivity to high-pitched sounds; aching in the area in front of the ears; a shooting pain in the face; and dizziness and nausea. This condition is known as *Temporomandibular Joint Syndrome,* or TMJ.

Caused by chronic spasms in the muscles attached to the jaw, TMJ is an extremely painful condition that originates from causes both physical and emotional, separately or in combination. Tooth misalignment can lead to TMJ, as can stress-produced teeth-clenching and grinding. Frequently, TMJ seizures are initiated by a minor misalignment, in conjunction with emotional stress and subsequent clenching or grinding. Caught in a vicious circle, the TMJ sufferer experiences stress and then pain, thereby creating more stress and more pain. The majority of TMJ victims go unnoticed or are diagnosed as having other maladies. Because of this it has been called the "hidden disease" and the "great impostor." Usually, the muscle spasms are mild and the sufferer adapts to their minor pain as a part of everyday living. More severe attacks may be so spaced that the condition appears to cure itself spontaneously, only to return again. People learn to live with this periodic discomfort without considering it to be of much consequence. It may affect the sufferer emotionally, however.

Whether accepted or ignored, a TMJ problem is still a chronic stress. Your nervous system is constantly affected, even if your consciousness is tuned out. Both body and emotions are involved. Going into a program of desensitization of external stressors when you have an existing internal stress such as TMJ may be futile. In fact, it can make things worse, because TMJ increases in intensity when the sufferer must deal with external stressors. This means that for an air-travel-anxious person, flying, or even thoughts of flying, can bring on an attack of pain or subtle dizziness.

In its more serious forms, TMJ causes patients to be hospital-

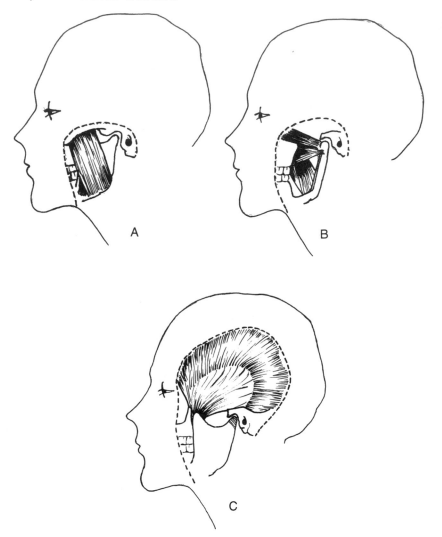

JAW MUSCLES INVOLVED IN TMJ SYNDROME

A. Masseter; B. Pterygoids (internal); C. Temporalis (attached to front prominence of jaw; rear prominence of jaw pivots near ear canal — indicated by black dot).

ized for intravenous feeding, because they can't open their mouths for food. Sometimes the severe cases lead to total debilitation and depression.

Remember, TMJ victims may experience dizziness, nausea, and disorientation without noticeable pain. This is probably because the temporomandibular joint is near enough to the ear to affect balance.

Before going any further in this program to clear your mind of air-travel anxiety, be sure you are free from vestibular disorders and TMJ syndrome. Regular or periodic dizziness, disorientation, or nausea may indicate that you should consult a physician or an ear, nose, and throat specialist. For TMJ problems consult a dental specialist. Once the proper medication or treatment has been prescribed, you can be sure that following the plan in this book will reward you with a comfortable flight whenever you fly.

Food for Thought

Less obvious than TMJ or vestibular problems, but an equally important obstacle to success in clearing your mind of fear, is the lack of chemical balance in your body. Eating habits have a profound effect on your ability to cope with stress. The reason should be clear: in order to cope with stressors and reestablish equilibrium, your body must burn off energy. This can only come from stored food, available blood sugar, oxygen, and other chemicals — all of which are affected by what you eat (or what you *don't* eat!). Food deprivation causes internal stress that results in muscle tension and overreaction to external stressors. That's one reason why starvation-type diets produce anxious, thin people.

It may seem unusual to discuss nutrition in a book about fear of air travel. I predict, however, that medical and psychological professionals will increasingly find links between food and feelings during the next ten years. A health book, William Dufty's *Sugar Blues,* has popularized — albeit a bit dramatically — the dangers of refined sugar. In *Psychodietetics,* Drs. Cheraskin and Ringsdorf relate poor eating habits to nervousness, irritability, memory loss, and our entire emotional lives. Another physician, H. E. Newbold, has produced an excellent study of food and emotions called *Meganutrients for Your Nerves*. A syndicated news story quotes Dr. Mary Jane Hungerford, a California family-counseling professional, as observing that "nutrition is involved in ninety percent of my cases — and in seventy-five percent of them *it is a major factor*." She says that many marriages improve immensely when couples are taken off their sugar and carbohydrate-rich diets.

Weakness, Powerlessness, Panic

Agoraphobia is the king of fears. Many agoraphobics cannot leave their homes. Others find it almost impossible to leave the safety of one room. Walking down a street, they may feel the pavement melt away and see buildings tilting ominously toward them. An agoraphobic lives under a constant threat of panic. In my clinical experience, refined sugar and irregular eating patterns occupy a significant role in the diet of over ninety percent of agoraphobics. This is not to say that refined sugar (sucrose) causes agoraphobia, but it may help maintain it. Agoraphobics tend to show the greatest degree of muscle weakness following the ingestion of refined sugar. The link between refined sugar, muscle weakness, and panic is speculative at present, but interviews with patients, after two weeks on diets high in protein and free of refined sugar, reveal a noticeable reduction of tension levels.

Although the phenomenon is not understood, it is a matter of record that ingestion of refined sugar weakens the muscles within ten to twenty seconds. Individual sensitivity varies. In some people, the loss of strength is negligible; perhaps in the neighborhood of five percent. I've found, however, that people who suffer from free-floating anxiety or chronic tension experience much larger losses of strength. Later in this book you will learn how to test the effect of refined sugar on yourself and others.

Jacobson, the same psychologist who developed progressive relaxation, observed that mental images can cause muscle tension and implicit movements in the areas subject to thought. For example, if you *think* of throwing a baseball, minute impulses will fire, causing muscle tension in your arm. These movements are translated into feedback to your brain, and you may say, "I *feel* like playing some baseball."

Now suppose you're a person with high sugar-muscle sensitivity. After swallowing the last bite of a sugar doughnut, you think about straightening up the house and doing the shopping. Thoughts of what has to be done run through your mind. Although you may feel energized by the intake of sugar, a subtle interoceptive feedback of weakened arm and leg muscles enters your brain, blending with the impulses of intended actions. The resultant thought may be, "These things all have to be done, but it just seems like too much effort. Maybe later." A subtle feeling of powerlessness begins in the body. Symbolically, the present feeling generalizes to, or may trigger feelings of, other times in your life when you have felt powerless or overwhelmed.

This feeling of powerlessness can be but a short step from panic, depending on the action you're thinking about. Contemplating a trip to the supermarket for ice cream may not create anxiety. But obsessing on a chain of negative thoughts while suffering muscle-sugar sensitivity can cause real trouble. Suppose you are in a plane and it encounters turbulence, or the seatbelt sign suddenly goes on while you are in flight. These are common occurrences, but a fearful or anxious flier may obsess on them, converting the innocent signal into an indication that something more serious will happen. This triggers anxiety. The result is shallow, thoracic breathing involving sugar-weakened chest muscles. Such labored breathing is often the beginning of hyperventilation, more anxiety, and panic.

For the agoraphobic, the situation is even more critical. Feelings of insecurity and a need for love (which is represented by sweets) drive many of these people to live on sucrose. Their muscles are often chronically weak and their tension levels high. Their breathing is almost constantly shallow and takes place in the chest (thoracic breathing). A simple act like leaving the house or entering a supermarket causes stress that demands body resources they simply cannot recruit. Shallow breathing accelerates to hyperventilation, weakness in the knees, and disorientation, driving agoraphobics home for security; there they find solace in poor eating habits.

Tina was a forty-two-year-old who had not flown for five years and could not drive an automobile unless accompanied. Her problem started on a trip to Las Vegas. Prior to that time she had had no difficulty with travel by any conveyance. The high pitch of active living, lack of sleep, and disorientation to time (many of the fine casinos have no clocks or windows) was a marked change from her ordered life. The circumstances underlying the trip were also a factor. The trip was her husband's gift to help console her, one month after her father's death. Tina was going through what is termed, in the book *Passages, a life crisis.* With the death of her father she became the head of her family, responsible for family finances, an ailing mother, and a depressed brother. She had always been a tense person and a thoracic or "chest" breather. Dieting was a way of life for her, as she prided herself on her attractive figure. In Las Vegas, on the day of her trauma, she did not eat anything before a dinner show. She has since recalled waiting in line to enter the room and feeling irritable and tense. She asked her husband to buy her a candy bar to tide her over till dinner. The wait for food soon became agonizing, and during the noisy show, seated at a crowded table, she began to hyperventilate. Trying not to make a scene, she struggled until she had to demand that her husband escort her out immediately. When Tina rose from the chair her knees gave way, and she had to be assisted from the room. She was seized with the urge to return home immediately, and her husband relented the next day. She lost her desire for food, drinking coffee and brandy to "quiet her down." The hyperventilation began again when the plane door closed, and it continued until she was halfway home. From that time on, she avoided air travel, automobile travel (escorted only) more than five miles from home, and crowded places. She responded very well to therapy, which included nutritional and breathing reeducation, relaxation training, and systematic desensitization to distance and enclosed places. Postural retraining had to be carried out behind the wheel of an auto, since she gripped the wheel and locked her chest muscles as she hunched forward. The use of a pillow in the small of the back aided her progress greatly. All proceeded well. Within three months she was able to drive alone and had flown in one of our class graduation flights.

Thinking herself cured, she slipped back into her poor eating habits. I received a call from her husband at five o'clock one afternoon. Tina was "on the floor hyperventilating." I promptly asked when she had last eaten. "Just a cup of coffee this morning," was the answer. I told him to give his wife orange juice and protein and call back in an hour. The "attack" subsided immediately, and since that day eight months ago her diet has been sane and so has she.

In the next chapter, you will learn a simple test that demonstrates the neurological muscle-weakening properties of refined sugar, and I will discuss its longer-term nutritional effects on the blood-sugar level. I must emphasize that the sugar-weakness-panic cycle I am hypothesizing and have observed clinically has not yet been tested in a laboratory. The weakening effect sugar has on the muscles is being tested more and more. Until all the data are gathered, then, you should at least be aware of this possible relationship, in order to increase your chances of successfully ridding your mind and body of the fear of air travel.

Body Messengers with Bad News

Through nerve links, hormones, and muscle feedback, the brain carries on a constant dialogue with parts of the body. Medical science has identified this communication process as an electrochemical one, the chemical part of which may be influenced by eating habits.

Remember Roy? Before he ate anything on the morning of his fear-conditioning experience, he reached for a cup of coffee and a cigarette. Both caffeine and nicotine send chemical messages to the adrenal gland. This is part of your personal early-warning system, and the stimulation causes release of another messenger, epinephrine (adrenalin). Without any real or present danger, coffee and a cigarette can set your brain's red telephone ringing, causing your body gradually to begin to prepare a defense of attack or flight. These stimulants also make the nervous system more irritable — that is, nerve impulses are conducted more frequently and erratically in the body.

Fearful fliers who smoke on a plane should be aware of what any physiology student discovers in a basic experiment — the cockroach-nerve preparation. It's a standard experiment in almost every college-level physiology course. A nerve from the insect is isolated and connected to an oscilloscope, which shows a picture of the impulses firing along the nerve. The rhythm is regular until cigarette smoke is blown into the vessel containing the nerve. Nicotine instantly does its work, violently increasing the nerve's electronic activity. Nicotine affects the smooth flow of nervous impulses, allowing them to surge more freely and actively. The sound of a ringing telephone is sharper than usual. A bump is reacted to more quickly and intensely by our muscles. There's only one problem: the warning is usually a false alarm.

This does not mean that you have to stop smoking or give up drinking coffee. But it is a good idea to cut down on both habits before and during a flight. It will also be helpful to keep this in mind if you experience difficulty in following a program of systematic desensitization: you may have preceded a relaxation exercise with a stimulant. Once you know the source of the difficulty, you can deal with it. Many of the people I've helped have continued to smoke and have still been able to overcome their fear. Many of those who have failed, however, have been unable to stop drinking ten to fourteen cups of coffee per day.

Alcohol by any other name is still a drug — one of the most dangerous drugs on this earth. Why? Because it works. It masks fears and releases inhibitions. How many times have you heard someone say, "Flying's no problem for me as long as I have a couple of drinks. I get bombed and it doesn't bother me." It *does* bother such people, but they don't know it does. What happens is that they require more and more alcohol the more flying bothers them. In the meantime, alcohol is speeding to the brain, attacking the frontal portion and the right hemisphere. This means a weakening of the ability to abstract, conceptualize, and empathize, to learn from experience and to sustain movement toward a goal. Your first line of defense is immobilized. Beware of false anesthetics, among which the principal ones are alcoholic beverages.

Unfortunately, the airlines have yet to realize the negative impact of alcohol. But they are in a dilemma. I am certain they feel that it has a tranquilizing effect, and in low doses it does. But in high doses it makes people drunk — and there's no room on an airplane for a drunk passenger. The limit is supposed to be two drinks, but I have personally witnessed airline employees serving more than the limit. I have also seen drunks seated aboard flights next to sober people, whom they have annoyed from takeoff to landing. This is inexcusable, because once a drunk is allowed onto a plane, little can be done with him. If the airlines are going to look the other way, they could at least isolate a "drunk tank" section, as they are now required to segregate smokers.

Auto Trips and Sugar Dips

Imagine what an automobile trip would be like if you had to feed gasoline to your car through the carburetor, a teaspoon at a time. Not much fun. Yet people fuel their bodies that way every day. The foods we eat break down into usable nutrients at different rates:

Fast: Sugar and Complex Carbohydrates

Medium: Fats

Slow and Steady: Protein

People who eat refined sugar and carbohydrate snacks between meals are taking in high-powered, predigested fuel. In chapter 4, you will see how this leads to a letdown. It puts you on a roller coaster of ups and downs in blood sugar and, in many cases, ups and downs in mood.

If you eat breakfast at 7:00 A.M., you probably want a snack about 10:00 A.M. After your noon lunch, a pickup at 3:00 P.M. seems like a good idea, and a 10:00 P.M. snack frequently follows a 7:00 P.M. dinner. These times correspond with the natural variations in the blood-sugar level that occur in many people. Blood sugar, a vital element in your ability to cope with stress, usually begins to diminish three hours after a meal. In fact, when it drops below a certain level you inevitably experience an upsurge of tension and irritability. Protein snacks such as sugarless peanut butter, cottage cheese, and hard-boiled eggs, which deliver a slow, steady supply of nutriment, will help you stabilize your emotions and use relaxation techniques even more effectively to deal with stress.

Before I became aware of the importance of nutrition in treating cases of anxiety, I was perplexed by the number of people who showed great resistance to therapy. I had tried almost every known behavioral and psychoanalytic technique. In reevaluating these patients, a startling similarity became apparent: virtually all of them habitually consumed large quantities of coffee with sugar, candy, pastries, and upwards of a quart of cola or pseudo-fruit sugar drink each day. Their food intake usually consisted of only one good meal a day — supper (the time when they least needed a large intake of food).

When these patients adjusted their habits, substituting proteins for carbohydrate and sugar snacks, the steady flow of nutrients throughout the day made effective therapy possible. These patients also became able to insulate their bodies against stress much more readily — almost automatically.

Breathing Naturally:
You May Pay a Price for Looking Fine

At the point where students learn diaphragmatic breathing in our classes, we always have to overcome their vanity by saying, "It doesn't matter how you look when you are relaxing." Why? Simply because all of your conditioning up to this point in life has focused on making you breathe the hard way so that you'll look thin.

Forget what your parents and drill sergeant told you. To be

an attractive person, you do not have to pull your stomach in and stand straight as an arrow. You may look like a ramrod and behave like an irritable wretch. Human beings were not made to walk or breathe that way. When you do, you distort the natural curvature of your spine, prevent your diaphragm from working properly, and cause stress in your body — long-term stress of which you are not even aware.

When we were toilet trained as children, we learned tension. We were taught to keep steady tension in the muscles around the anus, in order to retain the feces. Although that terrible, torturous time is long forgotten (a time when we were criticized, cajoled, and punished until we learned to maintain steady tension in the end of the alimentary canal), the tension is still unconsciously kept when we walk, talk, and live our daily lives. In a similar way, later in life, many of us learned to keep our bellies in and tight at all times.

The natural position for the body is with spine slightly curved, so that the diaphragm can do its work and the sheet of muscle that overlies the stomach and abdomen can expand and contract with the movement of the diaphragm. In chapter 5, you will find how this is done and learn why changing your breathing habits can change your outlook on a stressful situation. As you learn to breathe in this tension-free manner, you'll discover that you can get more air into your body with much less work.

Muscle Relaxation:
Hang Loose to Keep Yourself Together

Most people are not aware of the true levels of tension and anxiety in their bodies. Whenever tension hits they tend to ignore it. In a sense, they anesthetize themselves by inattention. When this happens, tension and anxiety are free to grow unchecked, causing the individual to raise the threshold of awareness — in other words, to ignore more strongly. Eventually, though, the anxiety bursts through (as it did in Roy's case) and panic takes over. If muscle tension predominates, pain, fatigue, and labored breathing may result.

In chapter 6, you will find muscle-relaxation exercises designed to confront tension actively — to go looking for it. You will learn to detect tension at very low levels, bring it up to a high level *under your control,* and then knock the bottom out of it and relax, still in control.

The term *relaxation exercises* may sound like a contradiction. But psychologists have proved that controlled tension, followed by relaxation of major muscle groups, can slow the heart rate and lower the blood pressure. Controlled tension and relaxation, when used as a "jamming technique" in a stressful situation, serves to work the tension out of the body. Instead of fighting the muscle urge to "fight or flee," the muscles are made to relax.

The Quiet Image:
Suggestion Power for Peace of Mind

It's an enchanting spring day. The grass is just beginning to show some green, and you wake to the sound of birds, as sunshine filters through the window. You feel just fine.

At breakfast your husband (or wife) casually says, "Gee, honey, do you feel all right? You look a little pale." This puts a hole in your euphoria, but the damage is not serious. Later a friend remarks that you've been looking tired lately. While making a purchase at the drugstore, you sneeze, and the clerk tells you he knows about the virus that's going around and hopes you'll get over it soon.

By this time you're beginning to feel terrible. Your system has been attacked, not by a virus but by the power of suggestion. Your self-image has been reversed from one of well-being to one of sickness. So it is with the relationship between mind and body. If we concentrate on a stressful scene, our bodies will follow. As we mentioned in our discussion of the weakness-powerlessness-panic cycle, a mental image will cause traces of appropriate emotional and muscle reactions. For example, stand and close your eyes. Picture that you are falling, and, without knowing it, your body will tense and your heart will accelerate a bit.

Fortunately, the reverse is also true. If you picture a relaxing scene, your body will respond with calm in the muscles and quiet in the emotional system. These body responses will in turn reinforce the tranquility in your mind. So the last part of your relaxation exercise will consist of concentration on a peaceful scene.

Your Emotional Tool Kit

Chances are you have faced the stress of air travel with the tools you've acquired up to this point in your life. They may be responses handed down to you by parents, teachers, or other authority figures; styles you picked up within your family group; or techniques you've discovered by accident.

In the remaining chapters of this book, you will obtain additional tools to help you construct a more solid defense, not only against your fear of flying but also against the many stressors you encounter in modern living. You may have to throw out some of your old tools. In return, you will learn to apply appropriate reactions to particular situations, instead of reacting to all stresses in the same way. "If you go through life with only a hammer," said the old Down East boat builder, "you treat everything like a nail."

Often, in working with fearful patients, I have introduced some of the simple techniques you are about to learn. The results of a little practice have been major gains in coping with fear. But you need to start with a firm foundation: an awareness that fear stylizes the body, and a determination to use your built-in power to restyle it. You need to learn to recognize the smallest improvement and reward yourself for it. Never criticize yourself, for *criticism is, itself, a stress.* If you make a mistake, compliment yourself for "catching it in time."

Understand that tension forces us to eat on the run, skip meals, and grab candy and pastries. Notice also that fearful people at times feel lonely and rejected, and that food represents love and sweet food represents a lot of love.

Every first-year psychology student learns about the three natural tranquilizers: food, sleep, and sex. It is comforting to know that aboard a plane at least two of them are second nature for fearless fliers.

3

Just How Fearful Are You?

WHILE YOU'VE BEEN SEATED in your comfortable chair, we have calmly looked at fear and discussed a method of clearing unwanted fears. In this chapter, the subject is you. Take a moment now to find a pad of paper and a pencil. Along with the material in this chapter, they will help break a few more of the bonds that are keeping you from flying with comfort.

In most ventures, we need numbers to succeed. The bathroom scale is essential to a weight-loss program. Blood-pressure readings tell a hypertensive patient when his diet and medication are correct. The same is true of Active Stress Coping. We need numbers to help quantify your fear and determine the part each of the three bodily systems plays in it, and to measure your degree of flight anxiety.

Measuring fear is not easy. Fear is a totally subjective experience. Our method of assessing it is determined by personality — hardly a standard of measurement. In the throes of fear, we are consumed with the struggle to maintain control; we have no time to concern ourselves with the application of some measuring technique. Later, in retrospect, we'd rather not think about our fears. These considerations, along with the fact that fear measurement is not included in our basic education, result in a society of people experiencing an undetermined amount of fear and anxiety. But how can we find any solution to this problem until we know the extent of the fear?

"I am *very* afraid," murmurs Joan, with palpitating heart, sweaty hands, and jumpy stomach. "I am *very* afraid," says Judy, sitting with her hands folded in her lap. These are two truthful descriptions of totally different conditions.

According to the general impression of the words *anxious* and *relaxed*, we are either one or the other. Actually, there are degrees of both. To further complicate the uncertain nature of fear, people use different methods of judging themselves, depending on the circumstances. Work anxiety in the conference room creates a different atmosphere for evaluation than does sexual anxiety in the bedroom.

How to Rate Your Air-Travel Fear

Air travel presents an array of stimuli, some of which may be stressful to one fearful flier but not to another. In this book, we will treat fear of air travel as a complex of fears classified according to the situation.

Some people may fear only one aspect of air travel while others fear several aspects. In this chapter we will introduce a method of ranking fear that is commonly used by behavior therapists — the SUDS (Subjective Units of Disturbance) scale. This will be your gauge for measuring fear, and, conversely, the absence of fear, in any situation, real or imagined.

To compare your fear of air travel with the fear of others, as well as to ascertain your level of fear, we will employ another measure: Sylvia Jane Solberg's Fear of Flying Survey (FFS). We have administered this survey to all our classes and private patients, from the time it was first made available in 1973. Dr. Solberg completed the research for her dissertation in 1974 at the University of Minnesota. It was the first major contribution to the group treatment of air-travel phobia. We will also use her Flight Symptoms Checklist to evaluate your past experience with flight and to monitor your progress in future flights.

Where Do Your Fears Occur?

As we pointed out earlier, each person responds to stress in a distinctive, patterned way that reflects a unique combination of responses in the three systems of the body — the autonomic, somatic-motor, and central nervous systems. We have developed the Self-Survey of Stress Responses to show you how to focus your efforts, during the relaxation exercises, on the most responsive system. Finally, we include a short survey of fears, to indicate the relative magnitude of your fear of air travel, with respect to other fears. We can compare your levels with the levels of others who were fearful of flying and who now fly confidently.

SUDS (Subjective Units of Disturbance Scale)

The scene is an airport waiting room. About fifteen people, pleasant looking and comfortably dressed, sit together in a section of upholstered lounge seats. Circulating among them, a psychologist and five trained assistants quickly ask, "What are your numbers?"

This is the prelude to a graduation flight for air-travel phobics. They are anticipating the whole flight process and feeling natural anxiety. At the same time, these students have mastered several powerful skills that will help them control and eventually eliminate their fear. One of these aids used in developing these skills, the Subjective Units of Disturbance Scale (SUDS), changes the way they talk (and hence the way they feel) about their fear.

"What are your numbers?" an assistant asks Judi, a young mother of three. Without hesitation Judi responds, "thirty-five." Knowing that this is too high on the scale for her to board a plane, Judi begins a relaxation exercise, guided by a staff member.

The SUDS technique, developed by Wolpe and Lazarus in 1966, has become recognized by behavior therapists as an evaluative instrument. One of its most important advantages is that it provides a new language to use under stress. When we use old words, our body slips into old behavior patterns, and treatment is more difficult.

The SUDS method allows quick assessment of interoceptive conditions and initiation of fast counteractive measures that will help people like Judi regain control. In addition, the use of numbers gives us a basis for keeping records and graphing our progress. But there is an added bonus. Dr. T. X. Barber, a researcher in the field of pain, found that when subjects in experiments objectively described pain sensations they were feeling, they could tolerate greater pain than when they simply experienced their discomfort silently. In other words, *the act* of ranking your own discomfort is a control procedure. It places the consciousness in an active encountering mode oriented toward mastering the situation rather than passively accepting or attempting to deny or escape feelings of discomfort.

The technique is simple. A score of zero SUDS means that no anxiety, tension, or disturbing thoughts exist in your body. A zero level is total relaxation, not sleep. Your mind can be active with pleasant thoughts, but there is either a lack of awareness of the body or an awareness of total freedom from anxiety and tension.

The zero level may cause difficulty for some people who fear. These are people who have mastered the art of denial and repression. They feel perfectly calm at all times, because they have learned to pay no attention to their body's emergency signals. In contrast to those for whom anxiety is unavoidable, these people will have to regain awareness of their feelings through active study of body responses to stressful situations. Blinding oneself to subtle variations in feeling gives immediate relief but costs drastically in the long run. If you are one of these people, you probably feel totally calm right up to the moment you board the plane or watch the door close: then sudden and immediate paralysis or panic takes over. This is the drastic cost — total powerlessness. For you, an effort must be made to reverse the control that fear has exerted on your perceptive processes. One can control nothing if one is unaware. The practice of rationalizing and finding excuses for your fear must be replaced by admission of it and an active attempt to monitor it.

At the other extreme of the scale is a score of 100 SUDS. This value represents the upper limit, the greatest terror that you have ever experienced or can conceive of experiencing. At this level, body functions are totally out of your control, and all rational thought is taken over by the emotions. For example, if you are reading this book and understanding what is written, you cannot be at a SUDS level of 100. On the other hand, you cannot be at a level of zero, since a certain level of tension is necessary to hold the book and focus on the pages. Most of the time we function at somewhere between zero and 100 SUDS. There may be instances of high levels, followed by a return to a low baseline. However, some individuals usually function at a high chronic baseline, around 60. They have become accustomed to a state of chronic tension. When stress hits, their level quickly jumps to near panic. Later, when we begin the practice of relaxation, you will be able to score your reduction in discomfort on this scale. By intermittently practicing the relaxation exercises, you will be able to tone the chronic level of tension down to more comfortable levels. You will notice at that time, incidentally, that your thought processes are clearer, and your awareness of the world around you will improve. Chronic tension and anxiety place an internal demand on your mental apparatus that robs you of full attention to the outside world.

The concept of the inverted "U," as presented by Robert B. Malmo in 1959, is very helpful in understanding this. In short, the relation between activation of the nervous system (anxiety or tension) and behavioral efficiency is described graphically by an inverted "U." At low activation, your performance is less than optimal. As activation increases, performance rises to an optimum point, then falls off as anxiety or tension increases further.

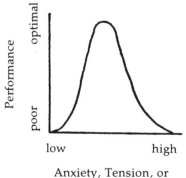

Anxiety, Tension, or
External Stimulation

Each human function has a "U" curve of its own, and the tension levels of optimum performance may vary. Tennis will differ from, say, writing a personal letter. But the one observation that holds true is that at high levels of tension, *all* constructive performance — thinking, feeling, creating, learning new skills — decreases. Performance that has destructive consequences appears at these high levels (fast, jerky muscle reactions, overreactions to sounds, insensitivity to others, regression to more infantile forms of behavior, or perseveration of the same behaviors regardless of their effectiveness). The ideal way to learn any behavior is to reach the optimal level of functioning at a low enough level of tension to be aware that your performance is, in fact, optimal. Later in this chapter, when we present the Self-Survey of Stress Responses, you will learn the body responses that enter into the accurate judgment of the SUDS level. For now, use your own criteria of tension and anxiety to rate your SUDS level.

Begin immediately to keep a log of your SUDS levels during the day, noting the SUDS level first thing in the morning, at noon (before lunch), at four P.M., and at eight P.M. List these four readings by date for two weeks. This will provide you with an emotional baseline against which you will compare future changes. In addition, each emotional peak that feels outstanding to you during the day should be noted, giving SUDS level and circumstance. In this way you will have a record of your peaks of emotion during the two-week period.

By using the SUDS scale during the two-week period you will learn the most important lesson that a fearful person needs to know to overcome fear: *It is erroneous to think that you must be either tense or relaxed. There are different levels of relaxation and tension, and by the simple act of monitoring the differences, you will automatically do things that lower your levels.* The only provision is that you not falsify your levels to fool yourself. It may be difficult in the beginning to admit to yourself that high tension levels exist, but only by confronting this fact will you be able to control your tension. If your tension levels are low during this two-week period, you will have important information indicating the isolated nature of your fear of air travel.

Roy's SUDS Levels Over a Two-Week Period

Day	A.M.	Noon	4:00	8:00	Peak	Circumstances
Mon.	25	55	55	15	70	Saw boss, discussed sales strategy
Tues.	20	50	50	20	65	Missed phone call
Wed.	15	45	50	10	50	Saw Dr. Forgione
Thurs.	15	40	45	10	70	Told boss of fear of flying
Fri.	12	30	35	10	50	Started diet; reviewed sales strategy with boss
Sat.	10	20	15	05	30	Had disagreement with wife
Sun.	10	15	15	15	35	Thought about work tomorrow
Mon.	20	35	30	10	35	Met important client
Tues.	10	25	25	05		None!!!
Wed.	10	25	20	10	35	Sales meeting
Thurs.	08	20	15	05	30	Prepared sales reports
Fri.	10	22	13	05	25	A great day!
Sat.	08	10	15	05		None
Sun.	08	12	10	08	25	Thought about work

Roy's record dramatically shows the effect of the change in his nutritional habits and his assertion to his supervisor that he fears flying (see chapter 4).

Fear-of-Flying Survey (FFS)

This is a modified form of the FFS as it was originally published (S. J. Solberg, 1975). Use a blank sheet of paper, date it, and make a column of numbers from 1 to 46. The items that follow refer to experiences that may cause fear or apprehension. Beside each item number on your piece of paper, mark the number under the column heading that most accurately describes how much you are frightened by the event. Work quickly but be sure to consider each item separately. If necessary, take a break between items, should your apprehension from one item affect your response to the succeeding item.

Example: If item 1 were to read, "Listening to a friend talk about a flight that he/she took that had mechanical problems prior to departure," you would mark a 3 next to the number 1 on your paper if you were much disturbed by the situation. Begin now to rate your fear on the items listed below. Try to respond to each item as an isolated situation without relating it to other items.

FLYING FEAR SURVEY

	Not At All	A Little	A Fair Amount	Much	Very Much
1. You have decided to take an airplane flight and you are at home making plane reservations and planning your trip.	0	1	2	3	4
2. Your plane tickets arrive in the mail, and you open the envelope and read the tickets.	0	1	2	3	4
3. It is the day of your flight, and you are at home packing and preparing.	0	1	2	3	4
4. You leave home and drive to the airport.	0	1	2	3	4
5. You arrive at the airport and go to the appropriate airline, where you check your baggage and are assigned a seat number for the flight.	0	1	2	3	4
6. You pass through the airline's security check, where all your carry-on baggage is searched by the security guard.	0	1	2	3	4
7. You are in the lobby waiting for your flight, and as you sit and wait you are aware of the activity of other people coming and going on other flights.	0	1	2	3	4

	Not At All	A Little	A Fair Amount	Much	Very Much
8. Your flight number is called, and you gather your carry-on baggage and get in line to enter the plane.	0	1	2	3	4
9. You walk onto the plane and are greeted by the stewardess at the entry. You notice the interior of the plane, with its rows of seats and small windows. You hear the quiet background music.	0	1	2	3	4
10. You walk down the aisle of the plane until you find your seat. You put your carry-on baggage beneath the seat in front of you and settle yourself in your seat.	0	1	2	3	4
11. You realize that the aircraft door is shut and that you cannot leave the plane.	0	1	2	3	4
12. Your plane is on the ground prior to takeoff. It is a stormy, rainy day, and when you look out the window of the plane you see the sheets of rain pouring down and see the puddles of water forming on the runway.	0	1	2	3	4

	Not At All	A Little	A Fair Amount	Much	Very Much
13. You feel the first lurch as the plane begins to move toward the runway.	0	1	2	3	4
14. As the plane rolls toward the runway, the stewardess demonstrates the use of the oxygen mask and other safety devices.	0	1	2	3	4
15. As you wait for the plane to take off, the stewardess walks down the aisle and looks to see if all seat belts are fastened. You reach down and check your seat belt.	0	1	2	3	4
16. Your plane has just been given the signal to take off, and the plane picks up speed rapidly as it accelerates down the runway. You feel the plane's vibrations and hear the engines roar.	0	1	2	3	4
17. As the plane lifts off the ground and climbs into the air, you hear the "thump" of the landing gear as it is retracted.	0	1	2	3	4

	Not At All	A Little	A Fair Amount	Much	Very Much
18. As the plane climbs, you are thrust back in your seat, and you feel the small changes in air pressure and the vibrations as the plane cuts through the air.	0	1	2	3	4
19. You are flying at a steady altitude in calm weather.	0	1	2	3	4
20. You are in flight and look out of the window and see the panorama below. Everything looks small from your view high above.	0	1	2	3	4
21. You are on a long flight, and, glancing at your watch, you figure that four more hours of flights are left.	0	1	2	3	4
22. While the plane is in flight, the pilot announces over the intercom that the plane is behind schedule and will arrive 30 minutes late.	0	1	2	3	4
23. You are flying in dense fog. When you look out the window, you can see nothing but thick fog; you cannot even see the wing tip.	0	1	2	3	4

	Not At All	A Little	A Fair Amount	Much	Very Much
24. While in flight, your plane encounters some turbulent weather. The flight becomes rough and bouncy, and you are required to fasten your seat belt.	0	1	2	3	4
25. Unexpectedly, your plane hits an air pocket, and you feel a great jolt as the plane suddenly changes altitude. The jolt causes confusion and disorder in the plane as the passengers are thrown off balance and loose objects are knocked out of place.	0	1	2	3	4
26. Your plane is approaching its destination. The "no smoking" sign and the "fasten seat belt" sign flash on. You feel the changes in air pressure as the plane begins to descend.	0	1	2	3	4
27. As the plane descends for landing, the wing flaps are lowered, causing the plane to vibrate a little. You hear the "thump" of the landing gear being lowered.	0	1	2	3	4

	Not At All	A Little	A Fair Amount	Much	Very Much
28. As the plane touches ground and begins moving down the runway, you hear a loud roar and feel the plane vibrate when the pilot reverses the thrust of the engines to slow down the plane.	0	1	2	3	4
29. Your flight is over. Your plane taxis to the place where you disembark.	0	1	2	3	4
30. Thinking about the flight three weeks before its scheduled date.	0	1	2	3	4
31. Thinking about a flight the weekend before its scheduled date.	0	1	2	3	4
32. Thinking about a flight one week before its scheduled date.	0	1	2	3	4
33. Thinking about a flight the night before its scheduled date.	0	1	2	3	4
34. Thinking about a flight the hour before its scheduled time.	0	1	2	3	4
35. Talking with friends about flying.	0	1	2	3	4
36. Going to the airport to see friends or relatives off on a plane flight.	0	1	2	3	4

	Not At All	A Little	A Fair Amount	Much	Very Much
37. In a plane flying over mountains.	0	1	2	3	4
38. In a plane flying over the ocean.	0	1	2	3	4
39. In a plane flying on a clear day.	0	1	2	3	4
40. In a plane flying at night.	0	1	2	3	4
41. In a plane flying in winter weather.	0	1	2	3	4
42. Watching a plane take off and land.	0	1	2	3	4
43. Eating a meal during an airplane flight.	0	1	2	3	4
44. Having my family on the plane with me during an airplane flight.	0	1	2	3	4
45. Flying on a plane by myself (no friends or relatives with me).	0	1	2	3	4
46. Flying on a plane with one friend on the plane with me.	0	1	2	3	4

Now that you have completed the FFS, add up the column of your responses to obtain a total score. There are 46 items in the survey, so the maximum score obtainable is 46 x 4, or 184. Of the 556 class members and private patients treated in our program, approximately 20 percent scored between 150 and 183. Only 3 percent reported a maximum score of 184.

The ranges of scores and the percentage of fearful fliers that obtain each range are shown below, along with the percentage distribution of 150 calmer fliers (employees and students of Tufts University who flew three or more times during the past three years).

	FFS Score	556 Fearful Fliers	150 Calmer Fliers
Phobia	184–150	21%	1%
Intense Fear	149–100	34%	1%
Moderate Fear	99– 50	16%	13%
Mild Fear	49– 25	28%	33%
Negligible Fear	24– 0	1%	52%

What we learn from this table is that a large number of calmer fliers have some degree of apprehension. Even though their FFS scores are in the lower ranges, certain items may cause extreme responses in calmer fliers; they may attain lower overall scores than fearful fliers by distributing lower scores for each item over a number of items (that is, in the "little" or "fair amount" columns). Seventy-one percent of the fearful fliers score above 50, while only 15 percent of all fliers score that high. These percentages take on greater meaning when we consider that national surveys indicate that because of fear, between 15 and 18 percent of the population of the United States avoids flying. This means that fear causes about 25 million adults — the range is between 23 and 28 million — to avoid flying. In these surveys, approximately 70 percent of the population has flown within the past three years. If we conservatively project our data, 15 percent of this group has moderate or greater fear.

The next step in your analysis of the FFS is to examine your responses to three types of items in the FFS: anticipatory (A), emergency (E), and common experiences (C). Anticipatory items are those that relate to thoughts or behaviors occurring prior to the actual flight. Common items are selected situations that deal with actual flight. There is only one emergency item, to determine whether you are responding sincerely. It is expected that the score on this item will be extreme (at least 3, if not 4). Code your Fear of Flying Survey answer sheet in the following manner: Place the letter A (anticipatory), C (common), or E (emergency) to the left of each item number, according to the following table. Then obtain a separate total of all A and C items.

FFS ITEMS LISTED BY TYPE

(A — Anticipation; C — Common; E — Emergency)

Question Number

A1	A6	C11	C16	C21	C26	A31	A36	C41	C46
A2	A7	C12	C17	C22	C27	A32	C37	A42	
A3	A8	C13	C18	C23	C28	A33	C38	C43	
A4	C9	C14	C19	C24	C29	A34	C39	C44	
A5	C10	C15	C20	E25	A30	A35	C40	C45	

Sixteen anticipatory items permit a maximum anticipatory score of 64. Twenty-nine common items permit a maximum flying score of 116. The one emergency item allows a maximum emergency score of 4.

You can compare your scores to those of the 556 fearful fliers and the calmer fliers by using the table below.

AVERAGE SCORE OF ANTICIPATORY, COMMON, AND EMERGENCY
ITEMS FOR 556 FEARFUL FLIERS AND 150 CALMER FLIERS

	Nonfliers and Fearful Fliers	Calmer Fliers
Average Anticipatory Score	41.3	5.8
Average Common Flying Score	51.1	21.4
Average Emergency Score	3.6	3.2

When you compare your scores to these average figures, remember that averages are affected by extreme scores, both high and low. What the average scores tell us is that fearful fliers (and nonfliers) report a great amount of anticipatory anxiety, while calmer fliers report very little. A surprising number of the "calmer" fliers, on the other hand, report scores indicating that they fly in apprehension. It has been a consistent finding in our work that, during the course of losing fear, the scores on common flying items diminish faster than the scores on anticipatory items. This point emerges clearly if we examine the responses of three classes of fearful fliers treated by the method outlined later in the book. The chart below compares the modal FFS class scores of three treatment groups, T-1, T-2, and T-3, before and after group treatment. (*The modal score is the most*

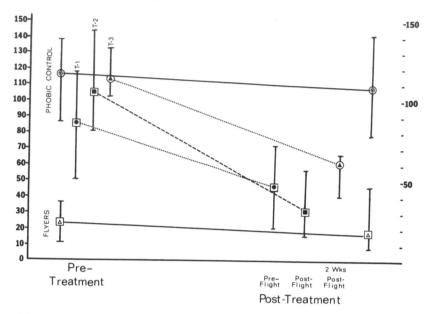

Most Frequent Scores on FFS Before Treatment and at Different Points After Treatment. Fear Scores Compared with Those of Calmer Fliers. Phobic control groups and calmer fliers' groups received no treatment but were tested before and after a ten-week period. Group T-1 was tested the second time before graduation flight. Group T-2 was tested immediately after graduation flight. Group T-3 was tested two weeks after graduation flight. Duration of treatment was approximately ten weeks.

frequent score. This score is used to prevent the distortion in report-ing data that sometimes occurs when the average score is used.) The symbol enclosed in either the square or the circle represents the modal score, while the vertical bar defines the range within which fifty percent of the scores occurred. Scores of the treatment groups are compared with scores of a group of fearful fliers who did not undergo treatment but were tested after the passage of the same amount of time required for the group treatment (ten weeks). The FFS was taken by a group of calmer fliers before and after the ten-week period, and their modal scores are included for comparison. Notice that before treatment the scores of the fearful fliers are significantly greater than the scores of calmer fliers; at their graduation flight, the scores of the treated fearful fliers are significantly lower than the scores of fearful fliers who were not exposed to treatment, regardless of when tested.

It is interesting that the treatment group which was administered the FFS *preflight* test (T-1) showed a reduction in reported fear even though members had not experienced the graduation flight. Further analysis of the scores shows that the greatest reduction in the FFS scores resulted from the lower reported fear attributed to common flying items by the classes that were tested for the second time *after* the graduation flight (T-2 and T-3 in the table below). The fear attributed to common flying items diminished, but not to so great a degree, in Class T-1, the class that was tested for the second time before the graduation flight.

REDUCTION IN REPORTED FEAR

	Anticipatory	Common	Emergency
T-1 (N = 180)	13.1	20.5	.9
T-2 (N = 196)	21.4	50.7	1.4
T-3 (N = 180)	24.1	43.1	.8

The table shows average difference scores of three treatment groups for anticipatory, common, and emergency items in the FFS. Difference scores obtained by subtracting post-treatment from pre-treatment responses for each individual. The higher the difference score, the greater the reduction in reported fear.

Flying with proper preparation and using Active Stress Coping techniques during flight results in significant reduction of reported fear. In no instance did a report of fear of any item increase after treatment.

It will be most helpful for you to retake the FFS after you have completed the program of Active Stress Coping and Systematic Desensitization that is presented later in the book. The reduction in your fear scores will be an important indicator of your readiness to fly. A final important indicator on the FFS is the

number of responses in the last two columns, the extreme responses of "much" and "very much." You will find, as the data
from those treated demonstrate, that the responses in the extreme categories will shift to the lower categories after desensitization and your graduation flight. As you continue to fly
using Active Stress Coping, the responses in the extreme categories will continue to diminish with successive flights.

REDUCTION OF EXTREME RESPONSE

	PRE-TREATMENT		POST-TREATMENT	
	Much	*Very Much*	*Much*	*Very Much*
Fearful Control (Untreated)	8.6	16.0	8.5	15.7
Calmer Fliers	1.5	.7	1.2	.5
Fearful Treated	8.7	13.2	3.8	1.9
Fearful Treated (Retest One Year Later)			2.7	.9

Table gives average number of responses in categories 3 (Much Fear)
and 4 (Very Much Fear) for groups of 150 untreated fearful fliers, 556
treated fearful fliers, and 150 calmer fliers before and after treatment or
ten-week period.

The Self-Survey of Stress Responses

Now that you have ascertained the degree of stress associated
with thinking about flying and with actual flying experiences,
we turn to determining your characteristic pattern of response
to stress in everyday life. As pointed out earlier, there are three
response systems in the body, each with its own feelings and
effects on behavior. The following survey will assist you in
determining which system deserves more of your attention
when you practice the control exercises that come later in the
book. Early in our work, we found that a battery of three control
exercises — diaphragmatic breathing for autonomic response,
muscle relaxation for somatic response, and guided relaxation
imagery for the central nervous system — had to be taught to
people with fear.

Over the years we observed that some people focused on
certain portions of the exercise battery to the exclusion of oth-

ers, and their selected portion usually worked quite well for them. We devised this survey to predict which portion of the relaxation battery they would select. It soon became clear that different people were discomforted by different physiological patterns, while other people were discomforted in all three systems. The portion of the relaxation battery that people tended to select was, in fact, the set of exercises designed to affect the response system that discomforted them. Take the following survey by marking your answers on a blank sheet of paper prepared as shown in the illustration on page 72; or photocopy the example.

SELF-SURVEY OF STRESS RESPONSES IN THE BODY

Each person has an individual pattern of physical responses to a stress or continued stress. This survey is designed to determine *your* pattern, to guide you in determining which portions of the exercises (that is, autonomic, somatic motor, or central nervous system) should be given extra attention. Write a number zero to five in the parentheses after the question. If there are two sets of parentheses, place the same number in *both*.

> Zero means never
> One means almost never
> Two means seldom
> Three means occasionally
> Four means frequently
> Five means almost always

	A	M	C
1. I tap my feet or fingers.		( )	
2. I clench my teeth or grind them.		( )	
3. I stammer or stutter.		( )	( )
4. My stomach flutters.	( )		
5. I kick my foot or bounce it.		( )	
6. I bite my nails.			( )
7. I pick at things (lint, hair, etc.).			( )
8. I feel nausea.	( )	( )	
9. I have pain in my chest or feel like a strap is tight across my chest.		( )	

SELF-SURVEY OF STRESSFUL RESPONSES IN THE BODY

Name:_____   Date:_____

	A	M	C
1.			
2.			
3.			
4.			
5.			
6.			
7.			
8.			
9.			
10.			
11.			
12.			
13.			
14.			
15.			
16.			
17.			
18.			
19.			
20.			
21.			
22.			
23.			
24.			
25.			
26.			
27.			
28.			
29.			
30.			
31.			
32.			
33.			
34.			
35.			
36.			
37.			
38.			

	A	M	C
10. My hands tremble or my head quivers.		( )	
11. My hands feel cold.	( )		
12. My hands sweat.	( )		
13. My heart beats very fast.	( )		
14. I feel distance from my surroundings.			( )
15. I continuously have the same or many thoughts running through my head.			( )
16. I move awkwardly, bump into things, or drop things.		( )	( )
17. I cannot concentrate.			( )
18. I must be aware of everything around me to keep control.			( )
19. My head aches, usually on one side (temple or jaw), with a steady ache.		( )	
20. My head aches with a pounding either behind my eyes or on one side of my head.	( )		
21. My forehead aches or the back of my head aches with a kind of pulling ache.		( )	
22. The muscles running from my shoulder blades across my shoulders to my neck ache on one side or both sides.		( )	
23. My face flushes.	( )		
24. I get dizzy.	( )	( )	
25. I want to be very close to someone.			( )
26. I tend to have lapses of awareness.			( )
27. I feel like I want to smash something.		( )	
28. I have to go to the toilet often.	( )		
29. I have difficulty eating or holding down food.	( )		
20. My calves, thighs, or feet get tense.		( )	

	A	M	C
31. I breathe rapidly and shallowly.	( )		
32. I have to check things again and again.			( )
33. I keep forgetting things.			( )
34. I want to retreat and sleep, safe at home.			( )
35. I busy myself putting everything in order.			( )
36. I have to eat and eat.	( )		
37. I produce gas (burp or other).	( )		
38. My mouth gets dry.	( )		

Upon completion of the survey, add the A, M, and C columns to obtain three scores. There are 14 items in each column, allowing a maximum score of 70 for each column. The higher the number in each category, the more you are affected by that system and the more you are aware of it. Let us briefly examine some sample response patterns.

	A (Autonomic)	M (Muscle)	C (Central Process)
Roy	45	38	15
Bill	24	3	7
Judi	40	20	29
Susan	62	38	46
Fred	42	36	57
Dick	8	15	6
Lou	9	27	10
Barbara	57	55	43

Roy, Bill, Judi, Susan, and Barbara show a pattern that emphasizes autonomic responses, indicating that diaphragmatic breathing should receive attention. But Roy, Susan, and Barbara show high scores in the muscle category also, so they should practice muscle relaxation as well. Dick and Lou are also muscle responders. Fred is an interesting case, his central process scores being higher than those in other categories. Whenever we see this pattern of scores, we interpret it to mean that denial and repression of anxiety have occurred. People like Fred obsess about many concerns (health, germs, failure) almost constantly. They are highly stressed people who, by habit, constantly feed themselves internal mental stressors. Fred did not fly on the graduation flight with the class. His perfectionistic tendencies triggered obsessing of negative thoughts (resulting in more anxiety) rather than initiating thought stopping (see chapter 7) and positive mental imagery. With more practice he was eventually able to stop his running thoughts and master his anxiety. He flew with the next class. Fred was the type of fearful flier who needs more attention than can be given in a class situation.

Perfectionism and the need to control are traits that always lead to anxiety and fear. When these signals occur in the body, the perfectionistic individual attempts to control them by rituals or thought processes that fuel the incompetence and anxiety even more. Self-criticism, for example, increases body tension automatically. When a child is severely criticized, his body learns a defensive pattern. Later in life, when he criticizes himself just as he was criticized, the defensive pattern becomes even stronger. If analyzed closely, obsessive mental patterns are little more than elaborated messages of inadequacy, vestiges of parental criticism, suggestions of failure and incompetence that have nothing to do with present reality. These mental word chains have to be broken if the vicious circle of anxiety–obsession–panic–avoidance is to end.

Central process scores will be reasonably high for all people who have fears, but Fred's score is unusual. Roy, Bill, Dick, and Lou are exceptions to this rule. Their history of fear is rather short, and their fear is specific to air travel. More pervasive patterns of fear, coupled with an anxious lifestyle, result in a pattern similar to Fred's. Should your pattern be similar to Fred's, you will need to practice the full battery of relaxation and thought-stopping exercises more extensively than the average fearful flier. You will need to monitor your obsessive thoughts and chart their reduction (see chapter 7) in addition to recording your daily SUDS levels. If after the initial program is completed you are still unable to fly, you may consider seeking the help of a psychologist. The therapy can be expected to go much more quickly, because you will have created a strong foundation for success.

It must be understood that, while self-management techniques of fear control are effective for the majority of fearful fliers, certain people need the added assistance of an experienced coach. The goal of coaching is to change the internal dialogue that turns every stressful situation into a feared one. A behavior therapist can provide this individualized service for anyone whose life is constrained by numerous fears. The approach to multiple fears is beyond the scope of this book, but the principles are the same. More often than not, once the behavior is closely monitored and control procedures are systematically applied to two or more fears, the entire fear pattern weakens. A behavior therapist ensures the systematic approach.

The Flight Symptom Checklist

This section is for people who fly apprehensively. If you have never flown, it will not be productive for you to use this checklist. Later, when you fly, it will be helpful in monitoring your progress. This checklist is a modified form of the checklist used by Solberg in her original research on air travel fear. It's a good idea to reproduce several copies of the checklist to use on each of your flights. It is divided into two major sections: the first enumerates specific responses while the second ranks SUDS levels at specific points in the flight experience. This checklist is to be filled out during actual flights.

FLIGHT SYMPTOM CHECKLIST (PART I)

Read each of the following statements carefully. After each item, indicate in the first column how you feel prior to the flight; then during level flight answer each item in the second column. Use the following scale values:

0 — The statement does not describe my feelings.
1 — The feeling (or behavior) is barely noticeable.
2 — The feeling (or behavior) is moderately intense.
3 — The feeling (or behavior) is strong.
4 — The feeling (or behavior) is very strong.

	Pre-flight	In-flight
My stomach is calm and free of tension.	___	___
I am thinking of all things that can possibly be pleasant about the flight.	___	___
I am so calm that I am able to think clearly about what is happening.	___	___
I find myself thinking of how much more calm I am about flying than other people.	___	___
I have an excited feeling, but it is not anxiety.	___	___
I am worrying less about the flight than I have about past flights.	___	___
I do feel confident that the flight will go well.	___	___
I feel very confident about taking this flight.	___	___
I am doing my relaxation exercises as much as I should.	___	___
I am less anxious than I anticipated I would be.	___	___

Please Rank the Following as They Apply to You in Flight:

Muscles Relaxed	___	No Tranquilizers Before Flight	___
Feel In Control	___	No Alcohol Before or During	___
Hands Dry	___	Heart Beating Normally	___
Dizziness Absent	___	Comfortable Breathing	___
Nausea Absent	___	Clear Vision	___

FLIGHT SYMPTOM CHECKLIST (PART II)

At different points in the flight mark the SUDS level you experience. (Zero is complete relaxation, 100 is panic and terror of the worst possible intensity.)

1. Taxi out to takeoff   ___
2. Takeoff   ___
3. Cruising at level flight   ___
4. Descent to landing   ___
5. Engines reversed on runway   ___

The first part of the Flight Symptom Checklist will assist the flier in monitoring progress made during successive flights. If you now fly with apprehension it may be helpful to fill out a checklist prior to beginning the relaxation program. With this level as a baseline, your progressively higher scores will be even more reinforcing. The twenty items allow a maximum relaxing score of 80. The higher your score on the flight checklist, the more relaxed a flier you have become. For those who are now avoiding flight because of fear, in-flight scores following the graduation flight will increase at a faster rate than the pre-flight scores. As you lose your fear, a phenomenon called back-chaining will occur. That is, the actual feared situation will lose its emotional charge at a faster rate than will the anticipatory behaviors. So expect the pre-flight scores to lag behind the in-flight scores on the checklist. From our experience, only twenty-six percent of fliers consistently score 80 on the checklist. Forty-four percent score 40 or higher, and the remaining thirty percent score below 40. As you can see by the nature of the items, a great deal of control is required to score in the 70s or higher. Patience and consistent application of the relaxation procedures will make this level attainable.

Part II of the Flight Symptom Checklist allows us to make some interesting comparisons. Solberg's research examined the effectiveness of lectures combined with automated desensitization procedures (slides and sounds of aircraft). She also included a control group that received no treatment at all. Her patients used Part II of the Flight Symptom Checklist based on a six-point scale. The scale we have used in our classes and recommend in this book is the 100-point SUDS scale. The differences between average ratings for traditional systematic desensitization with relaxation and those for nontreatment are shown in the chart below. Notice that when Solberg's data are transformed to SUDS values, the automated treatment results in lower fear values than does nontreatment, at all points of flight except takeoff. The data from a class run with twenty hours of training, nutritional preparation, desensitization, relaxation, and Active Stress Coping, as proposed in this book, are included for comparison. It must be understood that Sol-

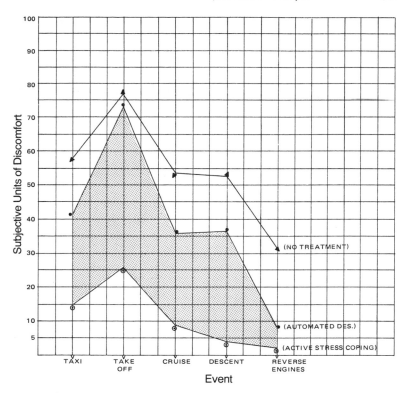

SUDS Levels at Five Points During Flight: Non-Treatment, Systematic Desensitization, and Active Stress Coping

berg's work was investigative in nature and was not designed to optimize fear reduction. At times the performance of scientific research limits the options of the researcher. The greater fear-reduction effects obtained with Active Stress Coping techniques result from the intentional massing of factors, all of which have been shown to be effective. As you progress, you will be able to compare your scores with Solberg's data on flight experiences. After the preparation outlined in this book, the scores on your graduation flight should fall within the shaded area on the chart.

Using SUDS scores becomes second nature to active stress copers. As I've mentioned, the very act of converting your feelings to numbers takes you a long way toward achieving control. After you've mastered the techniques of breathing, relaxation, and mental imagery described in this book, your first Fear-of-Flying Survey score will become a souvenir to show your progress. But above all, use your scores from the Self-Survey of Stress Responses to guide you through the techniques of Active Stress Coping.

Now that you know just how fearful you are, it's time to learn how calm you can become.

4

Air Travel, Fear, and Nutrition

Don't Eat Your Heart Out

TOO OFTEN, either for convenience or because of the pressures of the day, we are lured into a choice of diet that feeds fear and anxiety. Furthermore, psychological treatment for these problems may be rendered ineffective as long as a patient is literally eating his heart out. In our approach to fear and stress coping, a nutritional analysis should be the first step in changing behavior. Just what is the relationship between psychology and nutrition? What is the importance of good nutrition in learning to fly fearlessly? How can we distinguish the foods that feed fear from those that nourish relaxation? In this chapter, we will look at the internal imbalance — both chemical and physical — that must be stabilized before desensitization can begin.

To function properly, brain cells require a much greater amount of blood sugar and oxygen than do other cells in the body. Because of this greater need, maintaining critical levels of these substances and other nutrients is most important for a firm foundation on which to build psychological change. Moreover, external stress will cause fluctuation in the available amount of these essentials. The body must be able to reestablish critical levels quickly in order to cope with stress effectively.

Roy was waiting for me in our reception area. A handsome young man in his mid-thirties, outwardly sociable and pleasant, he offered a hand that was trembling and damp with sweat. Settling into the overstuffed reclining chair alongside my desk, he commented on the welcome comfort: "I'm a bit tired. I drove all the way in from Cleveland yesterday and had to be in the office this morning. My boss thought I flew in last night, so I had to keep up appearances. I often drive all night — just can't fly in airplanes, and I think it's about time I tried to do something about that."

Roy recounted a familiar story of air-travel panic; in fact, you read about his episode in chapter 1. He was involved in what psychologists call the traumatic onset of a phobia. Flying suddenly became more and more difficult. He began to lose sleep before a flight. One day, aboard a plane ready to leave for Tampa, Roy called the flight attendant and deliberately asked her when it would arrive in New Orleans, to give the impression that he was on the wrong plane. It was a clumsy ruse, but he was able to get off the aircraft before its doors were closed. That had been his last attempt at air travel.

"Nobody knows how I feel about planes — at least I don't think they do. For short trips I drive all night and keep my appointments. But the short trips are getting longer and longer."

Without early intervention, the fear of air travel, like any phobia, may come to affect almost every aspect of daily living. To preserve his social image of calm and confidence, Roy adopted a personality that was not his own. Outwardly he displayed composure and energy as in the past, while inwardly he developed greater and greater fear. Playing this role not only took energy but placed still another stress in his path.

Roy was now continually manufacturing excuses for taking shorter trips, and devising schedules for destinations within driving distance, to make it appear that he had flown. This was hard work, time-consuming and draining. In addition, he had to fend off pleas from his concerned wife, who was urging him to seek help. The widening spiral isolated Roy from his familiar supports and made him an increasingly stressed, defensive individual.

I suggested that Roy relieve some of the pressure on himself by discussing this problem with his superior, acting as if he had just been hit with this fear. Although risky, this maneuver would eliminate the auxiliary fear of accidental disclosure. Denial had been adding to the stress of his flying fear. By admitting his fear in this manner, he would accomplish two things: obtain relief from the strain of maintaining a lie, and form a supportive alliance with his superior. Considering his motivation and natural imaginative capability, I told Roy he could say that his doctor expected him to be flying in approximately ten weeks. (Later, Roy told me that the vice president in charge of his department had been more sympathetic than he had ever expected.)

By seeking professional help and confronting his fear, Roy had taken the first of the basic steps that can bring phobic behavior and affected life patterns back into harmony with reality. His act of assertion limited the widening effect the fear had on his professional life and prevented fear of an authority figure (his boss) from further interacting with his fear of flying.

I began to outline for Roy the next basic step in mastering his fear. I learned that he had recently undergone a full medical checkup, and that his physician had found no physical problems. Since eating patterns play a major role in both physical and psychological health, I asked Roy to describe a typical day's diet.

"Well, I have coffee with a couple of sugars at about seven," he said. "There never seems to be time for breakfast, and I don't miss it anyway, because I always break for coffee and Danish around ten o'clock. Lunch, when I have it, could be anything. It's generally with a customer, so I have a cocktail — which helps me relax a little. Then I drink a couple of coffees and have a candy bar or two during the afternoon. At home we relax with a drink before dinner and then the usual: meat, potatoes, vegetable, and dessert."

His eating pattern was characteristic of many phobics and anxious patients: high carbohydrate diet, with sugar and stimulants throughout the day. These patients are innocent victims of nutritional neglect. People who eat this way are physically stressed from within. They are creating a physical condition that makes it more difficult for them to deal with psychological conflicts and environmental stressors that are part and parcel of everyday life.

Roy was surprised to learn that everything in his nutritional profile was upside down. His best meal of the day was supper, followed by a relaxed evening at home. Upon awakening to face a demanding day, his body craved food and received none. Instead, it was hit with stimulants and deprived of nutrients. Each morning rush was a stressful experience, leaving him physically unable to deal with the pressures of his life.

We began with sugar and fear. "Sugar?" Roy looked amazed. "But I take sugar for energy. I get tired during the day and it gives me a lift."

People with Roy's eating habits become tired and depressed precisely because they *have* been eating sugar. In fact, that is frequently *all* they are eating. I suggested to Roy that he might suffer from occasional headaches during the day, combined with disorientation and irritability. He was surprised that I should know.

There are many sugars in nature, but only one of them feeds fear. It is refined sugar, or sucrose. "Refined" means that the sugar is extracted from large amounts of natural material, stripped of all nutrients, and packaged in a highly concentrated form. Unlike raw sugar, it does not contain any vitamins or minerals. Furthermore, when it is sold, it is in the form of a highly complex molecule that must be broken down, and the body requires B-complex vitamins and minerals to assimilate it.

Refined sugar, then, creates a "drain" on the body when it is ingested, drawing vitamins and minerals from the body system. We will detail its broad impact on the emotions later. But the most immediate effect of refined sugar, and the most devastating for the air-travel phobic, is its effect on the muscles of the body.

Muscle Testing for Sugar Sensitivity

Dr. George Goodheart is credited with establishing the discipline known as applied kinesiology. Those trained in kinesiology apply many tests to determine the effects of foods, jaw posture, and various chemicals on the muscle system. For our purpose, only the deltoid muscle in the shoulder and the sartorius muscle of the leg will be used as indicators of overall muscle strength. To check your sugar-muscle sensitivity you need:

- A friend
- One or two drops of honey (pure)
- 40–60 crystals of refined sugar
- A chair

Drop your jaw and do not allow your teeth to touch. Turn off fluorescent lights, remove high-heeled shoes, metal neck chains, and glasses with metal bridges. Stand facing your friend (as in the illustrations beginning on page 87). If you are right-handed, extend your left arm straight out in line with the shoulder, palm toward the floor (if left-handed, use the right arm). Have the other person push down on your wrist with a steadily increasing pressure while you resist with all available strength. Note arm movement and resistance.

Next, sit in a chair and cross your legs, with the top leg midway up the thigh of the lower leg. Again, the friend should test your strength. Grasping the top leg at the ankle, he or she should try to uncross your legs by pulling straight out from the body.

Stand again and on your tongue place one or two drops of honey, which contains unrefined, natural sugars. Wait 15 or 20 seconds and repeat the arm and leg tests. There is usually no appreciable difference.

Rinse your mouth with water, wait about five minutes to eliminate fatigue, then place the granules of refined (white) sugar on your tongue. After another 15 or 20 second wait, try the muscle tests again. This time have the friend test your strong, dominant arm as well as the weak one, and also test both ankles.

Roy, who was conditioned to expect strength from sugar, found, to his great surprise, that even his strong arm collapsed to his side after refined sugar was placed on his tongue. The pressure came from nothing more than my little finger against his wrist. He commented on the intense strain he felt trying to resist this slight downward pressure. A measuring device called a dynamometer showed that after the sugar, his shoulder muscles could resist only 10 pounds of pressure and his legs could resist less than 35 pounds. We calculated his overall strength loss at about 60 percent.

The calculations are rather simple: For Roy's Arm:

1) $\dfrac{\#\text{lbs. to yield after sugar}}{\#\text{lbs. to yield before sugar}} = X$ $\dfrac{10 \text{ lbs.}}{25 \text{ lbs.}} = .40$

2) $1.00 - X = L$ $1.00 - .40 = .60$

3) $L \times 100 = \text{percent lost}$ $.60 \times 100 = 60 \text{ percent lost}$

Actually, as done in the laboratory, we measure both the number of pounds pressure to yield and the rate of yielding; that is, how fast the muscles collapse. (See graph on page 89.)

The discovery that ingestion of refined sugar results in immediate muscle weakness is a recent one to the scientific community. All the available evidence points to the fact that refined sugar weakens, to some degree, every muscle we can test. The weakening effect is rapid, occurring from five to twenty-five seconds after sugar touches the tongue. At present, there is no known medical explanation for the phenomenon, but the direct pathway to the brain has been observed (Kare, Shechter, Grossman, and Roth [1969]). Roy's 60-percent strength loss is not too unusual for people who have fears; nor is it anything to worry about. The detrimental effects of refined sugar will presently become clear, but if you are determined to fly with ease, you can help yourself right now by beginning to avoid refined

Testing the arm for sugar sensitivity. Note that the palm faces downward. Jaw is loose, teeth are not clenched. This man is right-handed, so the test begins with the weaker left arm.

After a few grains of refined sugar are placed on the tongue, the arm is perceptibly weaker. Notice amount of movement with only slight pressure from one finger placed on the wrist.

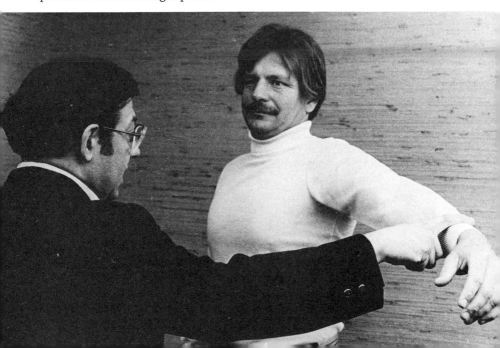

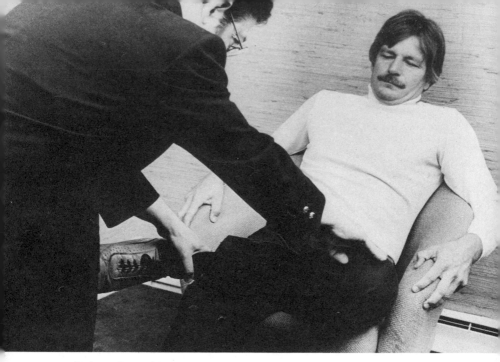

Before the subject takes sugar, the leg cannot be moved from this position.

Sartorius muscle loses strength, and leg moves easily under force of one hand, after ingestion of refined sugar.

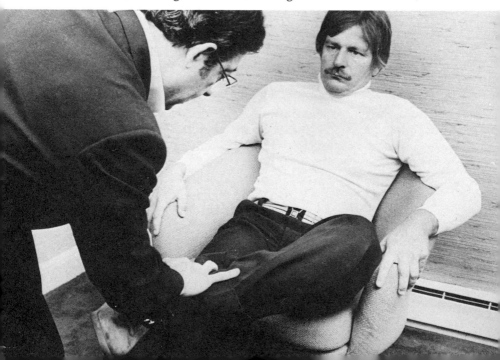

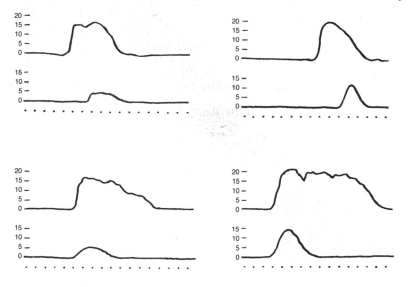

FORCE TRANSDUCER PRINTOUT OF DELTOID MUSCLE STRENGTH WITH AND WITHOUT SUGAR

Comparison of muscle strength of arms and legs, before and after one-half gram refined sugar placed on tongue. Vertical marks to the left of tracings indicate five-pound increments from baseline. Horizontal dots represent one-second time periods. In tracing the records, the pen moved from left to right. Upper left pair is the record of the left arm; upper right pair is a record of the right arm. Lower left pair is the record of the left leg and lower right pair the record of the right leg. The upper trace of each pair is the strength (pounds over time) before sugar; the lower trace is the strength after sugar.

sugar. It's in ice cream, cake, and soft drinks — the obvious foods. But it is also present in some not-so-obvious items like canned soup and ketchup. Instead of refined sugar, you can buy "sugar in the raw" (turbinado) at your supermarket, or purchase fructose or natural honey at a health-food store. Since fructose and honey are sweeter than sucrose, less is needed (a slight bonus in calorie reduction). If you test these unrefined sugars you will find that they do not weaken the muscles.

Baseball, Apple Pie, and Refined Sugar

Many Americans will be skeptical of the muscle-sensitivity test. This is understandable because what it tells us goes against accepted values. All through our lives, sugar has been pumped into our bodies. It was in the bottle formula most of us drank as babies. As children, our rewards were in the form of candy. Few things can rival sweets in delivering instant gratification and a feeling of security. How many desk drawers contain boxes of chocolates, to which many of us are so addicted that we must have them available all day long? Sugar symbolizes many things, not the least of which is love. To challenge all of this is, in a sense, to challenge a part of ourselves.

But muscle sensitivity to refined sugar also characterizes all the people I have tested. Some are affected only slightly, while others experience a dramatic loss of strength and endurance. The majority show a moderate loss of strength on the order of forty to sixty percent. The muscle-sensitivity effect caused by refined sugar is neuromuscular and not digestive. The change in the body is too rapid for the sugar to be absorbed into the blood.

However, the weakness itself is not half as dangerous as the subtle psychological reaction that may follow. In order to compensate for the loss in strength, our muscle system forces the muscles to work more and has to recruit other muscles to assist these weakened muscles. The brain cannot detect this weakness and compensation, but can detect the resulting subtle rise in body tension. These bouts of alternating weakness and compensating tension constitute a chronic stress. The tension is frequently attributed mistakingly to job pressures, the children, a difficult examination at school, low self-esteem, or psychological problems. At the end of the day, fatigue, irritability, or exhaustion may be greater than warranted.

Most of us cannot detect the changes in our body resulting from the ingestion of refined sugar. Any resultant drop in performance or feeling is likely to be attributed to more salient events of the day or targets of psychological conflict. With our perception deceived, there is fertile ground for even more distortions associated with our fear and anxiety. Events may seem too much to contend with. Self-esteem may suffer because we don't feel like doing things that others seem to take in stride.

A small percentage of the people I have tested are able to notice the effect of refined sugar on the tongue almost immediately. They break out in a sweat, and their hands tremble and become cold and clammy. They may experience slight disorientation and feel a weakening in the knees. These people are not prone to attribute the effects to fear or anxiety, because the association with sugar is clear.

At present, we are ascertaining the muscle-weakening effect empirically. Although it is still not clear to scientists how refined sugar crystals attack the body's neurological system, some have suggested that it may be through the nerves under the tongue, which are connected, to the deep parts of the brain. There are some scientists who reject this phenomenon outright, because the effect does not fit with their concept of the body and its nervous system. They attribute the effect to suggestion. Others tell us to ignore the phenomenon because no one knows *why* it works. In the history of science, discoveries have usually been made in the form of *functional relationships:* rubber falls on a stove and is vulcanized, or a block of wood sinks in water to the point where it displaces its own weight in water. In short, A plus B results in C. *Why* A and B result in C is in the realm of theory. We can utilize the discovery of the muscle-sensitivity effect and the implications it has on our everyday health while the scientists labor to determine the whys.

Once refined sugar has been digested, it creates energy that is potentially even more damaging for phobics and anxious people than is muscle weakness. The muscles may be inhibited in their ability to use the energy that suddenly surges into the body. Some may feel that the body is overwhelmed with emotion. A sudden charge in the system, accompanied by an undetectable loss of strength or a feeling that one is incapable of acting, may stimulate an anxiety attack. For others, *capability* is the key. Such people identify with their muscles, their ability to move effectively, to attack the environment. They need to feel in control at all times. When they have the energy and the urge to do something, they also have to feel capable of performing. With muscles weakened, feedback from the muscles following action may be diminished. Perhaps the most devastating result of sugar-muscle sensitivity for these people is the subtle feeling of incapability caused by energy in conflict with weakness. Generations have been brought up on the correct assumption that sugar will give a burst of energy. But now we are becoming aware that the muscle-sensitivity effect of sugar demands that a person recruit more muscles to produce the same amount of work, and that this may involve untold psychological and emotional consequences.

Roy was a jogger, and it was easy for him to see that a sugared drink could give him extra energy and then take it away. "With sugar-weakened muscles, it might take three quarters of a mile's worth of energy to run only half a mile." For the first time, Roy laughed. "I was just thinking. What's all this have to do with my flying problem? I certainly don't expect to go running up and down the aisles."

I pointed out to Roy that he kept his stomach muscles tight and breathed with the muscles of his upper chest (thoracic breathing) — something that would require attention later. For the time being, I asked him to consider what happens when the need for more oxygen occurs while one is under stress in an airplane that is pressurized to an equivalent of 5000 feet above sea level. Weakened by sugar, all of those upper body muscles have to work extra hard to expand and contract the chest. The extra work requires more energy and oxygen simply to move the air in and out of the body. At 5000 feet, the air is thinner than at sea level, so more air has to be moved through the lungs to obtain the needed amount of oxygen. In a person whose muscles are highly sensitive to sugar, the weakened muscles call for even more oxygen to do added work. Later, the metabolism of sugar calls for more oxygen too. As a result, many muscles use a lot of oxygen to get comparatively little oxygen into the body to meet its needs. People who are caught in this vicious circle feel that they are not getting enough air, a feeling that immediately causes anxiety, which in turn leads to a demand for even more oxygen.

"I know the feeling well," Roy said, "and it is one of the reasons why I don't fly. It's like suffocating."

Many people who breathe like Roy complain of tightness or heaviness in the chest on hot, humid summer days. I've noticed that these are the same people who feel tense and anxious in crowds, elevators, and closed-in places. There's a simple reason for this. On hot days, the air becomes thinner at ground level. These thoracic breathers, weakened by sugar or not, are trying to get oxygen out of oxygen-thin air. Add the humidity and you have heavy, water-laden air, which puts even more stress on the upper body muscles. The result is the feeling that a weight is pressing on the chest, or that a band of tension is extending across it. We will refer to this form of stressful thoracic breathing as *strap-tension* breathing. Because strap-tension breathing is frequently associated with anxiety, depression, and panic, its occurrence in response to environmental conditions may trigger these emotions. (The next chapter, incidentally, will be devoted to breathing.)

Returning to the trip during which Roy's fear of flying began, I asked him if he had eaten a snack in flight. It was becoming clear that what he had eaten had played a role in the events of that day. "The coffee with sugar and the Danish didn't really make up for my missed breakfast. I'm glad it's not all in my head."

I told him that a number of things had come together and that some of them were not "in his head." Not only what he ate but what he didn't eat, when he smoked, and how he breathed were factors that interacted with his psychological way of dealing with stress. I explained to him that the obvious factors could be changed without much effort. Once we had stabilized his diet and retrained him in relaxed breathing, we could deal with the psychological factors that remained.

Roy responded to this as many clients do in the early hours of psychological consultation. He became motivated to confront his fear problem actively, because there were relatively simple things he could do immediately: cut down on refined sugar, eat a balanced diet, talk to a superior at work, and learn how to use the SUDS level. Positive results, no matter how small, from these simple changes are of diagnostic value for the psychologist, but, more important, they convey a sense of mastery to the client. Rekindling the ability to control emotions is important in dealing with a problem such as inappropriate fear, because the feeling of powerlessness itself engenders fear. Relaxation training and desensitization proceed more easily on a firm nutritional foundation. There are fewer emotional fluctuations due to erratic diet; and a well-balanced diet results in a reduction in tension. The simple act of scheduling times to eat during the day (without television or newspaper, away from the desk and phones) is itself an act of mastery over the pressures that afflict your life. The act of eating is a natural tranquilizer that can both relieve the stresses of the day and fortify one for the stressors ahead. It usually takes two weeks to stabilize the diet before these benefits will be noticed.

A few of my colleagues have recently published books promoting quick psychological cures and easy routes to eliminating fear. (One book even purports to cure every major fear in one hour!) These, in my opinion, do more harm than good, because they engender skepticism toward more pragmatic psychological principles that, with practice, can help large numbers of people to help themselves. You can achieve comfort in flight, regardless of your level of discomfort; but in order to learn the skills involved, there must be a stable foundation and step-by-step preparation.

All the Caffeine Isn't in Coffee

I also asked Roy to avoid caffeine as much as possible in the two-week period before his scheduled return visit. Caffeine consciousness is a good habit for people with fears and anxiety. It's also important to remember that caffeine is present in tea, cola drinks, cocoa, chocolate, and some headache remedies. What is commonly known as "coffee nerves" is really the result of caffeine stimulating both your nervous and endocrine systems. In the endocrine system, two hormone "messengers" are released. They are epinephrine and insulin. Epinephrine makes the blood vessels constrict, raises the heart rate and the blood pressure, and increases the need for oxygen. The feedback of these reactions to the brain looks very much like a mild anxiety attack. "Caffeine can raise blood-sugar levels in diabetics; but, by stimulating insulin increase, it can lower blood-sugar levels in nondiabetics and hypoglycemics," according to Drs. Cheraskin and Ringsdorf in their book *Psychodietetics*. One cup of coffee contains 90 milligrams of caffeine, and just one to three cups can set up an emotional reaction. When a person skips breakfast, has coffee and a cigarette, and then drinks more coffee on a plane, he or she is primed for an even greater emotional reaction.

"I knew there was caffeine in coffee and tea," Roy responded, "but how much caffeine can there be in a chocolate bar?"

I showed him my copy of *Psychodietetics*, which mentions 20 milligrams of caffeine for each ounce of chocolate (or a little more than a quarter of the amount found in a cup of coffee).

Roy was beginning to learn that he had to put the odds for success in his favor by avoiding substances that feed fear. Not only does caffeine cause a stronger reaction in the anxious person than it does in someone of a more calm nature, the caffeine *habit* contributes as well. It frequently carries classic symptoms of addiction: tolerance, discomfort at withdrawal, and craving after its use has been eliminated. All of these are, in themselves, stressors.

Roy could reduce his intake from six cups a day to one or two cups. He could avoid using refined sugar in his coffee. And no withdrawal symptoms would be likely to occur if he stayed away from caffeine a couple of hours before relaxation exercises or, in the future, before boarding a flight.

With caffeine and anxiety, you're damned if you do and better off if you don't. Also, beware of headache remedies that contain caffeine. You'll do just as well taking aspirin without the 20 to 30 milligrams of caffeine. Learn to read labels and you'll be well on your way to comfortable flying.

If you, along with Roy, are wondering what you *can* drink to help prepare your body for desensitization, consider the whole world of *natural* fruit juices. All airlines serve orange juice, and many now offer apple juice along with the other beverages. I generally recommend decaffeinated coffee, herbal tea sweetened with honey, and lemonade with an artificial sweetener. You can always bring fresh fruit along with you — grapes and apples are ideal.

Cigarettes, Whiskey, and the Wild Blue Yonder

Roy noticed me looking at the burning end of his freshly lit cigarette. "All right, what about smoking and fear of flying?" he asked.

I reminded him that most of us who smoke are aware that it is a hazard. At best it's a calculated risk, but that's not our concern here. Psychologically, nicotine is a stimulant. Like caffeine, it increases muscle tension and heart rate and also causes constriction of the blood vessels.

In the lungs, carbon dioxide and carbon monoxide from cigarette smoke reduce the proportion of oxygen inhaled. This may interfere with your body's stress-coping ability. Carbon monoxide hinders the capability of your blood to carry its full measure of oxygen to the tissues. Nutritionally, nicotine lowers the level of vitamin C. This is the major vitamin for coping with stress. However, if you smoke, you can help yourself by eliminating refined sugar, steadily keeping your blood-sugar level high with proteins, and increasing your intake of vitamin C. Combined with cutting down on smoking, this program will help you tolerate the psychological effects of nicotine, even though the physical damage can never be eliminated.

While we were discussing the influence of dietary habits on Roy's ability to get rid of his air-travel anxiety, the subject turned to alcohol. Like most young executives, he sought relief from on-the-job pressures through an "occasional" cocktail or highball. The problem with this is that alcohol is an extremely strong drug with a treacherous psychological track record. Our national blindness to alcohol abuse is in part due to the widespread acceptance of drinking on social occasions.

In a pamphlet entitled "Alcohol: America's Most Widely Misused Drug," the New York State Department of Mental Hygiene, defining this drug, places the psychological emphasis properly: "We do recognize alcohol as a *mood-changing* substance. Most social drinkers use alcohol for this purpose, to some extent at least."

I will not even touch on the fact that more than seven million Americans have developed a destructive dependence on this drug. But I will say unequivocally that fearful fliers should not drink and fly, nor should they drink and attempt relaxation or desensitization exercises.

We are trying to create awareness of long-denied anxiety and tension, so that we can combat that anxiety with relaxation. Alcohol is, in many ways, a drug of denial. It masks both mental and physical processes. Thus, after a drink, anxiety may be boiling away in your system, yet you will not notice its adverse effects (except in the form of the need for another drink!). Physically, alcohol can go so far as to provoke an angina attack, while camouflaging the pain. Unlike anesthetizing one's feelings and rendering oneself chemically powerless in the face of emotion, confronting the emotion and mastering it pays off in increased self-esteem.

The Committee on Alcoholism and Drug Dependence of the American Medical Association further describes the real psychological effects of alcohol:

> Ingestion of small quantities of alcohol usually reduces feelings of anxiety and worry and causes a mild but general reduction of inhibitions. If drinking is continued beyond euphoria and exhilaration, dysfunctional reactions such as aggression, antagonism, depression and psychosis may appear, as well as disruption of speech and memory.

Just what constitutes "small quantities of alcohol" may vary from person to person, and, within each person, from time to time, depending on existing emotional state, nutrition, and environment. Bear in mind that drinking at high altitudes is deceptive. We lose our perspective, which is based on judgment of ground-level quantities. The AMA committee says that a 150-pound individual can metabolize approximately two-thirds of an ounce of straight whiskey or eight ounces of beer within an hour. Any drinking over the rate of two-thirds of an ounce an hour might cause symptoms of drinking "beyond the euphoria and exhilaration." But at cruising altitude and pressure, the two ounces of straight whiskey in each of those little bottles has the force of approximately three ounces. In flight, two drinks are equivalent to three at ground level. The more you relax in flight, the more potent the drinks appear to be. I treated a patient who would drink two manhattans before boarding, then drink constantly in flight. She felt no effects of the alcohol while in the air, because of her high anxiety level. Once the plane landed, however, she immediately became drunk and often had to be assisted from the plane.

I told Roy that he could learn to slow down his racing thoughts by thought stopping, and that he could control his fears and anxieties through diet, breathing, and relaxation. The self-control that he would come to enjoy would enable him to seek alcohol not for its drug effect but for its taste and social merit.

Vitamins: A Little Help from Our Friends

After our discussion about sugar, cigarettes, and alcohol, Roy was beginning to wonder what was left for relief. I told him that many authorities suggest the use of vitamins as natural tranquilizers, to help the body cope with stress.

Vitamin C is a good example. It has been described as "the stress vitamin." We need a constant supply of vitamin C, because humans are one of the few species that cannot generate their own. The only other animals with this deficiency are apes, guinea pigs, and fruit bats. The bodies of all other animals are designed to manufacture vitamin C from glucose.

At the University of Alabama, scientists measured the vitamin C in the blood of male goats. The amount was high, at twelve grams for each 140 pounds of body weight — 200 times more than *our* recommended minimum daily requirement. When they placed a female goat in a pen with a male, his vitamin C production almost doubled, apparently in order to cope with the stress. Sex is a stress — a positive one, but a stress nonetheless. Periodic electric shocks resulted in a similar increase in the goat's vitamin C level.

Books have been written on the benefits of vitamin C, and, today, this topic is an area of great controversy in the medical profession. Not all authorities are in agreement with what the animal data imply for human needs. The human need for vitamin C was dramatically demonstrated in the eighteenth century, when the eating of limes by British sailors prevented scurvy, an affliction that caused weakness, aches in the muscles and joints, shortness of breath, coarse skin, bleeding gums, and infections that would not heal. Scurvy is rare today, but some of its minor symptoms do closely resemble agitation and anxiety. To ingest the equivalent of 1000 milligrams of vitamin C, one would have to drink about eight cups of fresh orange juice. (Pasteurized orange juice may contain less biologically active vitamin C than fresh or frozen juice.) The recommended daily requirement in the United States is 45 milligrams each day, as opposed to 125 milligrams per day in Russia. Most authorities agree that doses larger than 1000 milligrams begin to approach medical treatment and should best be carried out under medical supervision, since doses above 4000 milligrams may cause blockage in the urinary tract and, in some, aching bones. Vitamin C is eliminated from the body if it is not utilized. It is helpful to distribute intake of vitamin C throughout the day.

Many nutritionists feel that smokers need even more vitamin C than normal, because vitamin C interacts with chemicals in the smoke and is thereby removed from the body. Also, stress, whether emotional or physical, uses up extra amounts of vitamin C. It probably will not be clear within the next few years exactly how much vitamin C is required by each of us for our particular needs; but drinking fruit juices instead of carbonated beverages and eating fresh fruit instead of pastry will probably supply you with sufficient vitamin C to begin coping with stress. Bell peppers and fresh strawberries are also rich sources of this vitamin. Some writers, such as Dr. H. L. Newbold (*Mega-Nutrients for Your Nerves*), feel that vitamin C has value in combating environmental and emotional stress. There are others who feel that the vitamin functions like a lid on the peaks of anxiety, holding it within more normal limits. Still others feel that B-complex vitamins and calcium are beneficial in canceling the effects of anxiety. Consulting with your physician, or one trained in nutrition, is a good idea, should you wish to use vitamins to assist in combating your fear.

Vitamins and proper foods are necessary ingredients in dealing with emotional control. We cannot go wrong if we increase the amount of fresh fruits, juices, and vegetables in our diets.

Hypoglycemic Reactions: Sweet Mystery of Menacing Proportions

I suggested that Roy might want to get an empty bowl and measure 30 heaping teaspoons of refined sugar into it. Then look at the pile.

That's what one day in the average American sugar eater's diet looks like to the average American pancreas. Every day a great many people in this country consume at least seven ounces of sugar, which is equivalent to a pile of 30 heaping teaspoonfuls. This adds up to approximately 170 pounds each year. The per capita estimate of sugar consumption has not changed since 1920 — approximately 100 pounds per person per year (according to the Retail Confectioners Institute). But that calculation includes every individual in the United States, young and old. Some are under five years old and eat less sugar than adults, and not all adults consume that much; many sugar eaters consume close to 170 pounds per year.

Roy said, "You're telling me that I may be eating more than my body weight in sugar every year?"

I told him that one of my patients drank eight cups of coffee per day, with two teaspoons of sugar in each cup (sixteen teaspoons), ate two jelly doughnuts before lunch (three teaspoons), had a piece of cake after lunch (three teaspoons), drank about a quart of cola a day (six to eight teaspoons), ate a candy bar at four o'clock (two teaspoons), and then had a pint of ice cream while watching TV (six teaspoons). With additional "hidden" sugar in ketchup and canned vegetables (another two teaspoons), her intake totaled to about forty teaspoons per day. She was a very anxious 120-pound woman.

The facts about nutrition and behavior have been obscured by appetite-appeal advertising and small-print packaging. The disclosure on packaging seldom gives the weight or percentage of each ingredient. For example, the U.S. Department of Agriculture released a study on breakfast cereals which showed that popular children's cereals average 42 percent sugar. Cheerios, on the other hand, has only 3 percent sugar. Nabisco Shredded Wheat (0.6 percent), Quaker Oats and Puffed Wheat (0.5 percent) and Puffed Rice (0.1 percent) have the lowest percentages. I handed Roy a bottle of ketchup I keep in my office for the purpose of illustrating small-print packaging, explaining that manufacturers list the ingredients according to quantity, with the highest first.

"Tomatoes, vinegar, sugar," he read from the label. "Salt, onion powder spice, natural flavoring — this means that sugar is the *third* highest ingredient after tomatoes and vinegar."

I then showed Roy a salad-dressing label that listed water, vinegar, sugar, and salt as ingredients, and a popular mayonnaise that indicated more sugar than egg yolk.

Acquiring the habit of reading labels will allow you to estimate your sugar intake. Awareness of sugar content can benefit all fearful fliers and is extremely important, because, paradoxically, the addition of refined sugar in the system can actually lower available blood sugar; the same thing happens to the body in a condition called reactive hypoglycemia (*hypo* = low, *glycemia* = blood sugar).

Blood sugar, or glucose, is the fuel that powers the brain and central nervous system. In hypoglycemic individuals, the fuel mixture is so lean that the physical-emotional engine can't run smoothly; it sputters and stalls. Irritability, depression, anxiety, and fear are some of the "backfires." Since our mental and emotional health is affected, all of us can benefit from a general knowledge of sugar and its effect on body chemistry.

Your body has a number of accelerators. We introduced them in chapter 1, where Oog, the Neanderthal man, had to step on the gas to escape the cave lion. One of these hormone accelerators, epinephrine, is involved in hypoglycemic reactions. It speeds up the heart, raises blood pressure, and — most important — signals the liver to release its stored glycogen, to raise the blood-sugar level for muscle activity.

You also have a brake system. It is controlled by a hormone called insulin, which burns off the excess when the blood-sugar level gets too high and causes the fuel mixture to become too rich.

Just as there are several kinds of knocks in an automobile engine, there are several kinds of hypoglycemia:

Fasting Hypoglycemia: Chronic low blood sugar resulting from a physical cause, for example from a tumor. A diabetic who takes too much insulin suffers from fasting hypoglycemia. This rare form causes headaches, mental confusion, personality changes, and even convulsions or coma.

Reactive Hypoglycemia: A more common hypoglycemic reaction, which occurs two to four hours after consumption of highly refined carbohydrates or sugars (breads with refined white flour, sweet desserts, candy). These foods cause an immediate sharp rise in blood sugar, and signal insulin to put on the brakes by burning off some of the excess. Refined carbohydrates characteristically are metabolized faster than the body can slow down the output of insulin, however. Insulin remains in the blood after the sugar level has begun returning to normal. A peak load of insulin attacking a normal sugar level inevitably causes low blood sugar. To the brain this looks like an emergency, so epinephrine is called on to muster more glycogen from the liver. As a result, one may feel nervous, irritated, anxious, light-headed, weak-kneed, or dizzy.

Idiopathic Hypoglycemia: For no known medical reason, blood-sugar level can drop. Symptoms are the same as in reactive hypoglycemia.

A person who under ordinary conditions would not experience the symptoms of a hypoglycemic reaction may react quite differently under chronic or acute stress (especially after skipping a meal). When the life histories of phobics and individuals suffering from free-floating anxiety and muscle tension are observed, simple patterns emerge. If not stressed, they can miss meals and feel fine. When they experience stress and suffer attacks of anxiety, they usually have not eaten during the preceding four to six hours.

I suggest that the term *stress-reactive hypoglycemia* be used to describe many patients who were formerly diagnosed as idiopathic hypoglycemic. Under conditions of stress, the body steadily releases epinephrine in preparation for an emergency. Obediently, the required blood sugar enters the blood stream from the liver. All may go well with proper nutrition, but when there is no quick replenishment of blood sugar, deficits occur. Most contemporary stress is not physical exertion (such as running from a lion). Instead, we suffer sedentary stress. We sit and fume after an argument or feel apprehensive about an office meeting. Contemporary stress doesn't burn sugar the way running does, so the amount of blood sugar goes up — accelerator, brake, accelerator, brake. The end result of this jolting ride is a series of blood-sugar dips and hypoglycemic symptoms. Add sugared coffee and cigarettes, and the ride becomes even more jolting. A typical phobic eating pattern like Roy's is actually an epic struggle between epinephrine (the accelerator) and insulin (the brake).

If we took a look at Roy's life from the perspective of his pancreas, here's what we might see: First thing in the morning, blood sugar hasn't been replaced all night and is low. Roy's pancreas is suddenly hit with stimulation and sugar at the same time. Nicotine from cigarettes and caffeine from coffee trigger epinephrine acceleration. Sucrose from the refined sugar Roy put in his coffee causes his blood-sugar level to peak. Roy slaps on the brakes by releasing insulin. This halts the rise in blood sugar, overshoots, and sends blood-sugar levels plummeting. Meanwhile, epinephrine is screaming for more sugar. Stress causes the release of more epinephrine. At ten o'clock, a huge dose of refined sugar from more coffee and a Danish comes barreling through. While Roy is pumping insulin for all he's worth, caffeine and nicotine go roaring by with epinephrine close in tow. Now glucose levels climb astronomically. This is a challenge to any self-respecting pancreas, and Roy reacts to the occasion with a mighty outburst of insulin (which, of course, again overshoots, reducing the blood sugar to a new level of deficiency).

By lunchtime, Roy's blood-sugar level is again low. He feels nervous, depressed, and tired. He has a temple headache and he "needs a drink." For the pancreas, the worst is yet to come. His liver has been steadily releasing glycogen to answer the repeated calls for glucose. Since carbohydrates and protein have not been readily available because of his poor diet, he begins to draw glucose and protein from his own muscle tissue. Roy's sales job is competitive, placing him under constant stress. Pressure and emotional strain combine with his nutritional habits to stimulate a steady flow of epinephrine, as well as associated physical symptoms of tension. In the drink rests a hope of calm. Interestingly, the first thing he orders in the restaurant is not food but a drink of alcohol. This is absorbed immediately. The liver now becomes occupied with metabolizing the alcohol, disturbing the blood-sugar balance even more. Cheraskin and Ringsdorf note that "Although alcohol by itself does not directly stimulate insulin release, an abnormally large amount of insulin will be released if the intake of alcohol is followed by an intake of refined carbohydrates." The pancreas, when primed by alcohol, brakes at the slightest instigation. Following his drink, Roy's lunch paradoxically results in a lowering of his blood sugar. Now begins his ill-prepared struggle with afternoon stress. A feeling of exhaustion may set in. Roy would like to go somewhere and lie down for a rest.

"So *that's* why I usually feel completely drained in the afternoons," Roy said.

I told him there might be other causes, but that stress-reactive hypoglycemia was a likely candidate, in light of his eating habits and the pressure of his job.

On the other hand, it is easy to prevent hypoglycemic reactions. First, we should think of food as fuel. That's really what it is. Like fuel, food burns at different rates. If you eat the way Roy does, you are jolting your body with a constant series of explosions. Sugar and carbohydrates burn too fast. A good diet includes plenty of proteins and fats for a slow, steady fire in your furnace.

Morning

The age-old advice about eating a good breakfast is still valid. Have some meat, eggs, and perhaps a slice of toast with margarine or butter. You've had no food in your system all night, and breakfast has to make up the sugar deficiency as well as prepare your body for its energy demands throughout the morning. Orange juice or any other fruit juice will get natural sugar into your body fast. If you are in a hurry, a slice of whole-wheat or natural-grain toast with natural peanut butter (made without sugar) and honey will serve as an emergency protein supply.

Instead of sweet rolls around ten o'clock, try a handful of nuts and raisins, cheese and crackers, or grapes. These slowly metabolized foods are much more likely to help you avoid fatigue, depression, and irritability. If you can't bring yourself to cut out regular coffee altogether, make every other cup decaffeinated. Remember to use an artificial sweetener, honey, or fructose — not refined sugar.

Afternoon

When you look at a luncheon menu, search for protein: meat, fish, cheese, and eggs. Many restaurants offer a hamburger with cottage cheese. If you want a drink at lunch or dinner, try having light wine with the meal rather than a strong cocktail before you eat. You'll enjoy the extra energy you have in the afternoon.

Most people need another protein snack around three o'clock. A hard-boiled egg or a couple of peanut-butter crackers is a good choice. Use imagination and any paperback diet guide that lists the protein content of foods. If you crave sweets, eat fruit instead of candy or pastry.

Evening

Dinner is usually planned around meat or fish anyway, but make sure you take it easy on the carbohydrates — potatoes, bread, macaroni, and noodles. Before you go to bed, have a protein snack to help your brain and nervous system while you're at rest. A glass of milk will do, although one doctor I know recommends celery stuffed with natural peanut butter.

Roy wondered if he would gain weight by eating so frequently. This is another common misconception. Protein energy is used, not stored as fat. This means that a diet high in protein is not likely to make you heavier. In fact, you may lose some weight as a result of the elimination of excess sugar and refined carbohydrates.

Before our first appointment ended, I scheduled another one in two weeks. I asked Roy to rate his daily tension levels on the Subjective Units of Discomfort scale outlined in chapter 2, so I could check on his progress. On the next visit, we would talk about breathing and relaxation.

After a moment's pause, Roy said, "You know, I think I'll begin carrying some candy around in my pocket — to give my competitors when we're selling against each other."

A Reminder

The milder psychological symptoms that have been documented as being associated with low blood-sugar level include:

dizziness	lack of coordination
headacches	tremors
fatigue	fast heartbeat
muscle pains	noticeable heartbeat
muscle cramps	irritability
inability to concentrate	shortness of breath
anxiety	noise sensitivity
depression	general restlessness

These symptoms may be associated with other medical problems; but a close look at your diet and some small changes in your eating habits may greatly improve your quality of life and help you fly fearlessly.

5

Autonomic Quiescence

Easy Breathing Equals Flying with Ease

In our bodies, some things just happen. Our pupils contract when we leave a darkened movie theater and emerge in bright sunlight. Digestive juices flow when food enters the mouth. The heart beats faster when we are frightened, and the breathing rate increases to take in added oxygen. These are unconscious acts, the work of the autonomic nervous system, a wonderful "automatic pilot" that controls involuntary body functions.

Breathing is one link between conscious, voluntary behavior and the involuntary behavior of the autonomic nervous system, which affects the emotions. Students of yoga and zen are well aware of this. They have mastered the skill of breathing to slow their heartbeat, lower blood pressure, and place the body in a state of autonomic quiescence. Autonomic quiescence is the emotional counterpart of muscular relaxation. When a person is said to be relaxed, the emotional system is calm (autonomic quiescence), the muscular system is relaxed, and central process activity (thoughts) is either neutral or focused on peaceful ideation.

In this chapter we will examine easy breathing. You will learn how to breathe in such a way that you will be able to settle those butterflies in your stomach, dry up sweaty palms, and quiet the wild pounding of your heart. Using breathing to achieve autonomic quiescence is the first step in Active Stress Coping.

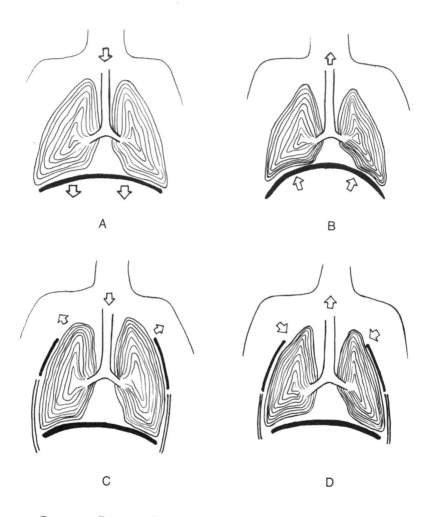

CONTRAST BETWEEN DIAPHRAGMATIC AND THORACIC BREATHING

Diaphragmatic breathing: On inhalation (A), diaphragm moves downward and air enters; on exhalation (B) diaphragm moves up, air is forced out.

Thoracic breathing: On inhalation (C), ribs move up and out and air enters; on exhalation (D), ribs are forcibly collapsed, and air leaves chest.

There are several fears associated with the fear of air travel that simply cannot be treated adequately without specific attention to retraining breathing. Claustrophobia, the abnormal fear of enclosed spaces, is almost always associated with a feeling of suffocation. People who fear elevators and crowds know this feeling well. Agoraphobia, the fear of being away from home, in supermarkets, theaters, and other public places, is also associated with breathing irregularities. Both of these fears are involved in air travel, when one is in an enclosed space, headed far away from home in the company of a large group of people. As air fares diminish, planes become more densely seated and the loading platforms more crowded. Effortless breathing, then, is *the* most important tranquilizing measure for air travelers who suffer from claustrophobia or agoraphobia. There are other fears that also can be reduced by breathing techniques. Among them are the fear of public speaking, the fear of driving an automobile on an expressway, the fear males have of urinating in a public restroom, the fear females have of suffocation during lovemaking, the fear of the dental chair, the fear of gagging when someone places an object in your mouth, and the fear of fear. With proper breathing, fear can be arrested.

"How am I doing?" asked Roy, who was lying on two pillows. We were midway through his second visit, and I was teaching him the fundamentals of diaphragmatic breathing.

Although partially under the control of the autonomic nervous system, the organs of breathing have an override feature. We can consciously control the speed, depth, and location of our breathing. The breathing apparatus resembles two balloons in a birdcage of muscle and bone. To fill these balloons with air, you can either pull all the bars of the cage outward or simply move the floor of the cage up and down. Pulling out the bars of the cage is called thoracic breathing. Thoracic breathing requires more energy, muscles, and oxygen than moving the floor of the cage, or the diaphragm. The diaphragm is a single sheet of muscle that separates the thoracic cavity (above) from

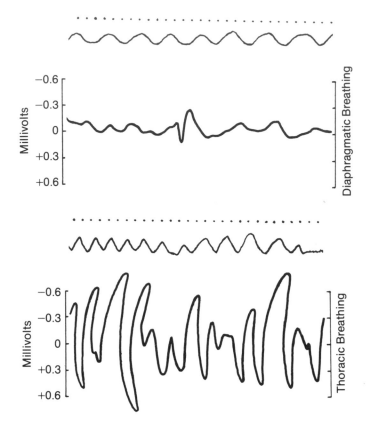

SKIN POTENTIAL RECORD

Record of a patient showing emotional arousal associated with diaphragmatic and thoracic breathing patterns. Horizontal row of dots
designates two-second time periods, as the recording pens move from
left to right. The uppermost continuous line is a record of diaphragmatic breathing. The continuous, irregular line immediately below is
a record of the skin potential, monitored from the palm of the dominant hand. The skin potential is an indicator of autonomic activity
(level of emotional arousal). The magnitude of the skin-potential
waves is given to the left of the record. The continuous line under the
middle row of dots is a record of thoracic breathing. Notice that the
skin-potential record immediately below is more active and contains
waves of significantly greater magnitude (greater autonomic arousal).

the abdominal cavity (below). Effortless, diaphragmatic breathing, which involves only this muscle, moves a great amount of air.

At the beginning of his second appointment, after Roy had settled into the easy chair, I asked him to take a deep breath. His stomach pulled inward and his chest expanded, indicating that he was a thoracic breather. Like all of us, Roy had begun life breathing in the natural way, using just the diaphragm while leaving his *rectus abdominus* muscle relaxed. (The rectus abdominus is a large sheetlike muscle that stretches from the groin to the ribs. The bellybutton is approximately at the center of this muscle.) Look at any sleeping baby and you will observe its effortless, peaceful breathing. The stomach rises and falls. This is diaphragmatic breathing.

As we grow up, our muscles become conditioned to thoracic breathing. Instead of the easygoing rhythm of "belly breathing," we adopt the more difficult chest action. To get a breath of air, thoracic breathers must coordinate several sets of muscles — the intercostals and transverse muscles that push against the upper girdle of deltoids, pectorals, and the trapezius. Thoracic breathing allows the extra breath normally needed only in an emergency. It is a labored breath. This is an emergency maneuver associated with a division of the autonomic nervous system called the sympathetic nervous system (the fight-or-flight response system). As a result, thoracic breathing sends emergency feedback along the interoceptive communication system to the brain. (See illustration, page 110.)

If in early life a child suffers from chronic fear, as the result of traumatic experiences, his or her breathing is characteristically thoracic, rapid, and shallow. Some children develop stammering or emotionally triggered asthma-like attacks that are characterized by shallow thoracic breathing.

Perhaps the golden age of thoracic breathing was the Gay Nineties, when women pinched their waists with corsets. So oxygen-starved were they that the slightest stress brought on loss of consciousness. When a horse ran away with a carriage, "strong" men stood by in loose-fitting pants held up by suspenders, while the wasp-waisted "weaker sex" swooned. Had

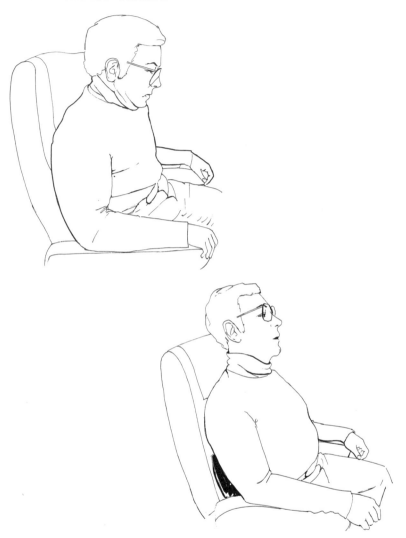

Top: The anxious flier sets himself up for trouble by grabbing the arms of the seat and tensing, locking the outer muscles across the thorax. Expanding the rib cage against this strap of tense muscles, as is done in thoracic breathing, renders a person almost incapable of dealing with anxiety. *Below:* Diaphragmatic breathing is probably the fastest method of relaxation.

the costumes been reversed, so, I suspect, would have been the reactions.

Today, we project the ideal of flat-stomached men and women, with thoracic respiration reaching the height of glorification in the centerfold of *Playboy* magazine. Slim is sexy, and so is chesty. Sex symbols, both male and female, always seem to be inhaling deep thoracic breaths. (In fact, they do hold their breaths in this fashion when photographed.) This social conditioning soon results in unconscious tension in the stomach muscle, blocking diaphragmatic breathing.

"First it was my high-school coach, and then my sergeant in the army, yelling, 'Pull in your gut!' " Roy said. "And all of those situps to flatten the stomach!"

I agreed that this was part of the conditioning that causes us to use an emergency system for everyday breathing. In an airplane pressurized to 5000 feet, panic and emergency breathing can lead to an unpleasant condition called hyperventilation.

The anxious flier sets himself up for trouble by grabbing the arms of the seat and tensing in typical "white-knuckled" position. Unknowingly, he has produced tension high in his arms and across his chest and upper back — the very muscles against which he must breathe. Expanding the rib cage against this strap of tense muscles across the upper chest, as one does in thoracic breathing, renders a person almost incapable of dealing with anxiety. The action itself creates an internal stress. Hyperpnea (labored breathing) begins.

During an anxiety attack, muscles don't act in a coordinated fashion. Thoracic breathing, because it requires the coordinated action of many muscles, quickly becomes inefficient. In order to make the chest heave, an inordinate amount of energy and oxygen must be burned. The anxious thoracic breather fights a losing battle: much oxygen is spent, very little gained. He feels suffocated, becomes more tense; the strap of tension across the chest becomes stronger, and breathing necessarily becomes more rapid and shallow, as the lungs attempt to move the air. Hyperventilation sets in, with symptoms that vary from one individual to the next.

Now the trouble begins. As his anxiety increases and his

breathing becomes faster, so he can *inhale* more oxygen, the thoracic breather *exhales* too much carbon dioxide. In the brain, a monitoring center normally maintains an ideal balance between oxygen and carbon dioxide. When this balance is upset by a drop in carbon dioxide, blood vessels in the brain are temporarily constricted, slowing the flow of oxygen and glycogen to the brain tissue. Simultaneously, blood throughout the body loses some of its oxygen-carrying capability.

A British researcher, Dr. L. C. Lum, has studied hyperventilation and found six types of symptoms:

Cardiovascular: irregular heartbeat, racing heartbeat, pains in the chest, numbness, tingling or burning sensation in the fingers.

Gastrointestinal: lump in the throat, difficulty in swallowing, stomach pains, a feeling of being "bloated."

Musculoskeletal: pains in the muscles, twitching or spasms, shaking or tremors.

Psychological: tension, anxiety.

Neurologic: blurry vision, difficulty in thinking, dizziness, creeping and crawling sensations, numbness and tingling.

General: weakness, exhaustion, fatigability, sleep disturbance, nightmares.

Both Dr. Lum and Dr. Herbert E. Walker of New York University School of Medicine maintain that hyperventilation occurs in men and women with equal frequency. June Carroll, a nurse at the Logan Airport medical station in Boston, reports that the most common complaint in the air travelers she treats is hyperventilation.

There are other effects of thoracic breathing. Squeezing the rib cage in and out places extra pressure on the heart, which is nestled in a little depression near the bottom of the left lung. Being squeezed and pushed around by interthoracic pressures makes the heart work harder. When we monitor thoracic breathers with a biofeedback machine that displays heart rate, we can clearly see that the number of beats increases with each inhalation and decreases with exhalation.

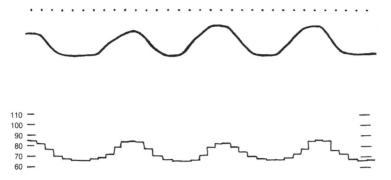

HEART RATE, THORACIC BREATHING

This graph illustrates the heart-rate fluctuations associated with thoracic breathing. The horizontal dots designate one-second time intervals, with the recording pens moving from left to right. The upper curved line is a record of thoracic respiration, while the lower step-like line is a record of the heart rate expressed on a beat-to-beat, beats-per-minute scale. The beats per minute are indicated to the left of the heart-rate record. Notice that the heart rate accelerates with every inspiration of a thoracic breath.

Reactions to this pressure may resemble the symptoms of a heart attack. For example, a young engineer became alarmed by sudden sharp pains in his arm and chest while working bent over in a cramped space below the deck of his boat. His breathing became an audible wheeze, like that of an asthma sufferer (which he was not). Three visits to an internist and a cardiogram later, he became convinced that his attack was not angina but hyperventilation. In my private practice, I find that thoracic breathers generally suffer from intermittent chest and shoulder pains that can be relieved by diaphragmatic breathing.

Dr. C. E. Wheatley of Northville, Michigan has studied the relationship between cardiac symptoms and hyperventilation. He discovered that fifteen of the ninety-five patients observed suffered chest pains from hyperventilation only.

"That happened in our office once," Roy remembered. "A woman went into a panic riding up in the elevator. She thought she was suffocating. Breathing fast and deep. The nurse put an ordinary paper bag over her face. Then she was sure she was

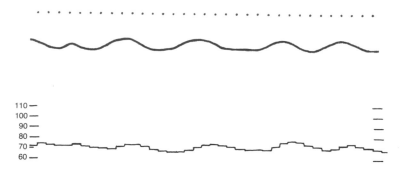

HEART RATE, DIAPHRAGMATIC BREATHING

This graph illustrates the heart-rate pattern associated with diaphragmatic breathing. This record was obtained from the same patient who demonstrated the thoracic breathing pattern above. The horizontal dots designate one-second time intervals, with the recording pens moving from left to right. The upper curved line is a record of diaphragmatic breathing, while the lower step-like line is a record of the heart rate on a beat-to-beat, beats-per-minute scale. The beats per minute are indicated to the left of the heart-rate record. Notice that the heart rate varies slightly (between 66 and 78 beats per minute), while with thoracic breathing it varied more widely (between 66 and 88 beats per minute).

going to die. But in about thirty seconds she was okay."

I told him that there are two ways to deal with hyperventilation. One method, the paper-bag treatment, increases the amount of carbon dioxide in the body by having the patient rebreathe exhaled breath. Incidentally, exhaled breath contains at least twenty percent oxygen, so the bag treatment is perfectly safe. Though good for emergencies, this is an extreme measure, since the last thing an air-starved patient wants is something placed over his or her nose and mouth.

The other way to manage hyperventilation is a long-term preventative measure: you can train yourself to breathe diaphragmatically. Diaphragmatic breathing is probably the fastest method of relaxation. It triggers a natural relaxation response, energizing the other half of the autonomic nervous system, known as the parasympathetic nervous system. While the sympathetic system prepares you to fight or run, the parasympathetic system helps you become relaxed and meditative. Heart rates slow down, the flow of blood to the brain is balanced at an efficient level, and little effort is required to gain a generous supply of oxygen by breathing. The heart rate of a diaphragmatic breather is slow and steady — with reduction of the up-and-down heart-rate pattern of the thoracic breather.

After about forty seconds of diaphragmatic breathing, you will feel a calmness within your body. This is a natural tranquilizing of the emotions. The feeling of peace and contentment seems centered in your midsection, where panic usually hatches butterflies. Hands and face become warm and comfortable.

"Sounds wonderful," said Roy. "When do I start?"

At this point I had him stretch out on the floor. To learn diaphragmatic breathing, it's best to begin in a position that favors free movement of the diaphragm.

Relax your stomach muscles by lying flat on the floor with a pillow at the small of your back. Place another pillow parallel to the spine, toward the back of your head. The two pillows together should resemble an inverted "T".

Lie back and let your shoulders droop over the second pillow. Keep buttocks flat on the floor. Place your left hand on your stomach, right hand on your chest. Throughout the diaphragmatic breathing exercise, the stomach hand should rise with each breath in and fall with each breath out. If the chest hand moves, you are going into thoracic breathing.

The two pillows together should look like an inverted "T".

The stomach hand should rise with each breath in and fall with each breath out. If the chest hand moves, you are going into thoracic breathing.

Now pick a spot on the ceiling and concentrate on it. Adopt the attitude that you have nothing else important to do. Don't feel rushed and don't worry about whether you'll get it right or not. Take a slow breath. Feel your stomach hand rise. Say the first syllable of the word *relax* to yourself — "RE . . ." Now s-l-o-w-l-y exhale and finish the word: ". . . LAX." Continue this action: "RE . . . [inhale] . . . LAX [exhale]." Make sure that your chest hand is not moving. Take your time. Breathe naturally, don't take forced, deep breaths. In time, you will learn to allow the air to leave your body without tension, like air coming out of a balloon.

After eight or ten breaths, the spot on the ceiling may be clearer to your vision than the surrounding area. In fact, your peripheral vision may become hazy and a little gray. This means your body is becoming quiescent. Soon, your eyelids may become heavy. If so, let them drift closed as you concentrate on the rise and fall of your stomach hand.

Practice soundless breathing. If you hear the air rushing out of your nose (you should not use your mouth during your early training in diaphragmatic breathing), then you are exhaling too fast. Slow down.

Some people may have trouble getting the stomach to rise and fall. If this happens, stretch your arms and place your hands over your head. This will so tighten the muscles in your chest that the only alternative, in your reclining position, is to breathe with the diaphragm. Another helpful position is with the hands at the base of the neck.

It was at this point that Roy had asked, "How am I doing?"

Roy was doing quite well. I suggested that he practice diaphragmatic breathing at least once a day, at a time when he could get away from the rush of business, when the phone wouldn't ring, and when he wouldn't be interrupted by the children.

Diaphragmatic breathing is important aboard a plane because of cabin pressurization. Air surrounds the earth like a shell, becoming thinner as we move away from the earth's surface. Breathing is easy when you're reclining in the sun on your favorite beach. At sea level, air pressure is about fifteen pounds per square inch. As you reach higher altitudes, the air thins out and breathing becomes more difficult. Modern jet planes have pressurized cabins. This means that some of the outside air is scooped into the cabin, where it builds up the pressure and makes breathing easy again.

The average pressurization in an airplane is eleven or twelve pounds per square inch, the equivalent of about 5000 feet above sea level. You generally don't feel the difference unless you become anxious and start breathing too rapidly and deeply. Diaphragmatic breathing allows you to move a great amount of air with little effort, to compensate for the reduced pressure. You can help yourself by observing a few precautions, however:

1. Drink noncarbonated beverages. The pressurization on the plane liberates carbon dioxide bubbles more quickly than usual, and holding a glass of sparkling soda under your nose can produce an invisible cloud of carbon dioxide around your head, making breathing more difficult. On the other hand, you should breathe over a carbonated drink if you begin to hyperventilate.

2. As I mentioned before, anxious fliers should not drink alcohol. A toxic substance, alcohol reduces the oxygen in your blood stream and makes you work harder to replace it.

3. Women should wear slacks or a full skirt. It is difficult to breathe diaphragmatically when your legs are tightly pinched

together for the sake of modesty. It is better to wear loose-fitting clothes, full skirts, or slacks. These allow you to relax with your legs apart, thereby facilitating diaphragmatic breathing. Avoid tight belts, bras, and girdles, which tend to restrict breathing and inhibit relaxation. For the same reason, men may need to substitute suspenders for a belt when they fly.

4. Cigarettes lower the oxygen-carrying capacity of the blood. Try to smoke less, or sit in the no-smoking section.

5. As soon as you take your seat, place an airline pillow in the small of your back. You'll find one in the compartment above your seat. Contoured airliner seat backs tend to hunch your shoulders forward, forcing the rib cage down against the diaphragm. The pillow frees this important sheet of muscle so that you can more easily relax by diaphragmatic breathing. A special orthopedic pillow is available for this purpose (and also to help you practice diaphragmatic breathing while driving your car).* In flight, keep the seat in a reclined position except during landing and takeoff. This will prevent cramping of the diaphragm by the rib cage.

* The supplier is Behavior Modification Associates, 25 Huntington Avenue, Boston, MA 02116.

ORTHOPEDIC PILLOW

When his appointment was nearly over, I told Roy he would soon learn how to breathe diaphragmatically in any position — reclined, seated, or standing. So that he could acquire this ability, I showed him how to get up from the floor while continuing to breathe easily.

First, Roy forcibly exhaled all of the air from his lungs. He then raised his body to a 45-degree angle, with hands propped behind. Arching his back and spreading his feet apart, he breathed diaphragmatically five or six times, making sure to arch his spine and push his stomach out with each inhalation. This position is an intermediate one that allows the blood to redistribute itself in the body. (An abrupt situp from a reclining position may cause dizziness.) It also holds the rib cage clear of the diaphragm sheet, so that diaphragmatic breathing can continue easily.

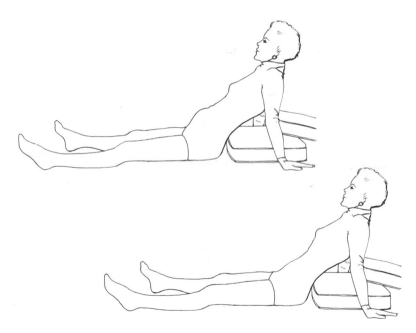

Raise body to 45-degree angle, with hands propped behind. RE (inhale) . . . LAX (exhale).

A full raise to a 90-degree sitting position was next, and Roy caught himself taking one or two thoracic breaths. This was the result of downward pressure from the ribs. With arms still propped behind him, Roy again took four or five diaphragmatic breaths before rising to his feet.

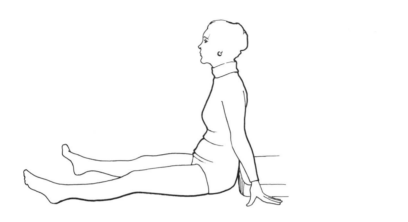

RE . . .

. . . LAX.

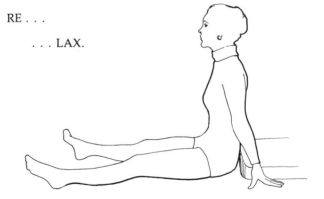

Take four or five diaphragmatic breaths from 90-degree sitting position before rising. RE . . . LAX.

Continue diaphragmatic breathing in standing position.

After Roy stood up, I had him place his hands behind his neck and continue diaphragmatic breathing. The next position for relearning diaphragmatic breathing is with the hands lowered to the hips, the forefingers extending around the belly, in order to monitor the abdominal breathing. The final position, most difficult for thoracic breathers, is to stand relaxed, with hands by the sides, and breathe diaphragmatically.

To join Roy in learning easy breathing, make a jellyroll out of a Turkish towel and place it in the small of your back as you sit watching television. Practice: RE . . . [inhale] . . . LAX [exhale]. Use the towel or a pillow at your back and practice as you drive to and from work. You may even discover new calm in the midst of creep-and-crawl traffic. Practice standing up, lying down, and sitting.

Gradually, you will make a habit of breathing as you did during the tranquil, secure days of infancy. Soon, diaphragmatic breathing will be automatic, second nature to you. Then you will be ready for the next step in Active Stress Coping — Deep Muscle Relaxation.

6

Your Relaxation Exercise

How to Muscle Out Fear

RELAXATION has become the Holy Grail of our time. Spending billions of dollars, Americans search for "relaxation" through jogging, bowling, and camping; they go to massage parlors, sporting events, and motion-picture theaters, and they consume alcohol and tranquilizers. So energetically do some pursue "relaxation" that they are overcome with tension, conflicts, and even cardiovascular attacks. Relaxation of this type, of course, is not true relaxation; it is distraction. We read about the tragicomic aspect of this type of relaxation in the newspapers. The golfer spending a "relaxing afternoon" clubs a duck to death because it quacks as he is making a crucial putt. The jogger who outruns his capacity in the first week of practice ends up in intensive care. The "vacation" in Europe includes five countries in twenty-one days. Competitive, hard-driving people do not change their style simply by doing something "relaxing."

Many of us tend to blame conditions outside our bodies for creating tension, then seek relief from sources in the external world. In the process, we ignore the role the self has in creating tension. This emphasis on external sources of relief is, of course, a mistake. No stress imaginable — not even flying in a plane, being watched by the boss at work, or disciplining a child — can tense our bodies to the degree they are made tense by our anticipatory thoughts and reactions.

Many people spend the weekend digging in a garden, mowing the lawn, and trimming hedges. They collapse into a chair Sunday night, thinking they are relaxed. The equation of relaxation with fatigue is a great American misconception. Relaxation and exhaustion are two entirely different physical conditions that may involve some similar feelings. But relaxation is next to impossible when we are too tired.

Most of us go through life never knowing we are tense until the tension level becomes almost unbearable. Yet true relaxation is only fifteen or twenty minutes away and costs much less than a drink of alcohol or a tranquilizer.

In this chapter, you will learn how to recognize muscle tension, bring it to a peak under your control, and then release it and enter a state of true relaxation.

On his third visit to my office, Roy looked more composed than on his first. Sinking into the familiar easy chair, he said, "Well, I'm learning to eat and breathe. What's next?"

He sat with legs crossed, hands clasped tightly over his knees — so tightly that his knuckles were almost white. I could tell from the position of his jaw and an occasional quiver of his cheek muscles that Roy was clenching his teeth. He was a living example of sensory adaptation, a beneficial and necessary body function that carries potentially disastrous consequences. The sensory system responds to change; we notice when a light gets brighter, clothes get tighter, or the shower gets hotter. We notice changes from an existing level of stimulation — a level to which we have become accustomed. If it were not for sensory adaptation, our conscious perceptions would soon become overwhelmed by the constant awareness of the tightness of our watchband, belt, or shoes; the pressure of the buttocks against a chair; the pressure of our elbows on the arms of the chair; and hundreds of other stimuli constantly affecting our bodies. When these pressure are first applied, we notice the stimulation; but it soon fades from our attention. The sense of smell, for instance, responds very quickly to sensory adaptation. We notice the odor of cabbage cooking when we first walk into the kitchen, but within one or two minutes it is no longer apparent.

This is a rapid change. Slower changes may go completely un-noticed because they take place below the detection level. Body odor may steadily increase without its owner being aware of its intensity — a situation that is not helped by others, since "even your best friends won't tell you." Sensory adaptation, then, is essential for life, because it frees the perceptual func-tions to scan our environment for new and important stimula-tion.

When we think of the senses we usually think of sight, taste, smell, touch, and hearing. There are more. For our purposes, the muscle senses of stretch and proprioception are most im-portant. The sense of proprioception tells us the position of our bodies at any moment, by the action sense receptors in the muscles. These sense receptors, like all others, are subject to sensory adaptation. They adapt to both external and internal stresses on the body. Unnoticed, tension levels gradually build. As a result of this gradual adaptation to increasing levels of tension, muscles can constantly be at a high level of tension without our knowing it. Many people customarily function at high levels of tension, accepting this as part of everyday life.

When the body is at a high level of tension, a person may be "touchy" — hyperreactive to noises and other stressors. It's al most as if the body were trying to protect itself. Rather than triggering sensory adaptation, some sounds such as aircraft en-gines cause irritation and annoyance. In addition, individuals who function at high levels of tension are constantly vigilant for potential stressors. They may become caught in a vicious circle: escalating tension levels (of which they are unaware) force them to anticipate stressors continuously. This action, in itself, increases tension.

By purposefully increasing and decreasing tension in the fol-lowing relaxation exercise, you will prevent the blinding effect of sensory adaptation from setting in and allowing tension to build uncontrollably. By actively monitoring tension levels you learn to relax muscles the easy way, at lower levels of tension, and at the same time avoid being overwhelmed by anxiety. By confronting tension rather than adapting to it people can take a major step toward learning to fly with the greatest of ease.

When I told Roy that we were going to go through a relaxation exercise and make him aware of the tension in his hands, legs, and jaws, he protested. "I feel perfectly calm," he said. "My SUDS level is no more than 20 right now."

Your Achilles Jaw

After telling Roy that by using a relaxation exercise he could lower his SUDS level to 5 or 10, I showed him the hidden effect teeth-clenching has on every muscle of the body.

The test we used is similar to the sugar test described in chapter 4. Roy stood facing me, arm extended straight from the shoulder, thumb pointing forward and palm out and horizontal to the ground. I pressed downward on his wrist while he kept his teeth parted. It took a generous effort to lower Roy's arm. Next, I repeated the action as he clenched his teeth.

Roy looked surprised.

Not only had he felt unexpected weakness, but also he was amazed that I could lower his arm with only my little finger. This phenomenon is demonstrable in many people. It is one of the manifestations of the complex temporomandibular joint that is still not understood by medical science. We repeated the test with Roy's other arm. It was somewhat stronger. His legs were tested in the same manner, one proving stronger than the other. Roy exhibited what dentists call the collapse of the vertical dimension of the jaw. In other words, his back teeth were slightly shorter on one side than the other, resulting in an overclosed jaw when he clenched his teeth.

Not everyone has this condition, but it is helpful to be aware of it when it exists. Overclosure of the jaw results in inefficient muscle utilization on one or both sides of the body. Muscles become inefficient as the result of complex compensatory effort. In addition, improper jaw relationships can set up chronic tensions in the muscles of the head and neck region, which, although not painful, affect dizziness, cause difficulty in swallowing, and produce sensitivity to sounds and susceptibility to headaches.

Humans have a tendency to clench their jaws when frustrated or anxious. If the jaw overcloses, they can, in fact, render themselves less able to cope with stressors. Anxiety and stress require more oxygen in the body. Weakened respiratory muscles have to work harder, adding to the stress. Knowing that over-closure of the jaw causes weakness, we can relax the jaw as part of the Active Stress Coping maneuver and gain more efficient muscle use. Relaxation of the jaw will also help in doing physical work, such as lifting suitcases when traveling, or walking through airports.

To improve performance, many professional athletes use bite plates that slip over their lower back teeth. Accurately sized to within a fraction of a millimeter, these devices set their jaws for maximum strength.

When the temporomandibular joint is viewed as a strength center, it is easy to understand why the history of mankind is filled with instances in which jaws have been opened to increase power. The Japanese karate practitioner cries out as he splits a board with his hand. Driving the spikes through the rails that spanned the country, the workers shouted "Hah!" as their sledgehammers descended. And the men of iron who went to sea used chantey singing to keep their mouths open as they heaved on the halyards and capstans of the old square-rigged ships. When I tore the cover of a matchbook in half lengthwise and inserted the two halves between Roy's back teeth, it was apparent that he became stronger with his teeth together. If you do not find a weakness when you are tested, your jaw relationship is probably fine. You can demonstrate the effect by inserting a strip of cardboard over one tooth on one side of your mouth and biting on it. You will find that you are weaker on the side with the cardboard.

Many times this weakness occurs if the teeth do not mesh correctly. A properly trained dentist can correct this situation. Many people have improper jaw relationships that cause great tension in the muscles of the face and neck. They may never show noticeable problems. However, should they undergo major stress or have their mouths open for long periods of time (as in dental treatment), muscle pain, headache, noises in the ears, or other symptoms of temporomandibular-joint syndrome may appear.

On the other hand, relaxing the muscles of the jaw can relax the muscles of the upper body. You can demonstrate this by sitting in a high-back chair that supports the head. Place a wooden pencil between the front teeth just behind the eyeteeth and gently close on the pencil without biting forcibly. If you have hidden tension in the muscles of the head and neck, you will feel them relaxing in four to five minutes. Keeping the lips together and the teeth slightly parted is a good way to maintain relaxed jaw muscles.

This test not only demonstrates the effect tension in one part of the body has on the balance of the muscles but also shows that we are unconscious of most muscle tension.*

Progressive Muscle Relaxation

The reason for practicing relaxation exercises is to create noticeable tension and make ourselves aware of it. Upon relaxing that tension, we condition in ourselves an Active Stress Coping technique that relaxes the skeletal muscles. The exercises utilize diaphragmatic breathing, so that the autonomic nervous system is quiescent. Thus, two of the three body systems are now under our control.

It is interesting to note that at least one foreign airline already offers a forty-five-minute isometric-exercise program on the entertainment headset channels during long-distance flights. Their cue comes from National Aeronautics and Space Administration recommendations, which are based on studies of astronauts who are confined to their seats for long periods of time. Exercising the muscles eliminates adapted tension and reduces swelling in the feet caused by steady pressure on the veins of the legs. But the key aspect of the exercise presented here is the cumulative relaxation of the major muscle groups. The two major sensations of fear are muscle tension and physiological arousal. By relaxing the large muscles, you ease tension and lower your heart rate, blood pressure, and respiration

* Other factors that markedly reduce muscle strength are metal-framed glasses, metal neck chains, metal waist belts, and high-heeled shoes. Have a friend test your muscle strength with and without these, separately and together (see test of arm and leg strength described in chapter 4). Any metal that crosses the head or spine horizontally will reduce muscle strength. High heels misalign the spine, causing compensation stress and reducing strength in other muscles. Think of these influences while carrying luggage and walking.

rate. Your condition changes from one of preparedness to fight
or flee to one of preparedness for observation and reality testing.

This is the second important benefit of learning to relax. You
will learn to associate flying with pleasure more quickly when
you are in a state of relaxation. This is the message of Wolpe,
Jacobson, and dozens of other professionals who have thoroughly studied people under conditions of both fear and relaxation.

"Why is relaxation so important to learning?" Roy wanted to
know. "I tightened up for every exam I took at school."

When he "tightened up," Roy immediately occupied his conscious mind with attention to a host of internal anxiety stimuli:
he was concerned with monitoring heart rate and respiration
and controlling the butterflies in his stomach. Little or no conscious capacity was left for scanning the test paper or recalling
answers to questions. Tension in the classroom diverts students
from attending to lessons, just as tension in the body of a fearful
flier hijacks his conscious mind and sends it into panic instead
of into a stress-coping mode.

Talking Yourself Into It

I told Roy he was going to learn to talk to himself. When he
looked doubtful, I assured him that internal dialogue plays an
important part in Active Stress Coping and that changing patterns of dialogue could help him change the way he felt about
flying. (There will be more about this in the next chapter.) In
the relaxation exercise, internal dialogue is recorded on a small
tape recorder. This not only helps you learn a new way to talk
to yourself under conditions that create fear but also frees you
from the burden of trying to remember the sequence of the
dialogue.

Soon the exercise becomes automatic. You will hardly need
to think about relaxing your muscles from head to toe when
confronted with a panic situation. If you practice as faithfully
as you would practice learning to ride a bicycle or learning to
ice skate, the art of relaxation will become just as natural and
twice as rewarding.

By this time, Roy was eager to begin the relaxation exercise. Before we started, however, it was important to establish the conditions best suited for learning to relax.

Urgency and relaxation don't get along too well, so I generally advise picking a time of day when you can be away from telephones, children, and the demands of the outside world in general. You will need fifteen or twenty minutes you can spend by yourself, without interruption. Roy ultimately chose two times, once early in the morning and once at night before going to sleep. This is a good plan, particularly if you are using the ten-week format. It allows you 140 practice exercises before you set foot on a plane.

Make sure your clothing is loose fitting. Slacken the knot on your tie, or take it off. Avoid trying the exercise while wearing a tight girdle or bra. Kick off your shoes and settle in an easy chair.

Beforehand, you will need to record your exercise on a small tape recorder equipped with auto-stop. Recorders with auto-stop shut off at the end of the tape. These are available for under thirty dollars and are essential to the success of the relaxation exercise. Get a one-hour tape, which will give you thirty minutes in each direction. The recorded exercise will take between fifteen and twenty minutes, leaving you plenty of time.

Relaxation is like a movie in slow motion; it flows the way a lazy river lolls along on a warm summer day. When you record, read the words s-l-o-w-l-y. The tempo should be easy and lazy. Don't try to sound like a professional announcer. Keep your voice calm and even. Speak softly, as though you were addressing someone sitting across the table in a small, quiet restaurant.*

Don't Try and You'll Succeed

Martha was a delightful student in our Logan Airport course. A school teacher who wanted to overcome her fear of flying in

* Prerecorded relaxation tapes and tapes of aircraft sounds are available from the Institute for Psychology of Air Travel, Suite 300, 25 Huntington Avenue, Boston, MA 02116.

order to enjoy world travel, she had a sense of discipline, including self-discipline.

"Doctor," she said at the beginning of one class, "this relaxation exercise is making me nervous. I feel that I have to have it down precisely and that I have to keep on checking. Will I finally relax when I have it down perfectly?"

An overzealous approach and a striving for perfection will prevent relaxation rather than foster it. If you try to relax by pushing yourself or being too demanding on yourself, you will automatically evoke arousal patterns that are incompatible with relaxation. When you push yourself you trigger defense reactions. Striving for perfection is an admirable trait, but when applied too early in learning any skill it can be destructive. In the early phases, most of the learning process involves the formation of unconscious behavior patterns. These are too complex for the conscious mind to monitor and control. In fact, if the conscious mind continuously interferes, the conditioned pattern of relaxation will be broken up. The feelings of relaxation are the emerging portions of the complex pattern of relaxation that is present in every body. They should be allowed to emerge, not forced. Early in training, your attitude should be that of a passive observer. Once the pattern is familiar to you and you have become expert in setting it in motion, then you can adopt the attitude of a director. To relax, it's best to start out fresh and carefree. Above all, do not *try* to relax. Just listen to the tape, and do what it says . . . let it flow. Learning to relax requires relaxing to learn. The effect of practice is cumulative. The first time you exercise, your state of relaxation may be barely perceptible; but it will be no less real. The more you do the exercise, the more deeply you will relax. If you keep at it faithfully, you will soon notice some of the signs of beneficial body relaxation:

- Arms and legs become limp and loose and feel heavy.
- Eyelids become heavy and difficult to keep open. Soon, they flutter and close.
- As you breathe diaphragmatically, breathing becomes slower and deeper.

- The outside world recedes into the distance.
- At first, the heart may seem to beat faster or make a pounding sound. This is because we become more aware of internal body sounds as we relax. In deeper relaxation even these body sounds will diminish.
- Feet and hands become warm and tingly, as relaxation causes blood to flow more easily to the extremities.

Some people allow themselves to be alarmed out of relaxation by these signs. Remember, you are always in control. Relaxation is natural, normal, and healthy. Deep relaxation is probably a new experience for you, with new feelings and sensations — all of them good. Usually people have to relax to a certain level, become accustomed to it, then proceed deeper.

Let's assume that you are ready to begin your first relaxation exercise. The world is out there somewhere. You are seated in your comfortable chair, fresh — not tired; the telephone is off the hook, and the children are out playing.

Progressive Muscle Relaxation

The relaxation-exercise narration is illustrated to show the correct body positions. You may wish to read it through twice at the outset. On the first reading, look at the illustrations as you go along. On the second reading, you'll be ready to make a tape recording. Read slowly and softly. Pause three seconds at each set of dots. The recording can then be used to guide you in performing the relaxation exercises.

Notice that the seated position requires the use of a pillow or jellyrolled Turkish towel in the small of the back, to facilitate diaphragmatic breathing. Always begin the exercise with at least three minutes of diaphragmatic breathing. Practice the exercise in a straight chair, in a recliner, and lying on pillows as described in chapter 5. The more positions you use in practicing, the easier it will be to relax in any number of situations.*

---

* The relaxation exercise originally appeared in *Fear: Learning to Cope*, by A. Forgione, R. Surwit, and D. Page (New York: Van Nostrand Reinhold, 1978). Reprinted by permission of the publishers.

Let your eyes drift shut . . . and settle down as best you can
. . . For the next few moments, begin to adopt an attitude . . .
that nothing is of much importance other than concentrating on
this exercise and relaxing . . . Begin by directing your internal
attention to the feet. Slowly, begin to bend both your feet at the
ankles . . . bending the feet upward so that the toes point upward toward the knees . . . building the tension slowly so that
you can study it as it builds in the area where you lace your
shoes . . . in the shins . . . and in the calves . . . Build it
slowly under your control . . . up to a point, equally in both
feet, where they neither shake nor hurt . . . You are controlling
the tension in that part of your body, building it under your
control to a level of rock-solid tension now . . . Hold it there,
study it, and when you are ready . . . think the word RELAX,
and slowly let the tension go . . . Study the relaxation as it
comes into those muscles under your control, pleasantly
deeper . . . and . . . deeper under your control. Smoothly allowing your feet to achieve their most comfortable position
. . . Letting the relaxed muscles find that position without your
stretching them in the opposite direction . . . That's good . . .

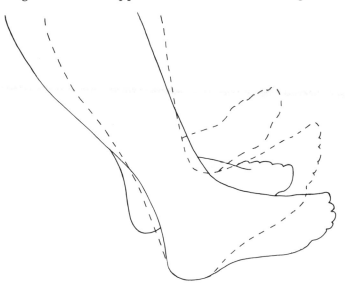

Now focus your attention on the muscles of the thighs . . .
Imagine that your two relaxed feet are heavy weights . . . Begin
to make a motion to lift your lower legs from the knees down,
as one unit. Slowly make the motion as if you were lifting . . .
Concentrate on the tension building, under your control, in the
thighs . . . Build the tension without actually lifting the heels
. . . hold it there . . . study the tension . . . Now think RELAX
. . . Slowly letting the tension go . . . study the relaxation as it
flows into your legs, under your control . . . deeper . . . and
deeper . . . that's good. As your legs continue to relax, they
will tend to roll outward, with the feet tending to spread, rolling on the heels . . . As your legs continue to relax . . . deeper
and deeper . . . focus your attention on the buttocks . . . Begin

to tense them by pinching them together and folding them upward and inward . . . rolling your relaxed legs even farther outward as you build the tension under your control. It's as if you were sitting on a block of concrete that's getting more and more solid . . . Feel yourself being lifted by the increasing tension under your control . . . Build the tension up to a maximum, now, to a point where the buttocks neither shake nor hurt . . . Hold it there . . . Now think the word RELAX, and let the tension go . . . Feel the relaxation coming into those muscles under your control . . . as if you were sinking into a soft cushion, pleasantly deeper . . . and deeper . . . That's right . . . Try to follow the flow of relaxation just a little deeper.

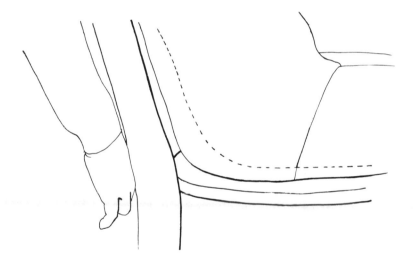

Now focus your attention on your abdomen . . . Begin to tense this sheet of muscle by slowly pulling the navel inward toward the backbone. Breathe . . . more and more with the upper part of the chest. Build the tension under your control. Continue breathing with the upper half of your chest, and notice that you can breathe regardless of where tension is in your body. Hold the tension at maximum now, and think RELAX, letting the abdomen sag, relaxing more and more under your

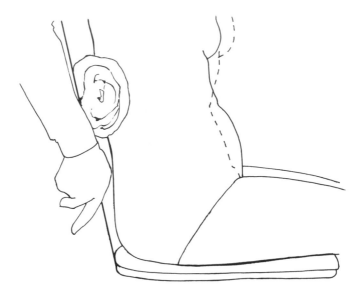

control . . . It doesn't matter what you look like when you relax; what is important is that you are relaxing deeper and deeper. Notice that your breathing moves downward as this muscle relaxes . . . abdominal breathing is relaxed breathing . . . that's good . . .

Now direct your internal attention to the hands . . . Begin to build the tension equally in both hands, by arching the fingertips and hands upward and backward, bending at the wrist, back toward the elbow. Building the tension under your control in the back of the hand and in the forearms . . . slowly up to the point where they neither shake nor hurt . . . hold that tension at maximum now; you are in control . . . study it . . . Now think RELAX, and slowly let the tension go . . . Study the relaxation as it flows . . . deeper and deeper under your control . . . you are relaxing your hands and arms, deeper and deeper. Allow the sensation of relaxation to flow to the rest of the muscles of your body . . . let the chair (or bed) support your body . . . relaxing . . . Now concentrate on the muscles in the back of the neck and the shoulders . . . Begin by slowly

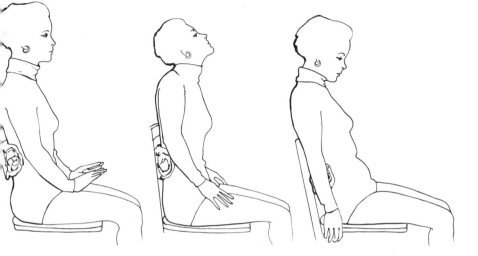

raising the shoulders . . . upward and slightly backward . . .
letting your arms roll outward . . . At the same time, begin to
tilt your head *slowly* backward, building the tension in the back
of the neck and right between the shoulders. Breathe . . . it is
very important that you breathe during this exercise . . . Continue to gently build the tension, as if you were going to stuff
your shoulders into your ears . . . *Do not force this exercise.* The
slow, gentle building of tension to a point where there is no
shaking or discomfort is what is important. Allow your mouth
to open, breathe as if you were breathing through a straight
pipe . . . upward. Hold the tension, now RELAX . . . let the
tension go. Feel the relaxation flow outward along the shoulders as they sag . . . allow your head to gently tilt forward . . .
Feel the relaxation up the back of your neck . . . spreading out
over your back . . . relaxing . . . deeper and deeper. Your
shoulders are drooping more and more, your head . . . tilting
forward more and more . . . relaxing. As your head comes forward, let it rest in whatever position is most comfortable . . .
Relaxing . . .

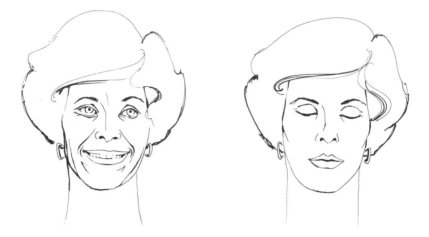

Now begin to drive the corners of the mouth deeper and deeper into the cheeks . . . building the tension in a tight smile . . . slowly up to a maximum . . . Each time you repeat the exercise, this maneuver will become smoother and smoother under your control. Hold it at maximum . . . Now RELAX, studying the relaxation as it flows, under your control, into the cheeks . . . As it flows, your lips slowly part . . . your jaw sags . . . relaxing deeper and deeper. Your tongue resting . . . Continue relaxing for a moment or two . . . Enjoy the pleasant feelings in your body, which you have allowed under your own control . . . Now focus your attention on your forehead . . . With your eyes still closed, begin to raise your eyebrows, wrinkling your forehead . . . in a frown. You are building the tension in that part of your body which is under your control. Slowly, build it up to maximum . . . hold it there . . . study it . . . now think RELAX, and slowly let the relaxation flow . . . like a piece of rumpled silk, smoothing, smoothing . . . over the top of your head and down over the upper part of your face . . . smoother . . . and smoother . . . Now without force take a slow deepening breath all the way to a comfortable depth . . . slow, unhurried, and smooth . . . The air is flowing in; you are getting all the air you need. There should be no force or jerkiness in the flowing. Hold it and think

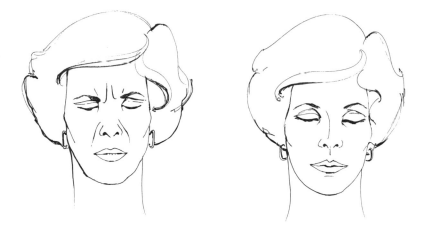

RELAX . . . letting the air flow like air coming out of a balloon
. . . Let the air do the work, not the muscles . . . Feel the pleasant, easy settling in your chest . . . relaxing deeper and deeper
. . . then let your body breathe for you at its own pace. At night
when you sleep, you breathe perfectly for the needs of your
body . . . slowly, easily. Your body knows how to breathe for
its own needs better than you do . . . so let it do so, and imagine the following scene.

You are sitting outdoors in a comfortable lounge chair . . .
Before you is a small, green field covered with lush grass . . . It
is neither too hot nor too cold . . . The sounds of the city are off
in the distance somewhere . . . In the middle of the field is a
tall, strong tree covered with broad green leaves. From where
you sit, you can see the tree comfortably . . . At the very top of
the tree, notice that one leaf becomes detached . . . and begins
to drift . . . from side . . . to side . . . drifting, settling effortlessly . . . so softly . . . so gently . . . that when it finally
comes to rest on the grass . . . it will hardly bend a single blade
of grass . . . Picture the leaf drifting, floating from side . . . to
side . . . soon coming to rest . . . as you are in the scene . . .
calming . . . resting . . . deeper and deeper under your control
. . . Allow the leaf to come to rest now . . . relaxing. Picture it
resting there . . . without effort, its own gentle weight sup-

ported by the grass . . . without the slightest bit of effort . . . an effortless balance . . . just as your body is supported by the chair . . . effortlessly . . .

Enjoy the deep calm you are providing yourself. Each time you do this exercise you become more and more familiar with the pattern of relaxation in your body . . . Your concentration becomes stronger . . . concentrating on the elements of the exercise that allow the pattern of relaxation to emerge more and more . . . When you feel ready, begin to think of reorienting yourself to the room . . . From time to time a desire to stretch will come to your muscles . . . Allow that feeling to remain . . . Notice how freely the breath moves in your lungs . . . Soon your eyelids will begin to flutter . . . allow them to . . . getting lighter and lighter . . . as if they want to open on their own . . . Any weight that was there dissolves . . . When they open, your eyes will be crystal clear, your senses crisp. As your eyes begin to open, notice that your body can be at ease while your mind is active. Enjoy the benefits of relaxation you have provided yourself . . . You can marshal your body for the tasks at hand any time you wish . . . but for a moment or two, reorient to the room, and enjoy the calm under your control.

Jamming

The full relaxation exercise is designed to relax you in fifteen to twenty minutes. After developing its use, and before actually flying, you will learn to use a 45-second version known as "jamming." This abbreviated exercise relaxes the major muscles of the legs, buttocks, abdomen, and neck. Jamming prepares the body to cope with gravity stresses during takeoff and landing. Properly executed, a takeoff jamming exercise begins as the plane accelerates down the runway, and reaches completion as the landing gear leaves the ground. Conversely, a jamming exercise for landing will begin when the plane is above the end of the runway and will end as the gears touch down.

Slowly, Roy began to orient himself to the room. I asked him to give me his SUDS level.

"Five," he responded.

In order to chart your progress in relaxation training, you should get into the habit of recording your SUDS level before and after the exercise, as well as your level at the deepest point of relaxation. You will then have three SUDS scores — before, during, and after — for each exercise you perform. Over the course of your training, you will notice two things. First, your pre-exercise SUDS level will diminish over time. This means that your baseline tension is reducing. You are becoming a more relaxed person. Second, your during-exercise SUDS level will show a greater reduction. This means that the exercise is becoming more effective in reducing tension. The more consistent the reduction, the more confident you will become that the exercise will relax you to the level of previous reductions, regardless of your level before initiating the exercise. You may also notice that your post-exercise SUDS score remains stable for longer periods of time following completion of the exercise. The pattern of relaxation will become stronger, gaining an inertia of its own.

The calming image suggested at the very end of the relaxation exercise is an important part of relaxation. Passive concentration on this image tones the brain and central nervous system and reinforces autonomic quiescence and muscle relaxation. In the next chapter, I will discuss mental imagery, internal dialogue, and assertiveness in more detail. For the moment, however, you may use any image that makes you feel comfortable. If the tree and leaf work for you, well and good. If not, here are two others:

It's a warm, sunny day. You are lying on a cushion in the bottom of a boat on a calm, shallow, crystal-clear lake. There are large fleecy clouds in the sky, and you watch them drifting, drifting slowly and lazily across a clear blue sky. A bird is gliding in circles; it rises higher and higher until it is a tiny dot.

Or you see a white dove in a silver cage against a soft black background. Slowly, the cage door swings open. In slow motion, the bird floats to the threshold. Then it begins to slowly fly away, getting smaller and smaller.

Or you can make up your own ending to the exercise. Just be sure that it is passive. You are an observer. It is important that you not participate in the scene and that it not be exciting. In the next chapter you will learn why. Once you have selected your image, use it *every time*, so that it becomes so familiar that you can concentrate on it automatically.

7

The Conscious Connection

Do You Think Who You Are?

IF A TELEVISION PROGRAM irritates, the viewer simply presses a remote-control button for alternatives. When a headache strikes, the sufferer can choose from a dozen sources of fast relief. A shortage of cash can be remedied by a plastic card and a 24-hour banking machine. Small wonder that many of today's fearful fliers expect to gain prepackaged courage at the speed of light! (Psychologically, instant gratification gives one a sense of control over events.)

But we are dealing with powerful attitudes; attitudes that have built up resistance to change during a lifetime of conditioning. To fly through the air with ease requires patience (to progress at a comfortable pace) and desire (to motivate and create a "practice habit"). Each reader will have a different speed and a distinctive style. Those who succeed will have the satisfaction of seeing in themselves an artist who has created a masterpiece in behavior modification. Along the way, they will learn to reject impatience as readily as da Vinci would have rejected a "paint-by-numbers" Mona Lisa.

Attitudes are made of strong stuff. Psychologists analyze them in terms of three elements. Your attitude about air travel consists of the following:

The Emotional Element — what your feelings tell you.
The Element of Behavioral Readiness — how you tend to act.
The Cognitive Element — your conscious thoughts, values, expectations, rationalizations, and perceptions.

If this trilogy sounds familiar, it's because the three elements of attitude are controlled by the three body systems we have discussed in conjunction with fear:

Element	System	Active Stress Coping Exercise
Emotional	Autonomic	Diaphragmatic Breathing
Behavioral	Somatic-Motor	Progressive Relaxation
Cognitive	Brain, Central	Passive Imagery, Thought
	Nervous	Stopping, Assertion

In this chapter, you will discover more new methods of coping with stress and anxiety. These will focus on adjusting your patterns of conscious thought. Passive imagery, when used with diaphragmatic breathing and progressive relaxation, induces the total relaxation response. Use of these exercises will protect you from fear and anxiety. Thought stopping is a valuable technique you can learn to play like a game. It serves the extremely important function of setting you free from the obsessive internal dialogues and images that tear at your physical and emotional strength. Assertion protects and preserves your well-being during times of confrontation with the outside world and the people in it.

Roy was clearly discouraged. "I really thought I could do it," he said, sinking into the soft chair. "Been eating protein, watching sugar . . . I practiced breathing and relaxation. I thought I was ready for just a little flight."

He told me that a company branch near New York City had needed his attention. Feeling brave, he had gone to the airport and stood in line for the shuttle. This flight was one a passenger could board without buying a ticket. You simply fill out a boarding pass and stand in line. The next thing you know you're on the plane. For Roy, it was like a shock treatment.

"I was third from the door to the ramp — you know, that tunnel leading to the plane. Standing there, I tried diaphragmatic breathing and relaxing," Roy recalled, "and suddenly all I could think about was the fact that there hadn't been any crashes lately, and maybe this plane was the one. Then I could see myself surrounded by flames. That did it. I went down to the parking lot, got my car, and drove to New York."

I explained to Roy that he had done something equivalent to venturing onto the ice with a professional hockey team before learning the game plan. After undergoing this experience, it was important for Roy to congratulate himself. I told him that he should be proud of himself for making a conscious decision to go to the airport, for experiencing the environment without a dramatic rise in SUDS level, and for practicing his exercises in an anxiety-provoking situation. He would soon learn how to gain control when feelings and imagination conflict with conscious thought, I promised.

Fears and Fish: Rational vs. Irrational

Control is elusive. Sometimes it seems that the harder we try to get hold of ourselves, the easier it is for self-control to slip out of our grasp. This is particularly true in the case of irrational fears.

An aquarium attendant drops his new electronic watch into a tank of piranhas. These carnivorous little fish have been known to eat a whole cow in a matter of seconds. No matter how much he wants to retrieve his watch, the attendant will not reach in the water because he fears losing a hand. This is a rational fear. Because he is in control of his thought processes, the attendant will probably devise a coping strategy, such as probing for the watch with a long pole.

By contrast, the film *Jaws*, which showed explicit scenes of a giant killer shark devouring innocent swimmers off the Cape Cod shoreline resulted in a series of false shark sightings up and down the New England coast. Many people, despite the summer heat and discomfort, avoided beaches because they feared an attack by a monster of the deep. Actually, sharks are seldom seen in the cold waters off the coast of Massachusetts, and attacks on humans are extremely rare. This was an irrational fear based on vicarious experience. It's a beautiful illustration of the way imagination can stoke the fires of fear.

Irrational fear pits feelings and imagination against the rational thought process. Even though his conscious mind told him that his life was *not* being threatened, Roy's imagination took over. Driven by his conditioned fear, he elaborated the fear image, and his autonomic nervous system began preparing his body for fight or flight. "I am powerless in the face of fear," he thought. And it was this feeling of powerlessness that sent him out of control.

This is the strength of the cognitive element — the mental control of a conditioned attitude. With no way to change this mental control, and years of practice in telling himself he was powerless, Roy's recently-learned relaxation and breathing techniques were overpowered. He regressed and bolted. I explained to him the reason why. His feeling of powerlessness was associated with the internal dialogue about crashing and the mental picture of fire. These, in turn, influenced his behavior. All three elements — emotional, behavioral, and cognitive — were then affected. His fear of flying was an entrenched pattern. Therefore, without skill in cognitive controls, his thoughts and elaborated images of fear were able to override his other new skills. Although he had begun to practice control of the emotional and behavioral components, these skills had not yet been formed into a new pattern. To compete with the old pattern, mental control of the cognitive component is essential. Now Roy was ready to learn the third and most powerful skill in Active Stress Coping: development of the mental control to ditch avoidance behavior in favor of a conscious coping strategy.

Strengthening the mental-control process also automatically prevents second-order anxiety arising from the fear of showing fear. The conscious acknowledgment that you may be "out of control" is a powerful fear-provoking stimulus. Is there anyone so unimaginative that he has not said to himself, "My God! I'm going to make a fool of myself in front of all these people!"?

While rational fear blends imagination and conscious thought, building a pattern of behavior designed to surmount an obstacle or solve a problem, irrational fear puts the conscious mind in competition with the imagination. When this happens, conscious thought (in the form of the "will") never wins. Imagination is too strong for conscious thought. The more we try to gain control over fear by combating imagination, the more we slip into panic and anxiety.

How to Succeed by Not Trying

While Americans were devising imaginative ways to outwit prohibition agents in the early 1920s, an unassuming French chemist named Emile Coué was showing people how to harness imagination and achieve goals. Coué believed that every thought had a corresponding physical impact. This he proved by a simple mental experiment.

> Suppose that we place on the ground a plank 30 feet long by 1 foot wide. It is evident that everybody will be capable of going from one end to the other of this plank without stepping over the edge. But now change the conditions of the experiment, and imagine this plank placed at the height of the towers of a cathedral. Who then will be capable of advancing even a few feet along this narrow path? Could you hear me speak? Probably not. Before you had taken two steps you would begin to tremble and in spite of every effort of your will you would be certain to fall to the ground.

There is strong evidence to suggest that Coué's work has a place in our modern world. Refinements in his concept of autosuggestion are commonly found in the treatment of conditions as diverse as dental pain and natural childbirth.

At this moment, your conscious mind is probably subvocalizing these words. It is used in everyday functions of thought, motor responses, and the formation and verbalization of conversations. Your silent subconscious, on the other hand, contains all the sensations you have ever experienced, from the burst of light that struck your eyes in the delivery room, to the words of your first-grade teacher and the taste of the food you had for dinner two weeks ago.

The body, Coué believed, is influenced when conscious ideas are accepted by the subconscious. By vocalizing positive ideas, which he called autosuggestions, Coué used thought as a curative force. Coué did not consider *himself* the healer; rather, he maintained that he taught people how to use the conscious and unconscious together. (In Coué's time, the terms *subconscious* and *unconscious* were used interchangeably.) For fourteen years, a steady stream of patients went to his home-clinic in a quiet part of Nancy, France. The cures were many and permanent. Most of the diseases — asthma, migraine headaches, rheumatism — were those modern medical science describes as psychosomatic. But cured they were, by nothing more than the application of Coué's principle of autosuggestion: "Every idea which enters the conscious mind, if it is accepted by the Unconscious, is transformed by it into a reality and forms henceforth a permanent element in our life."

Roy was somewhat skeptical of this principle, so I demonstrated one of Coué's experiments. While sitting in the chair, Roy extended his arms in front of him, folding his hands together. When this was done, I instructed him to concentrate on this thought: *No matter how hard I try, I cannot separate my hands. They are welded together as if they were one piece. In fact, my hands appear to be carved of stone; they are like the folded hands of a very old statue bound together tighter and tighter through the years. I cannot separate them.*

All other thoughts had to be removed from his mind, and there could be no equivocation. While he was concentrating on this thought, I had him try to separate his hands. His knuckles grew white, and the harder he tried, the tighter his hands held together.

Next, I had him think, "I *can* separate my hands." Instantly they came apart.

When the imagination says the hands cannot come apart, the will cannot separate them. But when the will and imagination are in agreement, pain can be conquered and dormant muscles will come to life.

This is why it is imperative for those who wish to fly fearlessly to focus on a peaceful, passive image when practicing the muscle- and autonomic-relaxation exercise. Trying too hard, or saying to yourself, "I will relax," causes your imagination to say, "You are willing it, but it is not going to be." Then not only will relaxation escape you but the self-imposed pressure to succeed will generate anxiety — the exact opposite of the condition you are seeking.

Keeping in mind that our subconscious contains all of the ideas pumped into our heads as children, it's easy to understand why close to 25 million Americans view air travel with emotions ranging from anxiety to outright terror. "I *will* take a vacation and have a good time," a fearful wife says to herself, while her subconscious, which determines her attitude, responds, "The hell you will! You are leaving home, and that's the same thing you did on your first day of school. Leaving home was dangerous and life-threatening then (your mother told you so hundreds of times), and it's dangerous and life-threatening now. You were powerless then and you are powerless now." In the meantime, her demanding husband, who cannot understand the reason for her fear, delivers the coup de grâce: "Look, I'm really tired and need a vacation. If you're so afraid, you stay here and *I'll* go." This means more separation, more fear and conflict (and perhaps more alcohol and tranquilizers).

We *can* reprogram ourselves. That's the hope for fearful fliers and for anxious and stressed people everywhere.

Based on what we now know, the term *will power* is a misnomer: there is nothing powerful about the conscious will. The imagination and the subconscious acceptance of conscious concepts win the day. You cannot will yourself comfortably aboard a flight to Bermuda, but you can breathe, relax, and think (or imagine) yourself there. These are the steps you need to take to desensitize fear, the strategy you can use to settle the approach-avoidance conflicts of air-travel anxiety.

Approach-Avoidance: All Alone on a Seesaw

Roy had, quite literally, experienced an approach-avoidance conflict. Standing at the end of the line, he was physically separated from the source of his fear. He was able to walk toward the ramp, until he reached a point — both emotionally and spatially — where his fear equaled his motivation to board the plane and fly to New York. It was as if he was walking up a seesaw, as many of us did when we were children. At midpoint, the board always threatens to tilt the other way. At an analogous point, Roy's imagination took over and he ran back down — off the ramp, off the seesaw, away from imagined danger.

The way to overcome an approach-avoidance conflict is to weaken the avoidance elements and increase the positive expectancies about the approach elements. When this happens, fear is not maintained by the emotions, and it gives way to new, stronger approach-oriented behavior.

In Active Stress Coping, we reduce our fear by switching the autonomic nervous system into a quiescent state, by relaxing all of the muscles, and by presenting the consciousness with a passive, peaceful, positive image that becomes accepted by the subconscious. When used together, these skills create a total relaxation response. Only after learning to set in motion this relaxation response pattern can you begin to destroy your fear by applying this relaxation pattern to the thoughts and images that formerly created the fear response.

Remember the fight-or-flight response? Originating in the autonomic nervous system, well outside the realm of voluntary command, it is this marshaling of the body's defenses that presents a barrier for fearful fliers. In his excellent book, *The Relaxation Response*, Dr. Herbert Benson cites the work of Dr. Walter R. Hess, who electrically stimulated the brain of a cat and thereby created bodily changes associated with the fight-or-flight response. According to Dr. Benson, Dr. Hess's most important discovery was the fact that by stimulating *another* part of the brain, one could produce physiological changes that were exactly the opposite: lowered blood pressure, slower heart rate, slower respiration, less muscle tension. In other words, there is a distinct possibility that in mammals, an autonomic response pattern exists that is exactly opposite to the fight-or-flight response. This pattern Benson termed the "Relaxation Response."

Whether you feel mild anxiety when flying through turbulence or suffer major tension at the thought of boarding a plane, the source of your discomfort is the fight-or-flight response. You can eliminate this unwanted stress by learning to summon the relaxation response, as you imagine various scenes connected with the flying experience. By so doing, you will be reconditioning your air-travel attitude. Total muscle relaxation and autonomic quiescence must come first.

At Harvard University, Dr. Benson tested a group of subjects who had high blood pressure. These volunteers were attached to biofeedback instruments that instantly measured changes in their blood pressures. With their awareness of a drop in pressure as their reward, the test group was apparently able to learn how to control this autonomic function. The key finding reported by Dr. Benson was this: "When we asked these subjects *how* they lowered their blood pressures, they said simply that they did so by thinking relaxing thoughts."

Here again, we can see the influence of conscious thought over unconscious body function. Just as agitated, negative thoughts and images summon the body's defenses, so relaxing thoughts produce feelings of well-being. This kind of relaxation, Wolpe suggests, is totally incompatible with fear. This is the kind of relaxation the fearful flier should seek.

Coué antedated current cognitive behavior therapists. He placed great importance on internal dialogue — the way we talk to ourselves. What you say to yourself also plays a vital role in Active Stress Coping. When frightened, you see yourself doing something in a negative way. You begin to expect failure. "This is it!" you tell yourself. "There's nothing I can do. I want to get out of here. I can't get out of here. I'm scared. I can't stand this. Trapped. Have to get out of here. Can't get out of here. Nothing I can do . . ." Over and over the same words reinforce the feelings of fear, powerlessness, and inadequacy. Some people summon up extremely grotesque images of tragedy that would frighten almost anyone!

In Active Stress Coping, we also tell the body what to do. But we learn to see ourselves acting in a positive way. Instead of trying to face fear without knowing the techniques to produce calm, our strategy, when we use Active Stress Coping, is to dispel fear. "I feel my SUDS level rising," you tell yourself at the first sign of discomfort. "I know exactly what to do. Concentrate on the feet, tensing them . . . and relax . . ." By immediately going into the relaxation exercise, you are practicing the principle that in every situation there is always something you can control: yourself. This habit strengthens with repeated practice. Remember, you should do the relaxation exercise at least twice a day. The reward is comfort in place of discomfort, confidence instead of insecurity, and inner peace where there was once turmoil.

Above all, decide on a peaceful scene that can become your personal property. Use one of those listed at the end of the last chapter, or create one that you can enjoy. This scene will be your link between your racing consciousness and your literal, childlike subconscious. It should be something you see in slow motion. You should always be the observer, never a participant in the scene. A fearful flier will probably be most relaxed with an event that takes place on solid, safe, secure ground — such as the tree-leaf floating image. Some find more calm in imagining a beach scene, watching a seagull soar, or thinking of waves rushing in and soaking into the sand. Still others prefer drifting in a canoe on a crystal pond, or recalling favorite locations from a happy childhood vacation. Whatever you choose, it should be a place that is associated with calm, a place you will enjoy imagining, free from all of your fears and frustrations, obligations and intentions. The calm scene is most important because it is the single coordinating mental event for the three body systems involved in the relaxation process. It is the cement that binds your breathing and relaxing exercises into a strong new air-travel attitude.

Thought Stopping

"On looking back, I think there were *two* things that kept me from taking that shuttle," Roy said. "One was an awful image that the plane would crash, and the other was a kind of shapeless, general panic about flying that took over. It was such a clear picture to me."

Roy's flight phobia was triggered by a phobic thought. The thought was followed by an obsession, a persistent and intrusive worry about an unlikely or implausible event, embellished by imagination. He had practiced this sequence before. When

Roy avoided flying, a safe means of transportation, he sought comfort in driving — in reality, a much more dangerous mode. The standard unit of measurement for determining transportation safety is the number of fatalities per 100 million passenger miles. In the period between 1972 and 1976, the fatality rate for air travel was .09 per 100 million passenger miles, while the fatality rate for automobile travel was 1.56. Roy's danger of being killed in a crash was 17 times greater in his car than on a plane!

But we can't reason with fearful thoughts. They arise spontaneously, out of habit or triggered by the sight of a formerly feared external stimulus. Fearful fliers walk around loaded with fearful thoughts and obsessional patterns, for these thoughts are organized, ready to surface at any instigation. Such thoughts and patterns can be triggered by a slight increase in emotion, or a verbal chain (cue words that we always associate with other words in patterns that have been practiced, sometimes since childhood). Each time you obsess you block the present and give yourself (your subconscious) a suggestion as to how you will act in the future. (See chart, page 156.)

Consider the case of Aunt Pauline, who had a classic obsessive personality. She was so afraid of lightning that she would religiously listen to weather reports. At the slightest indication of a storm, she had to take a little medicinal alcohol and retreat to the cellar. There was little chance that her house would be hit, and even less chance that she would be injured if it were. But Aunt Pauline spent every thunderstorm of her life, and a few too many overcast days, in the basement, drunk.

Fearful thoughts and their accompanying obsessive patterns take prisoners that way. They are self-starting and self-supporting. Typically, a fearful person pictures some imagined threat and holds onto a chain of related fearful thoughts, internal dialogues, and exaggerated images that have anxiety components. He or she strongly resists reasonable counterarguments, because anxiety blocks learning. Rationalizations and reasonable arguments that justify the phobic behavior further block new learning. In this way the fear becomes rigidly organized and defended. In some cases, the obsession comes to serve as an

Self-Statements without Stopping

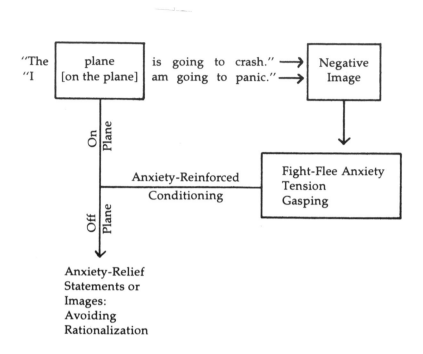

An obsessive thought not only suggests to the subconscious how to behave in a situation; it also conditions feelings of anxiety toward the symbol of the airplane. Consequently the thought or image of an airplane triggers anxiety. In the form of a vicious circle, the phobic conditions himself continuously. In contrast, thoughts of being off the plane result in relief from anxiety.

SELF-STATEMENTS WITH STOPPING

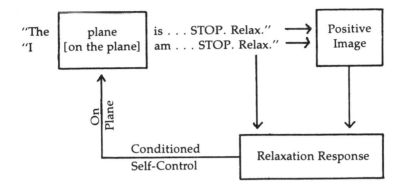

When the negative chain is broken, the new pattern of relaxation becomes conditioned to the symbol of an airplane. "Airplane" becomes a stimulus for self-control and relaxation.

anxiety-relief mechanism. For as long as the person worries, he exerts some control. The worry then begins to blot out any ability to work, play, and relax, however. Feeding on a vicious circle of fear and reinforcement, it grows larger and larger. Unreal though it may seem, many people walk around in a state of anxiety simply because they feel something is wrong if they're *not* worried.

While the object of a fear can be unreasonable, one can also obsess on a matter of legitimate concern. The irrational element in an obsession is the *degree* of worry. (I once asked a pilot at lunch if he feared crashing. "Sure," he said, and went back to his tuna-salad sandwich. This is a nonobsessive, normal reaction.)

Obsession is a chain reaction, but the chain can be broken by using a strategy called *thought stopping. Can* we stop our thoughts? How is it possible to interrupt these visions of impending doom and death that seem to crowd everything else out of our brains? Not only is it possible, but you have already done it, if you have ever read an entertaining magazine while waiting at the dentist's office. We can be extremely selective in directing our thoughts. Thought stopping involves the voluntary blocking of an initiated thought chain, and the replacement of that chain of behavior (fearful thought — image — obsessional pattern — increasing anxiety — worry) with another (fearful thought — "Stop" — "Relax" — relaxation image — relaxation response). (See chart, page 157.)

A word of caution: Do not start a thought stopping program unless you are committed to using the technique *every* time your fearful thought occurs. You will find that during the first one or two days of a program you will have to say "Stop!" fifty or sixty times, to break up the obsessional patterns. By the third or fourth day, you will probably be down to about forty. After a week or so you may be down to ten "stops" a day. In two or three weeks the frequency will be down to five times a day. The obsession will disappear, but you must attend to it *every* time it occurs. If not, you will be telling your subconscious that the obsession cannot be blocked. Recording the number of stops per day will be helpful in reinforcing your progress.

The thought stopping technique consists of three basic parts: (1) being aware of an intruding obsessive thought, (2) breaking the chain of thought and learning to direct attention to some other chain of behavior or aspect of your surroundings, and (3) developing a systematic program that strengthens this response until the frequency of your obsessive thoughts approaches zero.

Begin by settling in your comfortable chair. Choose a quiet time, when you are not likely to be interrupted. If you are one of the many people who obsess about the possibility of being in a plane crash, and this thought begins to intrude, say to yourself, in your head, "STOP!" and immediately create your special guided calm image: a tree, boat, or beach. Your reaction must be immediate and strong. If it is, you will find that you can indeed divert attention from an obsession, even if only for the second it takes to say "STOP!"

A few seconds may not seem like much at first, but it is a beginning. Don't forget to compliment yourself on your accomplishment. As you practice the technique, you will discover that the intervals between obsessive thoughts become longer and that the frequency of these thoughts, in any given period, diminishes.

In our classes at Logan Airport, I generally shout "STOP!" at the top of my lungs and jump up and down. Apart from surprising everyone, the purpose of this demonstration is to provide students with a "stop image." I actually want them to visualize my comical jumping and shouting when obsession begins to overtake them. You may want to create a similar image for yourself. Imagine a flashing red stop sign, or a policeman blowing a whistle — the more vivid and diverting the better.

Another addition you can make to the technique is to establish an immediate mental reward for stopping your thoughts. Some students reward themselves with a food image or a sexual fantasy. Once you have selected the image, become an expert with it. Above all, remember to compliment and reward your effort, no matter how tiny the success may seem at first.

In the beginning, obsessive thoughts may seem to occur more frequently than ever, as if trying to overwhelm you. This acceleration is normal and should not discourage you. If the acceleration is met with persistent stops, it will diminish. A conscious decision to cope with the problem of obsession serves to call attention to it. Although many people find that their first session yields substantial results, others require several sessions — up to a number of weeks — before they notice any progress.

To make thought stopping really work, play it like a game. Keep score with one of those little counters people use to count the stitches in knitting. Keeping this little device snug in your pocket or purse will remind you of the commitment to say (to yourself) "Stop!" every time an obsessive thought occurs. Each time you do, press the counter. Keep a daily tally. This will allow you to watch the number of obsession stops decline. When you drop from, say, 45 to 32 times per day, take yourself out to dinner, buy that book you've wanted to read, or go to a movie: you've earned a reward.

Not only will the counter give you an objective measurement of your progress, it will also serve as a diversion. The activity of keeping count is a new behavior, and it draws attention away from your obsessive pattern.

Soon, your obsession will be on the way to extinction. The sequence is simple: the key is consistency. The ideal stop sequence goes like this: "STOP! RE-LAX . . ." (Visualize your relaxing image, reward image, or both. Then reinforce it by relaxing a muscle group.) Soon you will find yourself automatically practicing diaphragmatic breathing, and your muscles will loosen the moment you "RE-LAX."

Even if you do not show an obsessive pattern in response to your fear image, the stop technique will jam the sequence of trigger followed by emotional arousal and muscle tension. The stop technique also allows cognitive shifting to occur. To avoid thinking of a tomato, for example, the best technique is to avoid saying "Don't think of a tomato." The negative statement acknowledges the tomato. The appropriate and effective technique is to STOP and think of an elephant. Saying "Don't be afraid" to yourself is as useless as saying "Don't think of a tomato."

You cannot think of anything other than "STOP" during the instant you shout "STOP" in your head. That split second is the wedge you need to break the chained thoughts of fear.

Assertion: A Word About Other People

Thus far we have focused on coping mechanisms you can develop within yourself to help establish control under conditions imposed by external happenings and by your psychological responses to those events. But the inner self and external events are only two dimensions of a three-dimensional situation.

The third dimension is other people. If diet, breathing, relaxation, thought stopping, and passive imagery are viable strategies for coping with fear, what is the strategy for dealing with family, friends, and fellow passengers?

Like most aspects of life, personal contact offers a choice. We can decide to be passive, hostile, or *assertive*. Let's look into a crowded elevator. The door opens and a large man steps in — right on the foot of another man. The second man now has a choice. If he opts for passivity, he will grimace from the pain in his foot and look at the floor indicator to see how long he has to wait before he can get out of the elevator. On the other hand, he may act with hostility, turning to the new arrival and saying, "Get off my foot, or I'll knock you into next Tuesday!" (He's then at a disadvantage and may be stepped on harder: hostility often begets counterhostility.) But if the foot-owner practices assertion, he'll simply state a fact, namely, "You're standing on my foot." Now the stepper has a choice. He can say "I'm terribly sorry," and get off the foot, or he can stay where he is (in which case the foot-owner has a good reason to be hostile). Assertion allows others to meet our needs voluntarily, by choice. In this way we gain recognition and self-esteem. By not telling others what to do, we allow them to decide how to respond to the stated need.

Selecting a strategy for dealing with people is critical. We have been doing it all our lives. As children, we experiment with the wide range of behavior available. Soon, through the reactions of parents, siblings, and peers, we learn what works — what results in ice cream, approval, and praise. As we grow into adolescence and maturity, the strategies available to us are further limited and refined. As a result, most of us grow up with a conditioned behavior pattern which dictates that we must react with either passivity or hostility, both of which present serious barriers to fear desensitization.

"I guess you might say I'm on the passive side," Roy told me. "It seems I give in too often."

I asked Roy if he ever felt that he'd "had it" enough to blow up in a storm of hostility.

"Yes, as a matter of fact. Just last week I lost my temper and told Sandy, my wife, that I was sick of the way she always waited until I got home and then made me discipline the kids for things they had done during the day."

When I asked Roy how he felt after the argument that ensued, he said, "Lousy." In fact, what he felt was guilt. This is a typical pattern of passivity, in which a passive person allows family or friends to bulldoze him into unacceptable situations without saying anything. Sooner or later, the passive person gets angry and reacts with hostility. This almost always results in deep feelings of guilt, which are followed by more withdrawal and passivity.

Those who lean toward hostility fall into a deeper trap of self-deception. Even though their persistently bombastic attitudes bend people to their wills, the price they pay is too high. It is not respect that the hostile person attracts, but fealty — an obligation that grows out of fear. This attitude, as many modern dictators have learned, is not too far from hatred and rebellion.

Every day you practice assertion, you enhance your ability to fly with ease. You prevent feelings from building pressure within you. Assertion is not a demand. It is simply a statement of your condition as known *only* to you:

A window is open: "I am uncomfortable in this draft."

A smoker sits upwind: "Your cigarette smoke is blowing in my face, and it bothers me."

To a waiter: "My soup is cold."

To a flight attendant: "This is my first flight, and I'm not quite sure whether I'm going to like it or not."

Remember Roy's first step? He told his superior that he had a flight phobia and was doing something about it. That act of assertion enhanced Roy's self-esteem. "I must be *somebody*, because my boss is respecting my needs," he thought. Asserting your fear removes the need to deny it, and denial is a major obstacle to overcoming the fear of air travel. Assertion allows you to control your environment rather than have it controlled by other people. Assertiveness is the key to self-esteem, because it counteracts feelings of powerlessness, feelings closely associated with fear.

Your world is divided into friends and enemies who all look alike, and neither perennial passivity nor habitual hostility will help you determine who's who. If you are always passive, enemies will brutalize you and friends will unknowingly bulldoze you. If you walk around with a chip on your shoulder, on the other hand, you'll never have any friends. People will act friendly out of fear but will actually reject you.

Assertion lets other people know how you expect to be treated without directly telling them what to do. Assertive behavior will place them in a position to act as friend or foe. What they do will tell you something about their attitude toward you and guide your future actions.

Entire books have been written for the reader who would like to pursue the subject further. An excellent one is *Don't Say Yes When You Want to Say No*, by Herbert Fensterheim and Jean Baer. You may also want to read the chapters on assertion in *Fear: Learning to Cope*, by Forgione, Surwit, and Page.

In addition to speaking up, there are nonverbal methods of assertion. Your judgment, the situation, and the people involved will all help you decide whether to express your assertion silently or verbally. Use either method, but practice assertion every day of your life.

Verbal Assertion

Be Heard. If "I prefer plain vanilla" becomes "Er . . . epfrpovaller," you'll probably wind up with pistachio. The point is that people have to hear your assertions before they can respect your needs. Speak clearly and distinctly, and look directly at them.

Be Sure. Pity the poor soul with tightly crossed legs and strained face who is afraid to ask the location of the bathroom. For an assertive person, there is no such thing as a stupid question. (This is especially true in an environment as strange as that of a modern jet plane!) Ask questions. What is that noise? Is there a peculiar odor in here? Do you have kosher food? (Most airlines do.) Be sure you understand the situation, so that you can control it. The people who write direction signs don't know everything. The information may be incomplete. Don't assume that your confusion results from stupidity. You have a right to know.

Be Communicative. Tell people how you feel. Let them know what you like and don't like. If they do something that meets your needs, reinforce the behavior as vocally as you would make an assertion. Consider the story of the launch operator at a yacht club near Boston: Plagued by yachtsmen who would call the launch for a pickup and then make him wait while they secured a hatch, or looked for handbags and wallets, he made a point of praising one couple who were always ready. The word got around the club, and soon there was competition to see who could consume less of the launch operator's time. People respond to praise of their behavior. Positive reinforcement can be more effective than criticism in asserting your needs. For example, "It would make me happy if . . ." is more effective than "Why don't you ever . . ."

Be Confident. Learn how to protect yourself, rather than putting yourself at the mercy of others. This isn't always easy, so rehearsing is helpful. Visualize situations that are particularly difficult for you. Imagine how others will respond, and plan answers to their questions or comments; decide how to tell them off as a last resort. When you assume this attitude, you will discover that you can be assertive in a more relaxed manner. Remember that *you are the expert on your feelings and preferences.* If you are ridiculed for your fear, inform the offender that it bothers you. If the ridicule continues, the person will have identified himself as inconsiderate, selfish, and insensitive (in other words, an enemy). You have a right to reject such people or attack them without any consideration for their feelings. Confidence is an expectation of positive outcome; it allows you to perform to the best of your ability. It results from planning and practice. Without these two elements, confidence is foolhardy.

Nonverbal Assertion

Act Calm. The poses you assume have a definite effect on your composure. If you sit in a relaxed position, feet on the floor, hands in your lap or on the table, you'll begin to feel calm. Others will think you are calm and treat you accordingly. Their actions will reinforce your feeling of calm and confidence.

Make Eye Contact. A calm, confident person who is not afraid looks others in the eye. You can accomplish more with this subtle but powerful act of assertion than with any other. If eye contact is difficult or uncomfortable at first, focus your gaze on another person's forehead or on the bridge of his nose. Anxious persons continually flee from situations by looking away. Without knowing it, they engender rejection from others, because the avoidance of eye contact is perceived as disinterest.

Take the Initiative. Encounters requiring assertion can occur at any time. You can remove much of the apprehension and suspense from these occasions by gaining the attention of people rather than waiting for them to get around to you. They may be engrossed in something and fail to notice you. If you tell ground personnel that you are an apprehensive flier, you often will be boarded first or given a choice seat.

You're Not Alone

You can learn much about your air-travel companions if you look around to see what they are communicating with their body language. That dignified, well-dressed man by the window, who is touching his nose between forefinger and thumb, may be fighting inner panic. This behavior, according to Desmond Morris, author of *Manwatching*, indicates that he is suffering from a schism between inner thoughts and outer behavior. A struggle may be taking place between fright and the need to appear calm. And notice the woman next to you who keeps moistening her lips. She's doing more than checking her lipstick. When the autonomic nervous system is activated, there's a reduction in salivation. (This is part of the shutdown of the whole digestive system.) She's scared, suffering from a racing heart and butterflies in the stomach. Even that plump fellow in the seat ahead gives himself away. You can't see his face, but you note a shiver now and then. This generally indicates the kind of cold sweat that accompanies the fight-or-flight response.

The point of all this is that self-admitted fearful fliers are far from alone. Look around and you'll see a host of people just as apprehensive as you are. My favorites are the suave business executive who calmly opens the *New York Times* and reads it — upside down; and the woman dressed like a fashion model who constantly flicks a nonexistent ash from her cigarette while consuming alcohol.

The reason for practicing assertion and gaining confidence through the knowledge that others feel as you do is to keep your desensitization program rolling along. Other people can slow your progress unless you let them know that you want to succeed. It is very important to observe three hard and fast rules:

1. There is only one person who knows when you should fly, and that person is *you.*

2. Do not fly until you *yourself* decide that you are ready. (For most of our readers, that will be at least ten weeks after opening the cover of this book.)

3. Fly under optimal conditions of your choice, initially, rather than waiting to be obliged to fly somewhere. Practice flights are not frivolous.

Fearless . . . and Frozen

People who can feel their anxiety in a stressful situation are lucky. Lucky because they can practice Active Stress Coping and feel a reduction in stress. Far less fortunate are those patients whom I have actually had to train (with biofeedback) to let their feelings of fear enter their consciousnesses. Only then could they begin to cope with the problem. It's a basic rule in psychology: you can't control an emotion of which you are unaware.

These people are not calm or comfortable, even though they look composed and report no anxiety. They have denied their fear for so long that it is not perceived. When asked, they give low SUDS levels, even in the lounge area waiting to board a flight. They get right to the door of the plane. And then they freeze. They can go no further, being literally seized with terror and not knowing why. Many professionals in high-exposure positions suffer this kind of flight fear: physicians, clergymen, lawyers, politicians, and actors. Because they must always appear to be cool and in control of the situation, they learn to deny and block their feelings.

You Are Ready to Desensitize . . .

. . . if you have practiced with Roy through chapters 4, 5, 6, and 7; if you have recorded the relaxation exercise, consciously made an effort to breathe diaphragmatically, and set aside some time each day to practice both; and if you can visualize your passive, relaxing image at will, exercise some form of assertion each day, and use thought stopping to halt obsessive internal dialogues and block negative images.

If you have accomplished these goals, you are ready for a rewarding experience — systematic desensitization of your air-travel anxiety.

As you progress, keep using the skills we have developed. Then something will happen: You will begin to think more of who you are. And for most people, that turns out to be an interesting person to know.

8

Taking Control

Self-Directed Systematic Desensitization, or Your Stairway to the Sky

To readers who have never flown because they fear the experience: Please observe these instructions, which are designed to help you succeed in clearing your mind of that fear. If you are skimming the book prior to reading it through, skip this chapter as well as those dealing with the graduation flight and advice for professionals. With proper preparation, this chapter can provide you with a rewarding experience. Without preparation, it may be a stressful self-test for which you are not ready. Remember, stress frequently occurs at levels you cannot perceive. The approach we employ in overcoming fear requires your ability to relax in the presence of triggering stimuli such as those presented in the following pages. Before you leaf through chapter 8, practice the relaxation techniques described in chapter 6 and learn thought stopping from chapter 7. You will then be able to read chapter 8 with positive goals in mind rather than with mere curiosity. If you elect to proceed and find that anxiety is building, reconsider these suggestions. Otherwise, you will be stonewalling your fear, a practice that is in direct contradiction to desensitization.

By carefully following the steps of systematic desensitization, you can build a stairway from that comfortable chair in which you've been sitting to an equally comfortable seat aboard your graduation flight. This unique stairway is not for climbing. You will relax your way up, at your own pace, one step at a time.

Desensitization will be a new and rewarding experience for

the majority of fearful fliers who have been trying unsuccessfully to use techniques that may have worked in other areas of their lives. Some of these techniques are:

- Denying the fear exists
- Ridiculing oneself
- Forcing oneself
- Dulling the senses with alcohol and other drugs
- Hanging on to someone
- Telling someone about one's fear
- Engaging in superstitious behavior
- Finding every possible reason to avoid flying

If you have been using one or all of these maneuvers, you most likely feel that it is impossible to effectively combat your problem: the fear is simply beyond your control. Psychologically, you are absolutely right.

Control is the key issue, because fear is learned under conditions over which we have no control. Emerging situations, physical conditions, and ways of thinking about ourselves in relation to the world around us have combined to create the fear patterns and thought maps described in chapter 2. Until now, there has been little information available about how to control these thought patterns. Now, however, it is possible to focus on fears and develop new behaviors that inhibit the fear response in the same way the fears themselves were learned. Through systematic desensitization we can learn how to regain control.

The principles involved are technically known as *reciprocal inhibition* and *exposure by means of graded intensity* — in other words, divide and conquer. Reciprocal inhibition is a theoretical principle proposed by Wolpe which is based upon the fact that a person cannot be anxious and relaxed at the same time. If a person can engage in relaxation response to a strong enough degree, the relaxation will inhibit the fear response. Generally, inhibition takes place only if a person experiences the feared thought or situation one segment at a time. This is because training has made the fear response too strong, and contemplation of the experience in its entirety is impossible to control. If parts of the feared situation, or symbolic representations of the feared situation, are entertained for short periods of time, however, the triggering of the fear response may not be as strong. This is the condition present in the second component of systematic desensitization, exposure by means of graded intensity.

There are different ways a feared situation can be graded in intensity: distance (either physical, temporal, or emotional); differences in theme or context; duration of exposure; and mode of exposure (fantasy or reality). The steps for overcoming fear, listed below, follow directly from the principles of reciprocal inhibition and graded.exposure:

1. Learning complete relaxation.

2. Building a hierarchy of fear-provoking situations.

3. Visualizing scenes from this hierarchy, from least fear-provoking to most fear-provoking, while in deep relaxation.

4. Actually experiencing the situations visualized, in the same graded fashion, while maintaining as much relaxation as possible.

5. Continuing to practice relaxation in these situations, even though fear and anxiety no longer occur.

Relaxation training, nutritional changes, and Active Stress Coping will be sufficient for those who fly with mild to moderate apprehension. But those whose fear is of such magnitude that they have not been able to board an aircraft will need to follow methodically the procedure outlined in this chapter. There is, of course, a level of fear intensity that falls between these two states of apprehension. If your fear is within this range, it is advisable for you to engage in desensitization.

Research has revealed that almost any neutral event can become feared if it is paired in certain ways with either a fear-eliciting stimulus or with the condition of fear in the body. In an interesting demonstration of this process, a psychologist imagined horrible thoughts and acted afraid every time he saw red-haired people. In a relatively short time, the sight of red hair caused him to be truly afraid. His fear could not be removed by the simple acknowledgment that he had purposefully

learned the fear. By systematically relaxing and gradually looking at images of redheads and then at real people with red hair,
he lost this fear.

There are other ways a learned fear response can be erased.
One way is called extinction. By the extinction method, the
fear-provoking thought is made to occur without pairing it with
other thoughts or events that elicit fear. Take, for example,
the simple thought, "I am sitting in first class while in level
flight . . ." In the extinction method, this image is held alone
— *not* paired with other fear-eliciting qualifiers that have been
linked with the image by years of practice, such as:

". . . wondering when the turbulence will start."

". . . so anxious I'm going to make a fool of myself."

". . . and I can't get out."

". . . but what if something happens?"

". . . wondering if the plane will drop like a piece of lead if
the engine stops."

". . . knowing that a calm *always* comes before a storm."

". . . having to be aware of every sound, movement, and
change."

As you relax in the comfort of your home, the image you project of sitting in first class will, if there are no fear-eliciting
qualifiers, gradually cease to elicit conditioned fear. If, however, the image is intermittently paired with any of the fear-
provoking qualifiers, the fear-eliciting power of the image will
become stronger and more durable, because the element of un-
certainty is reinforced. In this respect, thought stopping is the
most effective way to break up the linked thoughts that maintain a fear.

Some people nullify the extinction of conditioned fear by
minimizing this subtle accomplishment, through apparently
intelligent comments like, "But I know I'm not actually flying."
The statement of the obvious fact succeeds only in suggesting
that if one is flying one will act as his linked thoughts predict
he will act. Rather than practicing on the ground with neutral-

izing images of flight, this person follows the image, "I am flying in first class," with "but I'm really on the ground." In one intellectual stroke, the desensitization process is nullified, and the person retains mastery over the immediate situation but loses control of the flying situation. (This statement is usually made by achievement-oriented hypervigilant people psychologists call "controllers"; these people use physical and intellectual control as a defense against their feelings.)

A completely self-administered program of systematic desensitization is somewhat less powerful than one in which you have help in learning to relax and to assemble the hierarchies. The do-it-yourself approach is, nonetheless, effective; and enlisting an interested friend can provide the monitoring and assistance needed to increase the effectiveness of the technique. In the program that follows, you may elect to proceed by yourself or with the assistance of a friend. If your fear is severe, we recommend that you seek the assistance of a friend. Your selection will be most important.

Qualifications of Your Co-Worker

The person you select as a co-worker *should not be afraid to fly* and should:

1. Understand the program as well as you do;
2. Be able to direct you in the relaxation exercises when you regress to inappropriate fear-coping behavior;
3. Avoid pushing you beyond your level of readiness;
4. Be able to tolerate, even invite, your assertiveness;
5. Remind you of thought stopping should you engage in negative suggestions and fear-anticipatory behavior;
6. Monitor and reinforce your progress frequently and accurately, without giving false assurance;
7. Be able to fly with you, if necessary, on your graduation flight, to monitor your stress levels and to guide and time your relaxation and jamming exercises.

It is advisable that you not select a parent or a close relative. Usually these people are so emotionally involved that they have developed habits of interacting with you that are counterproductive. For example, one way people gain emotional support from others is by complaining and seeking approval. Another way is by acting helpless and drawing a person closer emotionally. Sometimes, husbands, wives, parents, and siblings have contributed to the problem by creating dependency in the person with the fear, or by trying to push him into flying, "for his own good." A common problem of many fearful people with claustrophobic and hyperventilative problems is that they are passive and unassertive, always trying to please others and conform to their expectations, to the point of rejecting their own needs. They are, in effect, already "closed in" by their lifestyles. When confronted by a real closed-in situation, they cannot deny their powerlessness, and the anxiety bursts through.

A clear example of the wrong way to choose a co-worker is seen in the case of Joan. A successful journalist, married to a less experienced journalist three years her junior, she denied the existence of the constant competition that was present in her marriage. She selected her husband as a co-worker in hopes that this task, and the successful completion of the program, would bring them closer together. Even though she did experience an overall sixty percent reduction in fear on the graduation flight, she recalled that her husband "recited the relaxation exercise to her while he leafed through a magazine or looked out the window." In addition, he "kept asking me why my anxiety level had not yet gone down to five, when I thought I was doing just fine at twenty." When at one point she had an anxiety surge (partially due to her increasing anger at his behavior), he explained to the adjacent passenger that his wife "was afraid to fly and acted like this at times." The husband's obvious attention to himself and others rendered him incapable of providing the assistance Joan needed. Joan improved in spite of his "assistance." Later, in marriage counseling, the husband revealed that it was important to him that Joan retain her fear. In so doing, she would continue to be dependent on him and allow him to avoid facing his fear that she would grow independent of him. Joan now flies alone and relaxed, while her husband is adjusting to the fact that he will not be abandoned as long as he continues to give her recognition and treat her with sensitivity.

Joan's situation is one to be avoided, and you can easily do so by following the guidelines we have discussed. With a supportive friend to help you, you are now ready to begin systematic desensitization.

Step 1: Determine the Exact Fear Triggers

You should now begin constructing your hierarchy of fear. You must first determine what the triggers of fear are, then rank them on a scale of intensity based on the SUDS scale.

Do you have fears that are triggered by situations similar to the flying situation? Determine your SUDS level when dealing with the following situations:

Confined places

Heights

Crowds

Distance from home

Being under the control of someone else

Loss of control of your emotions

Judgment by others

Being closed in

Death

Water

Relaxation

Dizziness

Loud noises

Conversation with other people

Loss of control of your bladder or bowels

If you have a SUDS level of 30 or greater for any one of these situations when they are dissociated from flying, or a total score of 100 points or higher, you need to begin forming hierarchies of these fears before starting to desensitize your air-travel phobia. The formation of hierarchies for feared situations is the same regardless of the fear. A hierarchy for air-travel fear can serve as a model for any of these other fears. More information on other fears and on the construction of hierarchies can be obtained from the following books: *Simple, Effective Treatment of Agoraphobia,* by C. Weeks (New York: Hawthorn Books, 1976); *Fear: Learning to Cope,* by A. Forgione, R. Surwit, and D. Page (New York: Van Nostrand Reinhold, 1978); and *Self-Directed Systematic Desensitization,* by W. Wenrich, H. Dawley, and D. General (Behaviordelia, P.O. Box 1044, Kalamazoo, MI 49005 [1976]).

A pattern of high scores on "distance from home," "confined places," and "crowds" indicates agoraphobia. This fear must be controlled before your desensitization of air-travel fear can begin.

Agoraphobia is a fear with so many ramifications that it affects almost every aspect of life. The most effective treatment for this fear is a combination of nutritional counseling, analysis of jaw bite, training in diaphragmatic breathing, muscle-relaxation training involving Active Stress Coping, thought stopping, assertion training, and real-life desensitization. In severe cases, antidepressant medication is prescribed in addition to the behavioral program. The typical behavioral approach is essentially the same as the one outlined in this book.

Fears of being closed in or confined are usually associated with breathing problems. Diaphragmatic breathing and real-life desensitization are effective against these fears. Fear of dizziness is usually associated with a physical problem in the organ of balance or the temporomandibular joint. In some cases hypoglycemia may be involved. Once these physical problems are corrected, relaxation training is effective. Fears and obsessions about death and about being judged by others usually involve deep-seated guilt that is not easily treated by behavioral methods alone. In such cases, analytic therapy, in combination with assertion and relaxation training, may be indicated. Fears of loud noises, of being under the control of someone else, of losing control of one's emotions, or of speaking to someone all diminish rapidly with the implementation of relaxation training, assertion training, and desensitization.

It must be made clear that this brief survey of fears and their treatment is in no way a prescription for the treatment of your fears. Often, fears are associated with depression and broader personality problems. A consultation with a psychologist is often very helpful in answering questions you may have about fear. Often people think one has to be severely disturbed to consult a psychologist. This is not true. Psychologists render diagnostic and evaluative services in addition to their treatment service. Like your family physician, psychologists answer questions and give suggestions for maintaining good health.

Usually, the desensitization of one fear results in the reduction of other fears a person has. If your SUDS total for the situations listed above is below 100, you may proceed to construct the hierarchy of your air-travel fear.

Although on the surface you want to overcome your fear, are you actually better off with it?

People have a way of avoiding stressful situations in their lives. This is a natural thing to do. But in order to avoid stress while overcoming your fear of flying, you will need to be as honest as possible with yourself before you proceed. Psychologists use the term *secondary gain* when analyzing problem behaviors. Secondary gain is the reward, usually hidden, that occurs because the problem behavior exists. This hidden reward factor usually maintains and reinforces the problem behavior, making its removal difficult.

A few examples may be helpful.

Mike was an intellectual man of fifty-eight. He ran a successful jewelry business. His wife was a strong, impressive matron who controlled the family while he engaged in business. Mike's fear of flying began when he was thirty, two years after his marriage. At that time, he and his wife were financially comfortable and could afford to fly and vacation anywhere in the world. Mike was a pleasant, unassuming man in his social life but a tiger in business. He prided himself on never having voiced an angry word in all the years of his married life. As long as his fear of flying continued, he did not have to go on trips with his wife and spend extended periods of time with her, away from his business, which was the major source of fuel for his masculinity. "She would always come up with places she thought we would enjoy visiting. Anyway, I can always take the train to New York or drive around New England to buy jewels." Mike's fear allowed him to keep some control over his controlling wife. He conceded that he was too old to learn assertive behavior, in order to protect himself from his wife. Moreover, at his age, what would his married children and the in-laws say if he left her? Boxed in, the only way he had of avoiding the critical issues in his life was to keep his fear.

Peter was an attorney for a large insurance company. He avoided flying after suffering an attack of hyperventilation en route to a major meeting in New York. He had reached a point in his career where more frequent flights to regional offices were required. Promotions and success in the company were ensured for him. Along with his ascent in the corporation, however, came increasing responsibilities. As he attained higher positions, he began to feel that he could not keep as tight a control over his surroundings as he had maintained in earlier positions. His fear of success could be avoided as long as his fear of flying continued. After acknowledging this hidden fear, he learned relaxation and then applied himself to the task of acquiring management training and better public speaking ability. Peter also underwent counseling, where he examined the significance of his belief that the higher you go, the greater the fall. Armed with the assertive ability to refuse promotions if he wished, the desensitization of his flying fear proceeded quickly. He later accepted promotions in stride.

Psychologists frequently find the secondary-gain factor in children who live great distances from demanding parents. On holidays, their fear of air travel saves them from having to decide whether or not to visit their parents. Furthermore, if they have difficulty being assertive (that is, if they lack the ability to refuse demands placed upon them by others), their struggle with an incapacitating fear will evoke sympathy, rather than anger, and they will not be made to feel guilty when they refuse a family visit. One must examine the effect this avoidance of deeper conflicts has on one's life. Quite often, acquisition of skills in assertion and relaxation eliminates the need for these sources of secondary gain.

One other common secondary gain, which women tend to pursue (possibly because of the cultural role they have been forced to adopt), is the attraction of attention because of their fear. Through restriction, fear is sometimes used to punish an inattentive mate. A common marriage is that of an independent male, who is not emotionally expressive, to a dependent female, who is free with emotional expression. These two types initially attract and complement each other; the male is attracted to the female because of her emotionalism, and the female is attracted to the male because of his strength and steadiness. Over the years, however, the emotional needs of the female are not met. Quiet strength becomes emotional rejection. The male views emotional demands by the wife as attempts to control him. Fears then develop in the female, requiring the attention and support of the male. In this manner, emotional support is obtained indirectly. This, however, has its price. "It seems unfair," said one wife, "that he pays attention to me and helps me with my fear of flying when he wins a trip for being a super salesman. But where was he when I needed help with the children or with other things that were bothering me?" I have frequently seen marriages lose their stability when one member loses a fear. The other member becomes threatened by having to adjust to the changing dynamics that result.

If you are using a fear of flying to gain a desired end, you must be prepared to deal with the growth and new patterns of social interaction that will result when you lose that fear.

Step 2: The Hierarchy

Hierarchy for Apprehensive Fliers

If you now fly, but fly in apprehension, you are already desensitized to many of the components of the air-travel experience. The list of items in the FFS on pages 59–65 can serve as a checklist of troublesome situations. Remember that in the survey, the emergency item, number 25, is supposed to elicit anxiety. It may be used in your desensitization hierarchy, but it is an event you will probably never experience. In all my years of flying, I never have. However, practicing (in your imagination) scenes of this nature, while maintaining deep relaxation, will reduce the anxiety produced by the thought of an air emergency. Once practiced, the behavior becomes part of your repertoire, and you can perform it without thinking. In an emergency, anxiety and immediacy block thinking, preventing a person from being creative enough to devise a coping strategy. The fearful person is even more unprepared than most, having engaged in counterproductive mental strategies such as: "Out of sight, out of mind," or "If I don't think of it, it will never happen," or "If it happens I'll be powerless." By refusing to think about it or programming his behavior with a response of panic, the fearful person trains himself to be ineffectual during emergencies. In fact, fearful persons become so sensitized to real emergencies that they respond to most normal events as if they were emergencies. Consider the parent who is afraid of fire. Terrified at the thought, the parent never trains the children in how to escape the home; the children never see how fire is properly managed, and when they see their parent's response to fire, they learn to be afraid, paralyzed, and helpless.

The jamming exercises mentioned in the muscle-relaxation chapter are the best way to cope with turbulence or rapid changes in the course of the aircraft. Most often, apprehensive fliers improve markedly after the changes that result from nutritional preparation, proper breathing, and muscle-relaxation techniques. With less anxiety, they can use their intellect to learn to adjust and creatively cope with immediate situations, rather than apprehensively wait for something to happen. With lower anxiety and practiced behavior comes a sense of mastery. But when defensive vigilance is the only coping strategy, the sense of powerlessness becomes strengthened.

A good approach is to master the information and exercises in the other chapters of this book. After five or six weeks of daily practice and recording your SUDS levels, take a short flight for diagnostic purposes. Record your SUDS levels on the Flight Symptom checklists and retake the FFS. If your scores are at or below the Active Stress Coping values shown in chapter 3, Flight Symptom Checklist II (refer to the graph on page 79), there is no need to go further with the desensitization. If, in addition, your score is 40 or higher on Part I of the Flight Symptom Checklist, you've done your work well. My only suggestion is that you should *continue to practice the techniques that led to your success.* Continue to score your next six flights, recording the scores to plot your progress. After you have continued to fly with ease during these flights, you may elect to ease off on the exercises. It will only be necessary to reinforce your control occasionally. Continuing to keep a record of all your flights will help you become aware of variations in your emotional state. In this manner you can maintain your stress level where you wish. Do not demand perfection of yourself in these early flights. Rather, look for gradual reduction in your tension levels.

If, on the other hand, your scores indicate more apprehension than the levels mentioned in the paragraph above, or if your anticipatory anxiety remains high, construct a standard hierarchy directly from the FFS in chapter 3.

The Standard Hierarchy

The simplest way to construct a standard hierarchy is to make a photocopy of the items in the FFS. Cut out each item and paste it on a three-by-five file card. You will then have a set of 46 cards.

If items that cause you apprehension are not included in the FFS, cards can be made up for them. For example:

In level flight on a clear day, you get up to go to the restroom. You enter the restroom and lock the door.

You are walking down the aisle and the seat-belt sign comes on.

You are walking down the aisle and the plane encounters slight chop (turbulence).

Rate each item on the SUDS scale and place your SUDS score on the back of the card. Try to do this carefully, not in a matter-of-fact fashion. One or two days later, rate each item again without looking at the score on the back of the card. Place your second score below the first on the back of the card. Repeat the procedure two days later, so that you have three scores for each item. Now add the three scores for each card and divide the total by three, to obtain an average rating for each item. Circle your average score and arrange the cards in ascending numerical value, from lowest score to highest.

After the cards are ranked in the manner indicated, turn them over and examine the items. You may be surprised to find that a pattern has emerged. Usually anticipatory items fall into a hierarchy determined by temporal distance from a flight. If common flying items are mixed in with anticipatory items at the low end of the scale, this means that these aspects of flying are associated with as much relaxation as being on the ground.

This hierarchy is sufficient for most apprehensive fliers. With this set of items you may now proceed to systematic desensitization.

A Personalized Hierarchy

If you have a SUDS score of 50 or above on any item, make up several cards, on each card expanding the scope of the situation by changing the temporal distance, context, or intensity. For example, Item 23 states, "You are flying in dense fog. When you look out the window you can see nothing but thick fog; you cannot even see the wing tip."

Changing the temporal distance and intensity, we might have:

> You are *thinking* of flying through spotty clouds on a sunny day. From time to time you pass through a cloud that obscures your vision from the window for two to three seconds at a time. You then have clear vision for a great distance.

The intensity and duration of the obscured vision can be gradually increased. You may elaborate the item as the duration increases.

> You are thinking of flying on a sunny day, and the plane enters an extended cloud formation. Since the view from the window is uninteresting, you begin to read an interesting magazine you have brought along. (You know that the plane is equipped with radar so accurate that it can guide the plane to the landing strip in a dense fog.)

The temporal distance is now changed on all the items.

> You *are flying* through spotty clouds on a sunny day. From time to time you pass through a cloud that obscures your vision from the window for two or three seconds at a time. You then have clear vision for a great distance.

And so on. Since you are creating scenes in your imagination, feel free to take artistic license. For example, change the context:

> You are on an airplane parked at the loading dock. As you look out the window, you cannot see the wing tip, due to the dense fog.

You can change the context even more.

> You are riding on a train through dense fog. It is so thick that the telephone poles along the track are not visible.

Spread out the temporal distance, intensity, and context so that you have items distributed from an average SUDS rating of 5 up to 50 or greater.

You will now have constructed a major hierarchy, with one or more minor hierarchies. When you begin desensitization, rank in order all items, from the lowest to the highest SUDS levels, and begin work on the lowest.

An Augmented Hierarchy

If you have not flown in a number of years, or, because of fear, have never flown, your hierarchy construction will have to be a bit more elaborate. Remember that you have two tasks at hand. First, you must familiarize yourself with a new, and in many ways totally alien, environment. Second, you must be desensitized from fear that is anticipated and triggered by real aspects of the air-travel situation rather than by distortions or imagined aspects of the air-travel experience that have themselves been influenced or created by fear.

From the moment you enter a terminal, your behavior is regulated. Signs direct you to various locations. You must be at the loading platform at a certain time. Machines and security personnel check your person and your belongings. Signs even inform you that in certain areas there are restrictions on what you can say. On boarding the plane, you will find that the visual patterns to which you are exposed are quite different from the stable verticals and horizontals that are part of your everyday life. Observe, for example, the photographs of the walkway and the door to the airplane. A tilted tunnel with no doors or windows opens into an area with curved surfaces and tilted edges.

For some this can be disorienting, resulting in compensating tensions in the body. To the inexperienced air traveler, these architectural elements subtly influence the body by inducing a feeling of being pulled forward or tilted to the side. The experienced traveler has unconsciously adapted to these influences and may not consider them important. But to the fearful flier, many minor stressors, mostly unnoticed, add up, increasing tension levels.

The series of photographs at the end of this chapter are intended to instruct and to serve as hierarchy items in your desensitization. The series depicts the scenes to which an air traveler is exposed in an average flight. Read the caption for each photograph, look at the scene, and rate each with a SUDS score. It may be helpful to cover the other photographs with file cards, so that you concentrate on one photograph at a time. Later, when you begin desensitization, examine the photographs in the series in the order in which they appear, unless there are some scenes early in the series that cause very high SUDS levels. If this occurs, desensitize to all the other photograph items before concentrating on these items.

Let's summarize the steps in constructing the augmented hierarchy:

1. Construct the standard hierarchy.
2. Expand this with one or more personalized hierarchies.
3. Look at the photographs and assign each a SUDS score.

Step 3: Desensitization

The instructions for systematic desensitization apply to *all* items, whether imagined or in photographic form. The procedure will result in lower anxiety levels in response to thoughts and mental images of flying and will provide you with a system for coping with the real-life hierarchy that comes later in your training.

Begin desensitization only after you have mastered the three components of the relaxation exercise: breathing, muscle relaxation, and guided imagery. Set aside a time of day when you will not be disturbed. Begin a complete relaxation exercise with five minutes of diaphragmatic breathing, then follow this with muscle relaxation. After holding the calm image you have chosen for two or three minutes, assess your SUDS level. If you have practiced properly, you should be at a level of 10 or lower. It is counterproductive to begin or proceed to an item higher in the hierarchy if your SUDS level is greater than 10. If you have not reached a relaxation level of 10, repeat the portion of the exercise that is most relaxing for you until you have reached 10. You are now ready to proceed.

Desensitization must proceed slowly. Remember, the goal is to associate the mental image with as much relaxation as possible:

1. Imagine the first item on the hierarchy (with the lowest SUDS score) for approximately five seconds.
2. Immediately after the five seconds think the word *relax* and imagine your calm scene for about twenty seconds.
3. Repeat the first item for ten seconds, ending with the thought *relax;* and then shift to the calm scene.

4. Repeat again for fifteen seconds, ending this period with the word *relax;* then shift your imagination to the calm scene.

If the first image, when kept in mind for different durations, does *not* result in an increase in SUDS level, proceed to the second image. At the slightest surge of anxiety (five or ten points), immediately think the word *relax* and shift to the calm scene. Continue to imagine the calm scene and breathe diaphragmatically until the level of 10 is regained. Then repeat the image, working up from the shortest duration to the longest duration. If the surge of anxiety occurs on your initial exposure to any item after the first, drop back to the previous item, imagine it at the shortest duration, and work yourself back to the item that resulted in the surge. The principle is similar to walking up a flight of stairs. If the step you take is uncomfortable, descend a step, compose yourself, and climb the step again. If you have experienced anxiety bursts of 20 or 30 points, you have not constructed your hierarchy properly. You need more steps (items) between the items you have included in your hierarchy.

In this manner, go through five items in your first session. Always end a session by relaxing to the initial SUDS level or lower. Never end a session with an anxiety burst, even if you have to end it without having completed five items.

Begin the sessions that follow by reviewing one or two of the items that you have most recently completed successfully. Then proceed with the five items targeted for the session. Try to schedule at least one session a day, without rushing through the hierarchy. After you have completed approximately a third of your items, begin each new session with an old item from the bottom of the list. Hold it in your imagination for thirty to forty seconds, relax, then proceed to the five items you have targeted for the day. Take one review item each session. As you become adept at the procedure and build strong relaxation with good mental control, you will be able to desensitize from five to ten items per session.

After you have completed the hierarchy, rearrange the order of the cards and rate each item without looking at your old SUDS scores. You should notice at least a fifty-percent reduction in score for each item except the emergency item. If you have not attained this reduction, repeat the troublesome items before proceeding to the next step. Upon completion of the hierarchy, take the FFS again and compare your total score to your initial score. Successful desensitization results in an average decrease of forty to sixty percent in the FFS score. By this time, you will find that you can much more comfortably entertain thoughts of flying.

Your success with the hierarchy may now be reinforced by desensitizing yourself to the photographs of an actual flight. Since the photographs are arranged in the same sequence they occur in an actual flight, it would be best for you to desensitize yourself to them in the order in which they appear. After having completed the desensitization with cards, most people can expose themselves to the photographic items for 30-second durations without much difficulty. As you proceed, try to place yourself in each picture. Again, the most important thing is to maintain your SUDS level at below 10. The same rules apply. If a surge of anxiety occurs, relax and shift to your calm scene. *These items are not tests of your ability to fly.* During the desensitization phase, your only task is to associate relaxation with each item. After having returned to a lower item, work back up to the triggering item and expose yourself to it for gradually increasing lengths of time. You may embellish the photographic scenes by listening to an audiotape of an actual flight,* while imagining yourself doing your exercise on a plane — being in control, looking out of the window and feeling relaxed, or lazily drifting off into a pleasant nap. Once the photographic desensitization is complete, it might be good to read chapter 10. You are now ready to experience real-life situations associated with air travel.

---

* This step is often not necessary but may be helpful in some cases. You can ask a friend to record a flight, or obtain a prerecorded tape from the Institute for Psychology of Air Travel.

Step 4: It's the Real Thing: Desensitization in Reality

To ensure complete control, it is important that all stressors prior to a flight be eliminated. This is particularly necessary for the fearful person who has avoided flight. By gradually allowing exposure to new sights and sounds, you develop relaxed confidence and orientation to the circumstances surrounding flight. This step is not as trivial as it may seem. We have measured the physiological responses of people who reported that they were apprehensive "only in flight," as they walked around the terminal or sat in a boarding area without intending to take a flight. Their emotional levels, as indicated by heart rate, skin-potential response, and skin resistance, were, on the average, higher than they would have been in another active environment such as a supermarket or bus terminal. Emotional levels may be elevated without our awareness of the fact. This finding is in agreement with the study cited by Desmond Morris in *Manwatching*, which found that people in airline ticket lines displayed significantly more behavioral indications of anxiety than those in bus-station ticket lines. Relaxing and desensitizing in the airline-terminal environment is an important precursor to flying without fear.

If you live in or close to a large city, short visits to an airport will pose no problem. Plan to arrive in time for lunch, or sometime in the early afternoon. Early-morning or late-afternoon rush-hour trips will be unsettling because of auto traffic. Those who live some distance away might plan a weekend trip to the airport. Reserve a room at the airport hotel and use the limousine service to travel to the airline terminals. You can use other times in the day for trips into the city. Traveling to the airport will familiarize you with the route and enable you to deal comfortably with aspects of the trip that may be stressful.

Over the years we have held our classes at Logan Airport in Boston. Numerous class members have related that their trips to the airport became less stressful as the class continued: some lost their apprehensiveness about going through the tunnel under Boston Harbor; others began to drive comfortably over the bridge across the Mystic River; still others became accustomed to the expressway traffic. Acquainting yourself with the approaches to the air terminal, even to the point of boredom, will ensure greater relaxation and more control over what is to follow.

On your first trip to the terminal, explore the facilities. Find out where the restrooms are situated. Locate the restaurants. If possible, select a restaurant with a view of the landing strip or loading areas. Visit the shops. After you feel at home, it's time to go to work. Find a comfortable seat in a waiting area away from the observation areas. People in terminals, as you will see, are occupied with their own thoughts and activities. They will not be too interested in watching you. Make sure your back is curved, to allow maximum diaphragmatic breathing (bring along a rolled towel or small pillow). Then begin the breathing exercise. Use only those components of the muscle exercise that are not too noticeable. Many students have learned to do the shoulder exercise in such a manner as to appear to be stretching. Let your eyes drift shut for a moment or two, and enjoy your calm scene. Once you have achieved deep relaxation, reorient yourself to the environment and do your assigned tasks. Apprehensive fliers will be able to proceed through the following hierarchy more quickly than those who have avoided flying altogether.

1. Stand in line at a ticket area and relax.

2. If there is no line, stand at the desk and relax. Should an agent ask to assist you, assert that you are working toward losing your fear of flying and are there to familiarize yourself with ticketing procedures. You will be pleasantly surprised by the amount of interest and conversation you generate. Ground personnel are most helpful in this respect.

3. Study the departing flights on the video monitors, and relax. Select a flight that will be departing soon, observe the departure gate, and ask directions to the gate.

4. Pass through the security post at the terminal. Walk down the hallway until you come to an area that does not have a parked aircraft. Seat yourself, facing in the most comfortable

direction (face the taxi strip or the hallway). Relax yourself to below 10 SUDS. Repeat this step facing the taxi strip. Observe the view through the window, while maintaining relaxation.

5. Repeat step 4 in a more crowded area that has a parked plane. Again, if SUDS levels dictate, face the hallway first. Then face the window and relax. Observe all the activity and the parked aircraft, while maintaining relaxation.

6. Walk to the window, support your arms on a barrier or column, and relax. Then study the view for longer periods of time.

These tasks may be accomplished in one session before lunch and one after. If you have to proceed more slowly, do not be discouraged. The idea is to associate relaxation with this phase of air travel. You are simply deconditioning the anxiety triggered by this environment. Congratulate yourself on the fact that you are discovering that this area is stressful and that you are overcoming the stress. Reward yourself with a healthy meal. After lunch, continue with your assignment.

7. Go to the gate of a flight that will soon depart. Relax and observe the boarding procedure. After the passengers have boarded, go to the window and watch the plane taxi away, while maintaining relaxation.

Remember, when performing these tasks, that you are simply an observer. *Do not* imagine yourself as a passenger.

8. Find an observation deck and watch planes taking off and landing. Relax for an extended period of time as you do this.

9. Go to the baggage-claim area and observe air travelers claiming luggage.

10. Repeat the first seven items with another airline, until SUDS levels are below 10 for each item.

11. Repeat each of the items above while entertaining the thought that you are an air traveler going through that particular phase of the air-travel experience. Entertain this thought for brief periods at first, relax, then try it for longer periods of time.

Continue your air-terminal familiarization until you are satisfied that your experience is controlled and relaxed. Avoid the thought "But I know I'm not flying" and other counterproductive self-disclosures. It will be most helpful to be accompanied by your co-worker at first, but strive to do the work alone when you go through it a second time. Do not push yourself to complete all the items in one day. Making two or three visits, in which a small number of situations are well-desensitized each day, is far better than exhaustedly completing one jammed session.

At some airports, those without tickets are not allowed past the security posts. Should you encounter this, asking permission from a customer representative (not a ticket agent) at the ticket desk will usually result in his or her accompanying you through. (It may help to show the representative this book, which you'll need to take along with you in any case.) You will find that these airline employees are selected and trained to help.

Once you feel comfortable in all parts of the terminal, you will have mastered the ground portion of the air-travel experience and will be well on your way to flying fearlessly.

You arrive at the airport and a Skycap asks if he can check your luggage.

Entering the terminal, you find yourself in a flurry of activity, including a passenger agent directing a young mother to her flight.

Now in line, you observe other passengers purchasing tickets.

The passenger agent looks up and asks your destination.

You watch while he punches a reservation into the computer.

As he fills out the ticket in your name, the flight becomes a reality.

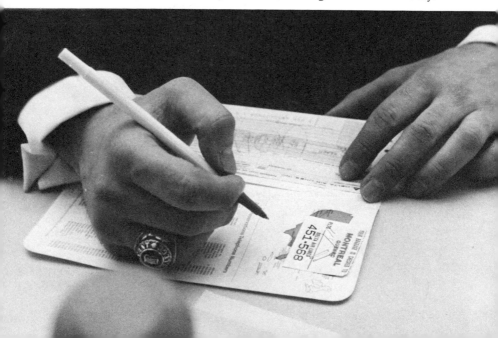

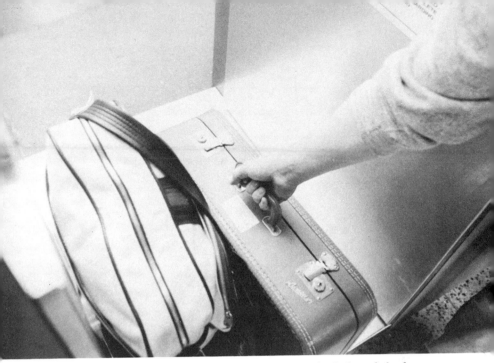

You leave heavy luggage at the counter to be checked aboard the baggage compartment of the plane.

All around you, signs are directing what must be done, in a serious vein.

PLEASE-NO JOKES

COMMENTS REGARDING DANGEROUS
ARTICLES OR ACTIONS
WILL BE TAKEN SERIOUSLY

WARNING
RESTRICTED AREA
Authorized Personnel Only
Beyond This Point
Approved Identification Badge Required

**OFFENDERS SUBJECT TO ARREST
AND PROSECUTION UNDER
FEDERAL AVIATION REG. Part 107**

Both your carry-on luggage and your clothing will be checked for heavy metal objects.

You walk through a metal detector before entering the boarding area.

And pick up your luggage from the security conveyor belt.

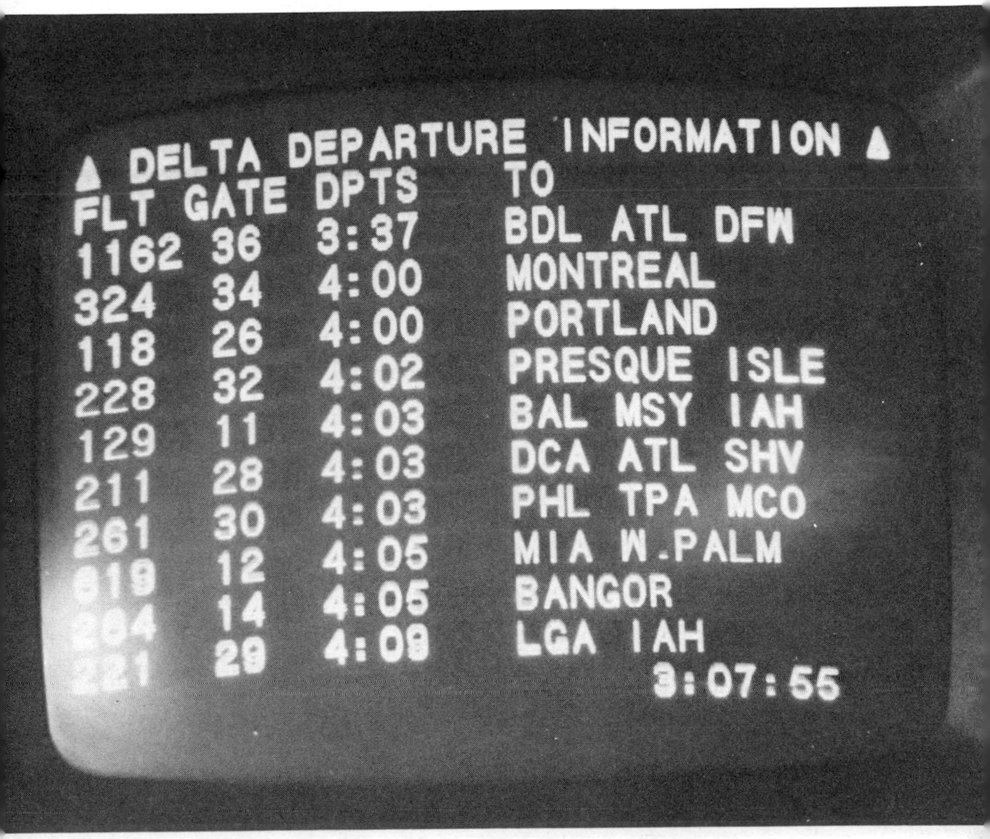
DELTA DEPARTURE INFORMATION
FLT GATE DPTS TO
1162 36 3:37 BDL ATL DFW
324 34 4:00 MONTREAL
118 26 4:00 PORTLAND
228 32 4:02 PRESQUE ISLE
129 11 4:03 BAL MSY IAH
211 28 4:03 DCA ATL SHV
261 30 4:03 PHL TPA MCO
12 4:05 MIA W.PALM
14 4:05 BANGOR
29 4:09 LGA IAH
3:07:55

You find a number of display screens listing your flight, your destination and gate.

As you approach the boarding area, modern jet aircraft seem to be growing closer . . .

. . . closer . . . and very close indeed.

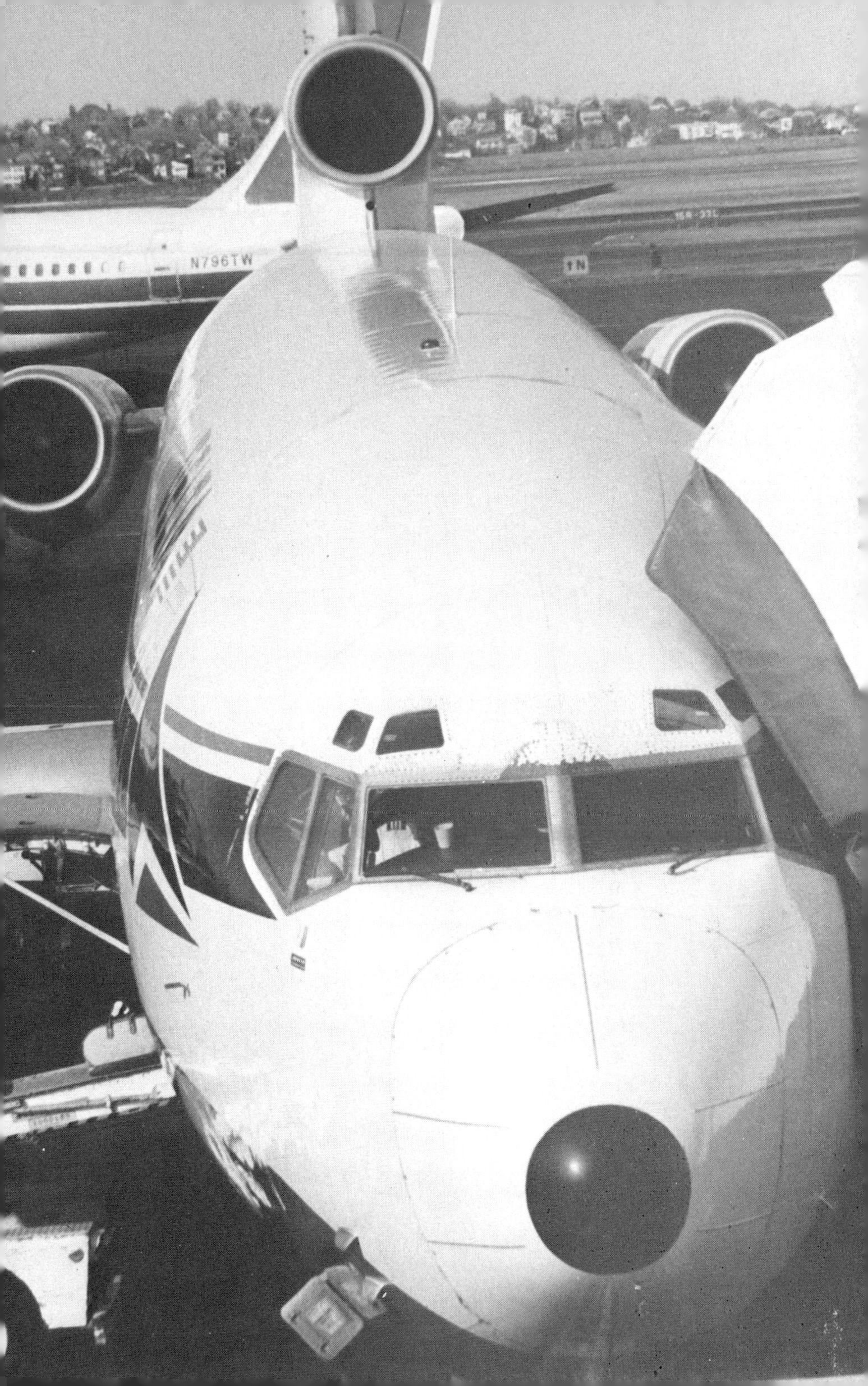
N796TW
1N

Standing in another line, you wait to receive a boarding pass for your flight.

With boarding pass in hand, you near the loading gate . . .

. . . which may simply be a walk across the field to a set of stairs leading to the plane, or . . .

. . . a tunnel you enter with other passengers.

This tunnel slants downhill and has no windows. To avoid disorientation, some of the passengers, like the man in the white shirt, trail one hand along the wall.

The entry tunnel sometimes seems like a lonely place for a fearful flier.

The doorway to the plane presents a conflicting array of horizontal and vertical lines.

As you pass through the door, being greeted by the flight attendant, you realize that you will soon be leaving the ground.

The flight attendant removes a portion of your boarding pass.

The Tourist Section has seats positioned six across.

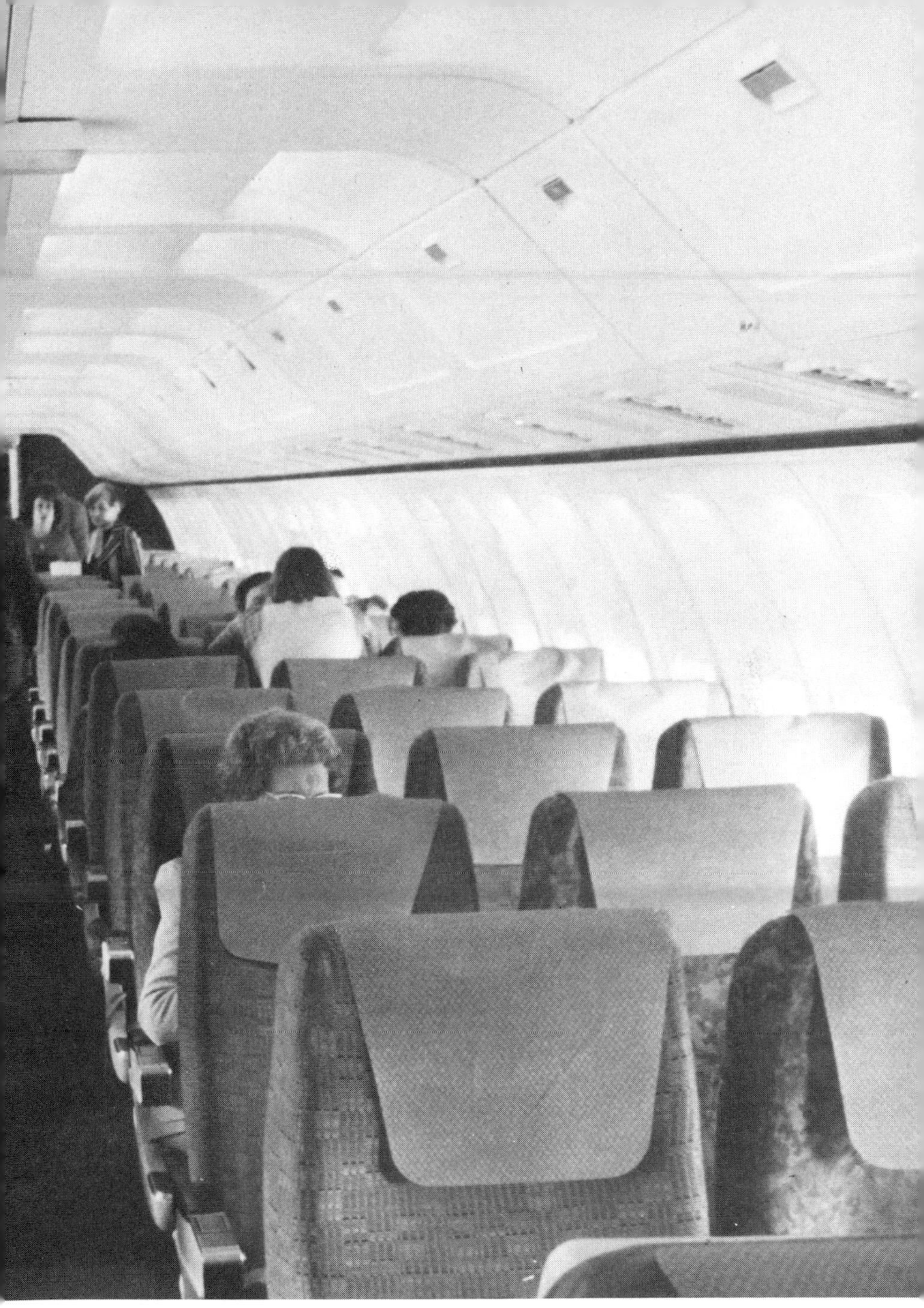

The viewpoint from your passenger seat is limited . . .

. . . and sometimes seems confining.

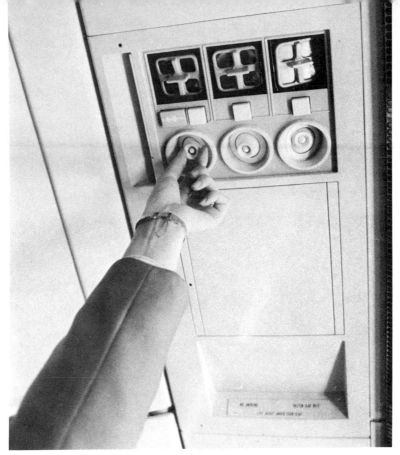

Above your head a control console offers air conditioning, a hostess call, and a reading light.

As you are examining this, a bell sounds and the No Smoking and Fasten Seat Belt signs both light at once.

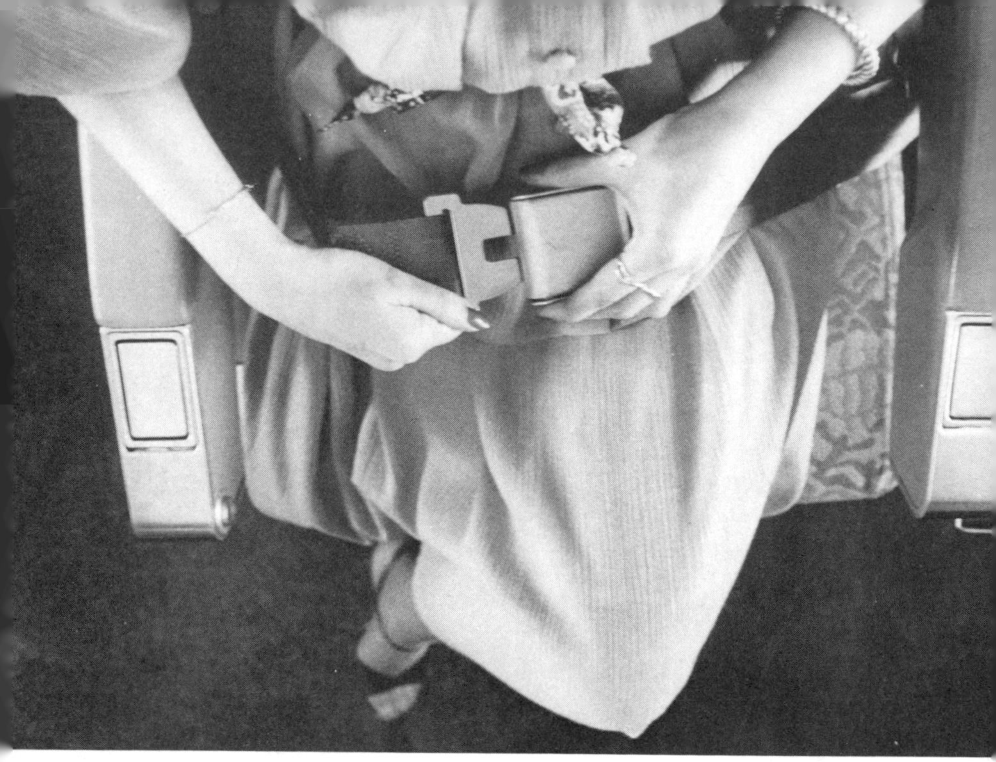

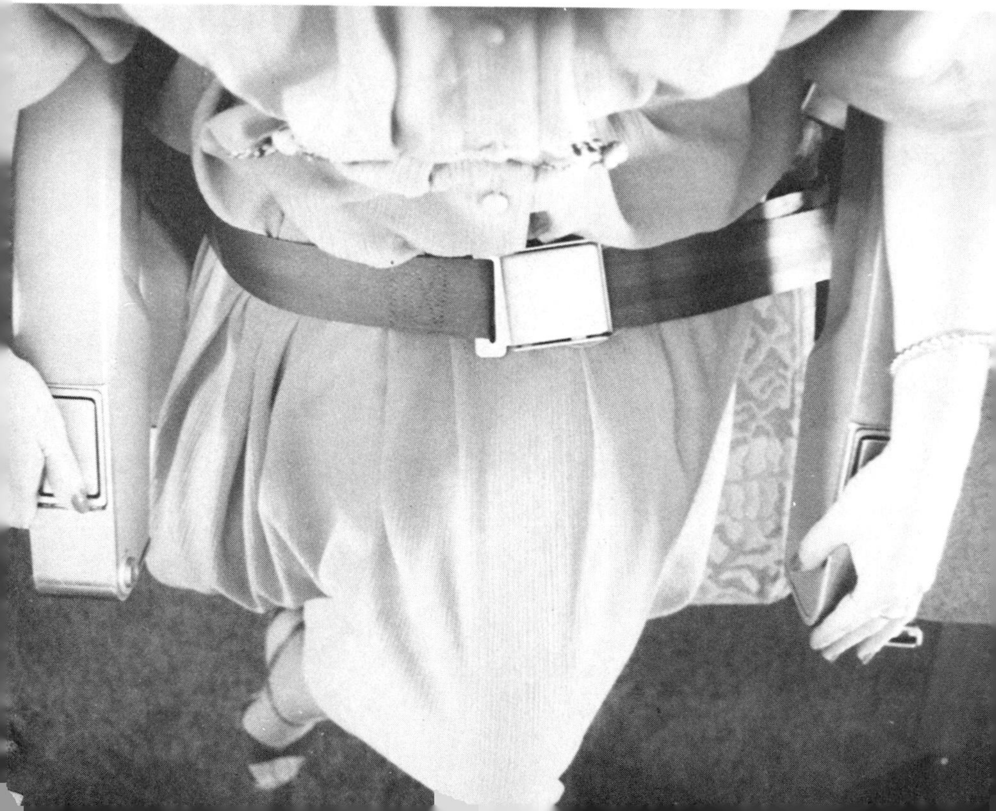

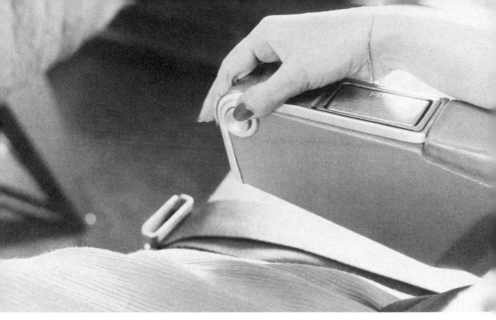

As you buckle up and press the button to straighten your seat back, you realize the plane will soon take off.

The flight attendant demonstrates the emergency oxygen breathing system.

The captain announces that your flight is next in line for takeoff. Your plane turns, and you catch a glimpse of the runway.

Pausing for only a moment, the engines roar and your plane lunges forward.

Faster and faster the plane rushes, until the runway marking lines seem blurred.

The plane lifts off the runway.

Prior to using the lavatory, you look inside and notice its smallness.

You extinguish a cigarette in the ashtray that is provided in every door.

By the ashtray is a sign that reads, "Vacant."

You enter the lavatory and slide a latch, which locks the door and

makes the sign read "Occupied."

As a fearless flier, you will learn to enjoy skyscapes — including other air traffic.

9

Aerodynamics for Fearful Fliers
Seeing Through Media Magnification

IF KNOWLEDGE ALONE could cope with fear, a standard physics textbook would be all a fearful flier needs. Even though I have seen a few rare cases in which fear was resolved by an explanation of flight and a discussion of the noises one hears in jet planes, the majority of fearful fliers need much more. This chapter has been designed to work in conjunction with our holistic program of nutrition, breathing, relaxation, and mental imagery to help air travelers master an unfamiliar environment.

Partial knowledge often strengthens flying fears. For example, a private pilot said to a friend at a cocktail party, "I told my wife she's a lot safer in my Cessna than in a big airliner, because if the engine goes out I can always find a spot to land, but those big babies drop like a rock." This, of course, is simply false. Jet planes have two to four engines, and the possibility of losing all power is quite remote. Even with no power at all, a modern jetliner can glide 150 to 175 miles from cruise altitude. Mass misinformation has led to the mistaken belief by many people that because a plane is made of metal, it will fall if power is lost. Since it has an aerodynamic form, a large metal aircraft is as capable of gliding as any small, light, private plane.

The news media also harm fearful fliers. Newspapers too often reinforce fears by generating dramatic verbal distortions, which appear to be written more for the purpose of selling newspapers than to provide information. Journalists should become psychologists for a day and see the effect their sensationalism has on readers.

A good example is an Associated Press story from the January 30, 1978 *Boston Globe*, under the headline, "As Jet Plummeted, Passengers Prayed." Apparently unmindful that he was creating the inaccurate image of an aircraft dropping straight down, the writer began this report with, "The jet plummeted downward and the pilot came on the loudspeaker. He said it was *plunging* toward the Atlantic." Even if the busy pilot had taken the time to make such a ridiculous announcement, which seems highly unlikely, it is doubtful that he would have used the word *plunge*. In the next paragraph, the writer distorted even the laws of physics. "For five minutes," the story continued, "the [plane], its engines out, fell — 8000 feet in all." A plane that takes five minutes to travel 8000 feet straight down is descending only 18 miles an hour — hardly "plummeting" or "plunging."

The only possible explanation is that the plane was doing what a plane is supposed to do: gliding *in* the sky, not falling *out* of it. Unfortunately, this story places more emphasis on near-disaster than on accurate reporting of the event. Unless the reader carefully analyzes the story as we have, another flight fear is reinforced.

Media magnification contributes to air-travel anxiety, because in news reports the general public only learns about flying through reading the particulars of air tragedies. We receive such distorted images of flight easily and without effort. This material is delivered to our homes. When we approach the subject of flight from the point of view of a description of a crash, we learn only one thing: a fear of flying.

Tens of thousands of perfect flights, in which the pilot touches the craft down like a feather, are never reported by the press. Figures from the National Transportation Safety Board, comparing the period from 1971 to 1975 with 1976, show a *decrease* of 82.6 percent in passenger fatalities. Your chances of being killed are almost fifty times greater when you're walking to the corner store than when you're flying to Europe.

Unfortunately, most of us learn about flying from news reports of air tragedies or from "heart-in-mouth" accounts of presumed near-disasters. These make exciting stories. Such reports are emotionally upsetting experiences for most readers. And learning anxiety is hardly the way to learn facts about anything!

The effect of media magnification is to generate fear through an imbalance in proportion. This imbalance is often unknowingly created. Perhaps an exercise in visualization will help clarify the point, not only for phobics but for the media as well. Imagine that this page is completely blank. If the white space represents all the safe flights in a year's passenger airline service, a microdot (about the size of the period ending this sentence) would symbolize the proportion of accidents. The news-media coverage of those accidents, however, would be represented by a large black circle about the size of a fifty-cent piece. Interestingly, if the media gave proportionally the same space and time to fatal automobile accidents involving drinking drivers, the reports would probably occupy five or six hours of television time and fill your Sunday newspaper, from cover to cover, for several weeks.

Inevitably, readers of sensational media reports about airplane disasters visualize the passengers, then identify with them and end up imagining what the experience would be like from a personal point of view. A fear that blocks further learning has then been created. Recognizing this, our version of aerodynamics for fearful fliers begins with flying objects that don't even contain people — paper airplanes.

Why Ben Franklin Was Smiling

At the Franklin Institute in Philadelphia, there is a magnificent marble statue of the scientist, philosopher, statesman (and behaviorist, although he didn't know it), Benjamin Franklin. In a rotunda called Franklin Hall, this huge seated figure smiles down beneficently on contemporary scientists and museum visitors.

Some say the statue actually looked amused one fall day in 1967, during what was perhaps the most unique event ever to occur in Franklin Hall — a regional semifinal in *Scientific Amer-*

ican magazine's "First International Paper Airplane Contest." Certainly, it was the kind of scientific sport that would have been thoroughly enjoyed by the editor of *Poor Richard's Almanack,* the man who flew kites during thunderstorms. A museum assistant, positioned high above the floor, on the mezzanine, committed one paper airplane after another to flight, while staff members below took precise measurements of time, distance, and maneuverability. Before it was over, this contest attracted more than 12,000 entrants from all over the world. You can read a full account and find a number of winning paper-airplane designs in a volume entitled *The Great International Paper Airplane Book.*

Although this was a promotional contest created more for fun than for the advance of technology, I mention it here because anxious fliers have much to learn from paper airfoils and paper airplanes. The most basic of aerodynamic forms, they serve to disprove the "plummet" image incorrectly attributed to airplanes by both the amateur pilot and the overzealous journalist.

First, let's make an airfoil, which can become the wing of a paper plane. Fold an 8½-by-11-inch sheet of paper in half, lengthwise. Before you do anything else, hold this flat surface with the fold facing you and blow on it. You'll find that aside from a little fluttering, nothing happens. When you have formed an airfoil, the same piece of paper will act quite differently.

Now slip the top edge of the folded paper toward the crease about a quarter of an inch (figure A). This will cause a "hump" to be formed, technically known as the *camber* of your airfoil. To make this camber permanent, tape the edges of the paper together at the ¼-inch location mentioned above. Now you're ready to demonstrate lift. With the camber facing upward, grasp the taped edges of your airfoil between the thumb and forefinger of both hands. Blow directly on the fold (figure B).

The paper will rise in a stream of air. This motion is the result of different air pressures against the top and bottom of the airfoil. Air must travel farther over the curved top section than it does over the flat bottom section. This creates a lower pressure on the top surface than is present on the bottom surface.

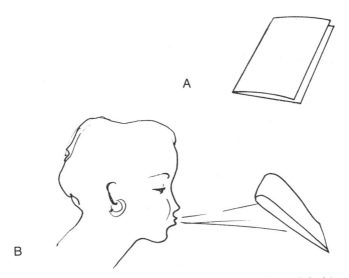

High pressure below and low pressure above produce lift. Your breath serves as air speed, and an aerodynamic form always has lift as long as it has air speed.

Multiply this pressure by the thousands of pounds of thrust produced by modern jet engines and the wingspans of contemporary aircraft, and it's easy to understand how tremendous forces are created to hold a plane aloft. Remember that the greater the air speed, the more powerful the lift. To prove this, stick your hand out of the window of your car when making turn signals. With your palm down and fingers together, tilt the edge of your thumb slightly upward. Notice the strong lift forces as your car travels at twenty or thirty miles an hour. Imagine the force and relative amount of air that would flow by at 600 or 700 miles an hour.

How to Make the *Fearless Flier*

You have created a wing. Now for the plane to go with it. Again take a piece of paper — preferably a stiffer type than used for the wing — and fold it in half. Cut out the silhouette of the rudder and body (figure C). Then fold vertically at a point just ahead of the "cabin," and cut a slot to hold the airfoil wing (figure D). You can stiffen the fuselage of the *Fearless Flier* with a drinking straw taped along the inner crease. Finally, slip the airfoil into its slot, center it, and add two or three paper clips to the nose, for weight (figure E). Fold down the stabilizer, since this model needs no rudder (figure F).

The *Fearless Flier* is designed to be dropped from a horizontal position. After a little adjustment (sliding the wing forward or backward, or adding or removing paper clips), notice how it glides when released from shoulder height. Next, take a pebble of approximately the same weight as the plane and drop both objects at the same time (figure G). The next time you read a newspaper report or hear someone talking about a jetliner plunging, plummeting, or "dropping like a rock," you will have the right to be scornful. You have performed an experiment, with an aerodynamic form, proving that planes do not plummet; they glide.

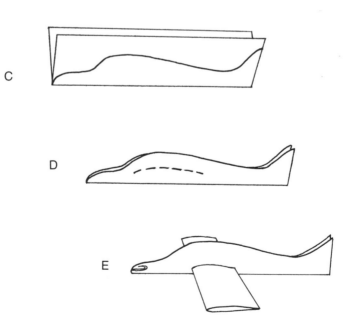

C

D

E

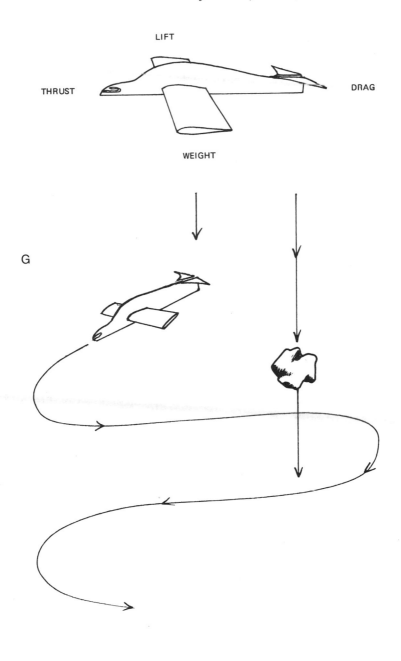

LIFT

THRUST

DRAG

WEIGHT

G

Heavier Planes — and Maneuverability

Hundreds of years before the Wright brothers flew their plane at Kitty Hawk, men leaped into the air attached to various types of gliders. Many times these flamboyantly designed contraptions reacted by creating lift. Indeed, mastery of manned flight often seemed tauntingly close to being achieved. Yet one of the most basic elements of air travel was missing from all of these early experiments. Before men could create powered flight, they had to learn how to turn an aircraft to the right and left.

Today, nearly eighty years later, it is difficult to believe that the Wright brothers began their experiments not knowing how to turn and bank a plane. Their discoveries about the lateral control of aircraft created a whole new body of knowledge that still holds true. Until Wilbur's glider flights in August, 1901, experimenters had theorized that airplanes could be steered with a rudder, much like a boat. By bending parts of the wing surface for control, the Wrights proved that another feature is necessary to ensure stable turns: rolling to one side or the other. A move to the right, they found, required lowering the right wing and raising the left.

Turns on land or water are one-dimensional maneuvers. A car or boat simply pivots one way or the other on its axis. Wilbur and Orville learned that their airplane, on the other hand, turned in two dimensions. *Yaw* — a pivoting motion — and *roll* — a tilting action that lowered the side of the plane toward the turn — were both required.

Today, no one would think of flying from New York to Los Angeles in the flimsy plane the Wrights built in 1902, with its structure of cloth, wire, and wood. Modern aircraft are skillfully assembled out of lightweight yet strong aluminum-copper alloys and super metals like titanium and molybdenum.

Airframes are designed to have unbelievable strength in relationship to light weight. Most of us think of metal as iron or steel. Metal used in transportation may even suggest to us an image of railroad tracks and engines. But metal no longer has to be heavy to be strong. The combination of copper and alu-

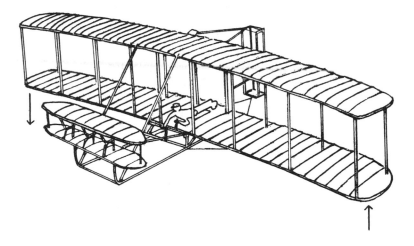

WRIGHT BROTHERS' AIRPLANE TURNING RIGHT

minum that comprises more than 95 percent of each modern jet is able to withstand thousands of pounds of pressure for each pound of its own weight.

These strong lightweight bodies are driven by a power plant that pilots call a marvel — the modern jet engine. The emergence of the turbojet in 1939 revolutionized aircraft propulsion. Planes had traditionally used complex piston engines with propellers (a form of rotating wing), to develop enough air speed so that the wings could create lift. One only has to read a description of the operation of an old piston engine to understand why these machines required constant vigilance and maintenance:

> Aviation piston engines are similar to car engines, but larger and more powerful — usually with six or eight cylinders . . . arranged in horizontally opposed pairs. Each pair drives one crankpin, via two connecting rods, and the front of the crankshaft is geared down to a slower running propeller. The rear end of the crankshaft drives accessories and may be geared up to a faster running supercharger which pumps extra air (to burn more fuel) into the engine as the aircraft climbs into thinner atmosphere . . .

Today's jet engines contain few moving parts and require minimum maintenance. They basically have three sections: a compressor, a combustion chamber, and a turbine. Up front, the compressor sucks in air and sends it to the combustion chamber. A kerosene-like fuel (much heavier and safer than gasoline) ignites in the combustion chamber, creating a stream of hot air. This high-energy air flows over a turbine, and performs two functions: it runs the compressor and shoots a high-velocity jet of hot air from the rear of the engine. Jet planes are pushed through the atmosphere at high speeds by thousands of pounds of thrust.

The combination of strong, lightweight metal wings and tons of thrust produces hundreds of tons of lift. In principle, it all works the same way your paper *Fearless Flier* works, but with a bigger push. Here, for example, are the thrust values and wing spans of four popular planes:

Plane	Approximate Total Takeoff Thrust	Wing Span
Boeing 747	104 tons (four engines)	196 feet
Boeing 727	24 tons (three engines)	108 feet
Lockheed 1011	63 tons (three engines)	155 feet
DC-9	14 tons (two engines)	93 feet

All jet planes are designed to fly and land safely on just one engine. Once every year, commercial airline pilots must go through a safety exercise that requires them to demonstrate the ability to handle a jet plane under two conditions: with half their engines working, and on one engine. Of all the pilots interviewed for this book, however, none had ever flown a scheduled flight during which the plane had lost power or all but one engine had failed. Whenever pilots talk about jet engines, they say more or less the same thing: "The reliability is remarkable."

Today's jet planes must prove their ability to withstand stress and strain under even the most punishing conditions. No other product must undergo as much regulation; their designs are tested for years before they are certified by the Federal Aviation Administration. Even before an airplane undergoes the strin-

gent and expensive certification process, the aircraft manufacturer spends at least 2 billion dollars for its design and tooling. A single Boeing 747 takes six months to build and costs between 45 and 65 million dollars.

A huge banner hanging in the Everett, Washington, plant, where the Boeing 747 is assembled, reads, "We are recognized by our quality. (What kind of recognition do you want?)." Standing on a balcony high above the production floor of this, the largest building in the world, a visitor can almost feel the deliberation and precision that separates aircraft manufacture from every other enterprise, except perhaps the manufacture of surgical instruments. There is movement, but no rushing. Typically, an employee selects a tool and then checks it before performing some assembly operation on a wing or body. The unforgettable sound rising from a production area the size of forty football fields is steady and, in its own way, precise. One wonders why this vast area seems so unusual for an industrial plant, and then realizes that it is because of the unbelievable cleanliness — of the floor, the machinery, and, above all, the aircraft being assembled. (Readers interested in enjoying this experience should contact the Boeing Company, P.O. Box 3707, Seattle, Washington, for information about plant tours.)

When you board a modern aircraft for your graduation flight, you will be stepping into a structure that is more carefully built, tested, and proved to withstand stress than your home is; a machine far more safe — by any standard — than your automobile.

In order to become airborne, a plane must accelerate to a speed at which the lift created by the wings overcomes the weight of the aircraft. For a Boeing 747, the takeoff weight will probably be more than 366 tons, requiring a ground speed of 180 miles per hour for liftoff. Its 196-foot wings (and, in fact, the wings of any aircraft) will bend, not only on takeoff but at various times during the flight. This should not alarm you — they're designed that way. The bending action means that the wings are doing their job, lifting the plane and absorbing shocks, just like the springs and shock absorbers in your automobile. The average time of liftoff for most commercial jets is forty-five seconds.

During the runway acceleration, which presses you against the back of your seat, the thrust of the engines cancels out the drag (the tendency of air to "stick" to the plane's body and control surfaces). When this happens, the jamming exercises you will learn in the next chapter are appropriate.

While in flight, your captain may turn to the right or left. During these banks, the cabin will not remain level. It will slant toward the direction of turn. If you are sitting on the left side of the plane during a left turn, for example, your seat will be lower than that of someone sitting on the right. You will see the line of the horizon move upward, as the ground fills the window view. This may seem strange if you are accustomed to turns on land or sea, which are basically flat. If you are accustomed to riding a bicycle, however, you may recognize the motion and view as similar to what you experience when turning a corner.

Movements in an aircraft seem exaggerated. As we have previously mentioned, most normal turbulence (which pilots call *chop*) causes less bumpiness than does driving on a country road at 35 miles per hour. "The most dangerous thing that can happen in clear air chop," a major airline captain says, "is that you may spill your coffee on your new tie."

The frequently used term *air pocket* is a total misnomer. There is no such thing as an air pocket. Turbulence, or chop, is caused by weather conditions, such as a mass of warm air meeting a mass of cold air, or a high-pressure front crossing a low-pressure front. On the airplane's radar screen, pilots are constantly watching weather conditions as far as 100 miles in advance of the plane. They carefully avoid any system that looks as though it might involve risky flying. Planes always carry enough fuel, and there are so many alternative routes that flying through rough air rarely occurs.

Charting Your Chop

One of my notebooks is filled with black felt-pen lines drawn over the blue guide lines. Most of these dark lines are smooth, while some look like a tiny child's first scribbles. The book is my "chop-chart log," a very handy device for keeping an informal record of flight conditions. It provides me with an objective frame of reference. You can start a similar log for car travel, even before your graduation flight. Keep a record of riding in an automobile under several types of road conditions — on highways, secondary roads, and dirt roads.

Use any convenient-sized spiral-bound notebook. At the top of the lined page, write the date, the nature of the trip, and the kind of vehicle. (Before you fly, your entry might be something like, "May 11, 1980 — Marblehead to Logan Airport — in 1979 Buick automobile.") Someone else will have to drive. Hold the log book in your left hand (if you are right-handed) and place your left elbow on an arm rest. As the car moves along, slowly trace the blue guide lines on the log book with a felt pen. When the car hits bumps, the motion will be transferred to your book, the page will move, and the pen will record the shock.

It's interesting to monitor air travel in the same way. Taxiing and irregular motions of the plane show up as peaks and valleys on your chart. The roughest marks on our chop charts are cre-

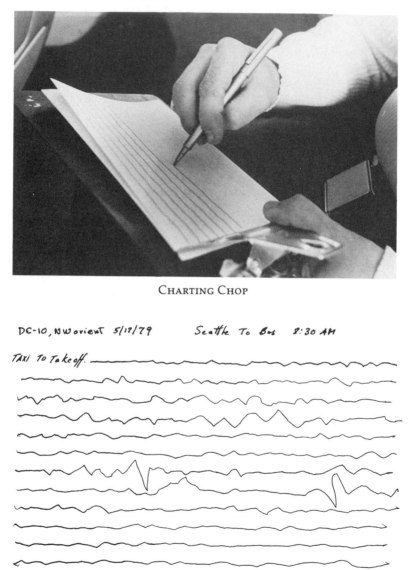

CHARTING CHOP

CHOP CHART — PLANE TAXIING TO TAKEOFF

ated as the plane taxis to the runway. In-flight charts are usually smooth. A chart made in the first-class section looks different from one made in the rear tourist cabin. Plan to take a log book and chart your graduation flight, and make sure to chart your automobile ride to the airport as well!

How a Plane Slows for Landing

Your plane will enter a glide path miles from touchdown, as it approaches the landing runway. In order to maintain lift at lower speeds, the captain extends slats from the leading (front) edges of the wings and flaps from the trailing (rear) edges. At a carefully calculated time, the landing gear is lowered to further slow the aircraft. Each of these operations is accompanied by characteristic noises, such as "thumps" and the sound of rushing air.

Passing over the end of the runway, the plane noses up and power is reduced. This gently lowers the craft until the landing gear touches the ground. Sometimes there is a slight bounce or skip when a large jet touches down. While it may seem like more in the cabin, the actual height of the bounce is usually only six or eight inches. Once all the landing gear is on the ground, the captain begins to slow the plane's speed. Slats and flaps are lowered to increase drag, while additional surfaces called "spoilers" rise from the wings. With an imposing roar, reverse-thrust buckets emerge at the rear of the jet engines, directing their blasts of hot air forward and outward. Use of the full wheel brakes is reserved for emergencies, but part of their stopping power is added to the action of the control surfaces and reverse-thrust buckets.

Many pilots will tell you that the most dangerous part of their job begins after they dock at the boarding ramp and leave the plane, for then they must face the perils of automobile travel to their ground destinations.

This chapter is meant to be an overview only. Its purpose is to familiarize you with a few scientific principles. For readers who would like to learn more about airplanes and the aerodynamics of air safety, several books are listed in our bibliography. The important information for you to pack with your luggage is:

1. Rocks plummet, airplanes glide.

2. From cruise altitude, a modern jet plane can glide 150 to 175 miles.

3. Engines provide thrust that pushes the airfoils, lifting the plane.

4. Aircraft are built to withstand far more stress than they will ever receive in service. Even one engine provides sufficient thrust to fly and land an aircraft. Most jets have three or four engines. Loss of power from one engine, which happens rarely, is of little consequence. During level flight the engines are not at full power; there's plenty left to spare.

If you have been practicing Active Stress Coping and feel comfortable with these aerodynamic facts, you are ready to fly. In the next chapter, we will plan your graduation flight.

10

Your Graduation Flight

THE PLANE eases up to the accordion-pleated end of a loading ramp at Logan Airport. As the cabin door opens, passengers disembark. Among them are about seventeen people who seem more enthusiastic, more ebullient than the others. Moving as a group, they disappear behind the doors of a Delta Airlines function room.

If you open one of those doors and enter, you will find yourself in the midst of a jubilant celebration. It is a graduation party for fearful fliers. For ten weeks these people have persistently practiced proper diet, diaphragmatic breathing, muscle relaxation, thought stopping, and passive mental imagery. Each made the decision that only he or she could make: when to fly.

Now, with glasses of champagne, they toast the new skill they have practiced and developed. Silver wings on lapels and dresses proclaim the ability to fly fearlessly.*

There is only one person in the world who knows when you should take your graduation flight, and that person is you. Most readers will find they are ready to take this flight no less than ten weeks after sitting down in a comfortable chair with this book. If you have reduced your intake of sugar, cut down on coffee, alcohol, and cigarettes, and filled your diet with nutritious food, your body is in the best possible condition for coping with stress. By this point, you have learned how to switch from thoracic to diaphragmatic breathing at will and

* If you would like your own set of Fearless Flier's wings, write the Institute for Psychology of Air Travel (see page 269).

have practiced the relaxation exercise at least 140 times (twice a day for ten weeks). You can create a passive scene, stop obsessive thoughts, and use assertive behavior. In short, you have prepared all three body systems — autonomic, somatic-motor, and central nervous. Taking a graduation flight without systematic desensitization and relaxation practice can only lead to disappointment and reinforcement of your flying fear. There are no shortcuts to flying with ease. You must practice, practice, practice.

When you feel you are ready and your scores are in the proper range, this chapter will help you plan a comfortable graduation flight.

Roy didn't even wait to sit down. "I'm ready to fly," he said. Having observed his increasing composure and ability to deal with stress situations, I agreed. When he settled into the office chair, Roy no longer hunched forward, with legs tightly crossed. His hands rested leisurely on the arms of the chair, his trunk was curved slightly backward, and I could see that he was breathing diaphragmatically. He looked strong. When he greeted me, his palms were dry and he wasn't clenching his teeth as before.

We chose a morning flight from Boston to Portland, Maine. This is an ideal choice. A graduation flight should be a round trip that totals no more than 800 miles. Many airlines offer flights to cities 400 miles or less away from your home, on planes that return within an hour. Recalling Roy's experience with the shuttle, we eliminated that flight as a possibility. It is also a good idea to avoid commuter flights on propeller craft. The objective of a graduation flight is to associate as much relaxation as possible with the kind of large jet aircraft used on longer trips.

"How about Saturday morning? Is that okay with you?" Roy asked.

Since Roy was a private patient, I would be flying with him. If you have selected a co-worker, as suggested in chapter 8, that person should accompany you. Remember, your companion should be the person who has worked with you on systematic desensitization and who understands SUDS levels and relaxation exercises. Throughout the flight, there will be SUDS-level readings and relaxation exercises. It is your co-worker's responsibility to remind you of the steps in the strategy, so that you will not have to be concerned with that aspect of the flight.

Mornings are best for graduation flights, and weekends offer an opportunity to fly on planes that are generally less crowded. The fearful or first-time flier should not schedule a graduation flight at night. Mastery of the stresses imposed by darkness should come only after the completion of a successful daylight flight.

Before his San Francisco flight, Roy had reserved seats on planes many times, so he knew how easy it is. The transaction is usually handled by telephone, the earlier the better. In fact, some airlines offer discounts for advance bookings. Also, if the airline you call does not have a flight that offers immediate return to the city of your choice, its ticket agents can often find one for you on another airline. Reservation clerks will even book a seat for you on another airline.

The Graduation Flight Plan

To ensure that Roy would stay in control of his anxiety, he and I planned the flight carefully. He would pay extra attention to nutrition for at least three days prior to the flight. Before going to the airport, he would have a good breakfast, with no coffee. Timing is essential. The unnecessary stress caused by rushing (as well as the possibility of being "bumped" because of lateness) is not advisable, so we agreed to meet at the ticket counter forty-five minutes before flight time. (When traveling, allow even more time, because security checks can be time-consuming.)

Even though the actual trip was several days away, we planned Roy's relaxation-exercise strategy to match the feelings and sensations that occur during various phases of flight. Let's take a look at the plan.

A. When the captain receives tower clearance, he or she turns

STAGES OF FLIGHT

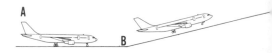

the plane on the runway and begins acceleration. Three chimes will usually be sounded, or the flight attendants will be asked to take seats. At this time, we need to use the jamming exercises: relax the feet, buttocks, and shoulders, then commence the breathing exercise. The procedure is timed to last forty-five seconds, which corresponds to the average time necessary for takeoff. In a properly jammed takeoff, the release of the shoulders and neck coincides with the moment of liftoff. Loose muscles symbolically give the body over to the airplane at liftoff. Relaxed muscles become shock absorbers, while tense muscles make the flier feel even the most subtle vibrations of the plane. This principle will be discussed later.

B. At liftoff, the friction of the wheels on the runway suddenly disappears. The flier experiences a quick, smooth feeling of uplifting support, which some describe as a gentle "oomph." Almost immediately, a series of thumps and bumps occur as the landing gear retract. The plane angles sharply upward in a climb, at maximum power, and some pressure may be felt in the ears. To relieve this we will swallow, chew gum, or yawn, while making a yawning sound. This will equalize the pressure on either side of the ear drums. While the plane is climbing to cruise altitude, it may also bank, causing the horizon line to move up or down in the window view. During a climb is an excellent time for a full relaxation exercise of ten to fifteen minutes. As soon as the No Smoking sign goes off, recline your seat. The Seat Belt sign will remain lit, but the belt may be slightly loosened.

C. When the plane reaches cruise altitude, a new engine sound will occur that is lower in pitch than previous engine sounds. The speed will be slower, but since the passenger's body is still moving at climb speed, the G forces of deceleration

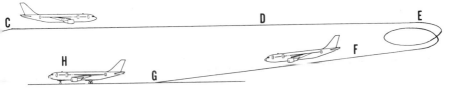

are not felt. Instead, one gets a brief sensation of floating. A portion of the jamming exercise will counteract any discomfort this feeling might cause. After this point, the captain will turn the Seat Belt sign off.

D. During level flight, a jetliner offers comfort and luxury away from telephones, television, and the cares of an earth-bound world. Flight time offers a fine opportunity for additional relaxation exercises, listening to music (either from the plane's system or from a small portable tape machine with an earplug), reading, catching up on correspondence, enjoying skyscapes, or meditating. To many, the gentle, throbbing "white sound" of the engines is an invitation to sleep. One can also play backgammon or card games. Things the flier should *not* do include engaging in games, if he or she is an extremely competitive person; using the time to mull over family problems; reading mystery stories or other tension-producing literature; engaging in self-analysis; drinking alcohol; or trying to make a date with the flight attendant. From time to time, the plane may encounter chop. Today, pilots usually know about this condition ahead of time and make an announcement to the passengers. On-board radar can tell the pilot about weather 100 miles ahead of the plane. When the announcement is made, one should start a jamming exercise. If chop is encountered, it should be counteracted instantly by another jamming exercise. On a recent flight from Atlanta to New Orleans, one fearful flier who practiced this procedure reported no sensations of tension and actually got off the plane refreshed, while several of her male friends who tried to anesthetize themselves with alcohol left the plane exhausted. Alcohol plus chop generally means nausea.

E. The captain usually will announce when the descent of

the plane begins. This may be as far as sixty miles from the airport. To create additional lift at slower speeds, the flaps will be extended from the wings, causing a series of whirring and grinding sounds. The decrease in speed at this point is subtle and may go unnoticed. As the plane enters the airport traffic pattern, there will probably be a series of banks, as the plane circles. This is the cue for the initiation of another complete relaxation exercise.

F. At the point of final approach, the No Smoking and Fasten Seat Belt signs will be lit. Flight attendants will tell passengers to bring their seats erect and lock the tray tables. With a series of thumps, whirrs, and groans, the landing gear will be lowered. When this mechanism hits the air stream flowing under the fuselage, the flight becomes less smooth, and a perceptible slowing of the plane will occur. Each of these events is an opportunity to use jamming. As the plane settles into its approach to the runway, begin a full relaxation exercise. At lower altitude there are more air currents. Since the plane is moving slower and adjusting to the approach, the ride will not be as smooth as at cruise power.

G. Modern jet planes are designed to land on their wheels amidships (at the wings), then tilt forward onto the front wheels. Frequently there is a slight skip or bounce as the first set of wheels touches down. The height of this bounce seems greater than it really is. The plane generally goes four to six inches off the ground and then settles back again. When the nose wheels touch down, reverse buckets over the engine jets create a tremendous roar. A sudden deceleration presses passengers forward, away from their seats. For this reason, a jamming exercise should begin as soon as the roar is heard. Pulling the feet back counteracts this forward motion.

H. At this point, flight attendants give some very important advice, which often goes unheeded. All passengers should remain seated during the taxi to the boarding ramp. There are times when a plane's brakes must be applied suddenly, and standing passengers, particularly those crouching under the overhead compartments, could be thrown off balance and seriously injured. This is a good time to practice diaphragmatic breathing to prevent feelings of claustrophobia. It's also a good time to relax and to indulge in self-congratulation. Notice how eager many passengers are to get up, only to stand in line and wait to disembark.

The Liberation of Roy

Roy met me at the ticket counter, on time and dressed as I had recommended. He wore a pair of loose-waisted casual slacks and an open-collared sport shirt. On his feet were comfortable, rubber-soled shoes. Tight clothing, such as girdles, should be avoided when you're flying; and many travelers carry slippers to wear on longer flights. (Tight shoes become a discomfort because feet have a tendency to swell slightly at reduced levels of air pressure.)

"I've already completed one relaxation exercise at home," Roy told me as he bought his ticket.

The actuality of the flight, combined with his excitement, had raised Roy's anxiety base level. His SUDS score stood at 45 — much too high to board a plane, but typical of fearful fliers at this point.

We walked to the loading area and checked in, so we could make our seat selection. Roy chose an aisle seat in the No Smoking section forward of the wing. This is a good seat for a graduation flight. If there had been a first-class section on our flight, we would have chosen seats there. The most comfortable flying is usually over the wings or in front of them. In addition, the more spacious accommodations in first class offer larger seats and more room for carry-on luggage; also, the ratio of flight attendants to passengers is higher, resulting in better service. One serious precaution: most first-class tickets include free alcohol. Just because something is free is no reason to accept it. One drink of alcohol can cancel ten weeks of faithful relaxation practice. In this case, something free may be far too expensive! It is important that you master the situation on your own, without dependency on chemicals. Drinking alcohol in order to cope is really an admission that the situation is too much for you to handle. (Think about occasions in which people have said, "I need a drink.")

While seated in the lounge prior to boarding, we decided to

do something about Roy's SUDS level. I guided him slowly through a relaxation exercise, and when we were finished, he looked at me and said, "I'm not sure that helped."

I told Roy that it had helped, but that his perception of the change in his SUDS level was being hampered by the intensity of his anxiety. This condition is governed by Weber's Law, which states that as the base level of any stimulation increases, a greater change in stimulation is necessary before one can notice a difference. In other words, as anxiety increases, the ability to detect a reduction decreases. It is essential that fearful fliers understand Weber's Law, because it explains why they should repeat relaxation exercises over and over again under conditions that are highly stressful. Remember that during practice, exercising always reduced your SUDS level somewhat. That reduction always occurs, whether you perceive it or not.

You can demonstrate Weber's Law with room lights and a book of matches. First, turn all the room lights up to full brilliance. Put on ceiling lights, table and floor lamps — everything. Then have someone turn away, facing a wall, and ask him to light a match, then blow it out. You will perceive no change in the room illumination, even though the match flame has provided additional light. This is exactly what happens after you do a relaxation exercise when your SUDS level is high. The exercise works, reducing anxiety, but you can't perceive its effect.

If, at this point, you say to yourself, "My God, it's not working," you are actually suggesting that you are powerless. This misconception turns anxiety into panic. Rather than working against anxiety, you are calling for surrender. The statement means that your anxiety is not the slightest bit affected by any of your efforts. Our experiments show that doing an exercise, regardless of the anxiety level, always reduces physiological stress levels, even though subjects cannot perceive the reduction. A recent study shows that the reverse is also true. Saying negative things about oneself will increase physiological activity even though one may not notice the increase (Schuele, 1980).

Now turn down the lights. Make the room dim, but not dark.

Again, have someone face a wall and strike a match and blow it out. You will see a glow against the wall and then notice a reduction in light. Similarly, at low levels of anxiety the effect of the relaxation exercise becomes more obvious. At a lower level it is easy to say to yourself, "I feel more relaxed. I am in control."

The lesson to be learned from Weber's Law is that the more relaxed you are, the more sophisticated your ability to detect change in your body. When under stress, you should repeat relaxation exercises until you detect a drop in SUDS level. If you detect a reduction from a high SUDS level, you will know you have reduced anxiety by a large amount. Once you notice the change, you will be able to do the exercise again with an even greater drop in anxiety.

In all, Roy went through three relaxation exercises in the boarding lounge. "I'm down to about twenty-five, and I'm really glad we got here early so there was time to do this," he told me.

A fearful flier should have a SUDS level of thirty or lower before boarding a plane. From the material in chapter 3, you have learned that some of the highest SUDS levels occur just prior to takeoff. This is because the anticipation of a fearful experience is often more stressful than the experience itself. Moreover, the normal excitement of this time is usually perceived as anxiety by the fearful flier. Working on tension reduction and thought stopping during the period from ticket purchase to boarding helps the graduate see that he or she can bring the anxiety of anticipation under control. Waiting until you are on the plane to exercise, denying anxiety, or quitting after one exercise can lead to boarding the plane with a SUDS level that is too high.

Our departure was announced, and we approached the door to the ramp. After showing our boarding passes, we entered the boarding tunnel. Roy remembered to trail his hand along the wall for orientation. He had remarked to me earlier that this confining, downward-pitched environment, in which noises are distorted, had never seemed to bother him. Now, however, he turned to me with a knowing look.

"It works," he said.

The flight attendant tore off half of our boarding passes, and we went to our seats. Immediately, Roy opened the overhead compartment and removed a pillow, which he placed at the middle of his back as he reclined his seat. In the erect position, airline seats are designed for safety, not comfort. Roy was now in a good position to breathe diaphragmatically. With his seat reclined and a pillow in the small of his back, he did a full relaxation exercise as the other passengers filed past.

When Roy finished his relaxation exercise, his SUDS level was fifteen. Because he had been in the midst of a relaxation exercise, he had not noticed the thuds and bangs as the baggage was loaded into compartments below our feet. The flight attendant began making her welcome and safety announcements to a full plane. Except for an elderly lady, two teenagers, Roy, and myself, she might as well have been talking to herself. It always amazes me that people can converse or read while important safety information is given.

Here is a typical pre-flight announcement, much like the one Roy and I heard:

> At this time please check to see that your seat belt is fastened, your seat is upright, and your tray table is closed. May we also remind you to place all your cabin baggage under the seat in front of you.
>
> A safety-instruction folder has been placed in the seat pocket in front of you. We ask that you review the information contained in it. On our [plane], the emergency exits are the doors on both sides of the airplane. Please familiarize yourself with the exit nearest you.
>
> Our cabin altitude is controlled for your comfort but should it change, an oxygen mask will be automatically released from the unit above your seat. Pull down sharply on the mask, place it over your nose and mouth, and secure it with the strap, as your cabin attendant is now demonstrating. Continue to breathe normally until you are advised that the masks are no longer needed. We ask that you do not smoke while oxygen is in use.

With some variations, every flight must begin with these announcements. This is required by federal law. Listening to them — they are different for each type of aircraft — is not only a matter of courtesy but also a matter of safety for the air traveler. A word of caution: If pre-flight announcements cause an increase in your SUDS level, immediately perform a relaxation exercise.

The flight attendant passed our seats on the way to the back of the plane, as it was taxiing to the runway, and asked Roy what he was doing. Roy, who was busy charting the light bumps and jiggles in his chart chop log, looked up and told her that he was a fearful flier on a graduation flight. (It is important to assert yourself. You may find that others are more interested in what you are doing than you would expect.) With the dramatic increase in the number of passengers per flight, many more people have to be served by each flight attendant. Consequently, he or she has less time to devote to individual passengers. Fearful fliers, first-time fliers, and graduates should always identify themselves but should also inform attendants that they have a set plan to follow.

There were squeaks and groans, as well as a few rattles, as the plane taxied. I told Roy that these sounds were all normal, since a plane is designed to fly smoothly through the air, not roll along a concrete strip like an automobile on a highway.

From somewhere in the cabin, three chimes sounded. The plane wheeled sharply to the right. It hesitated for a second, and with an increasing roar lunged forward. At exactly that moment, Roy lifted his toes to begin the jamming exercise. As the plane gathered speed, we were pressed against the backs of our seats. Roy tensed his feet, pushing himself back farther into the seat. Rather than allowing the takeoff to cause unfamiliar feelings in his body, he was causing even more intense feelings on his own. Relaxing his feet, he tensed his buttocks. Some trays in the galley rattled, and the plane roared down the runway. Relaxing his buttocks, Roy hunched his shoulders. As his shoulders relaxed, the plane lifted off the runway. Roy took a deep diaphragmatic breath and relaxed even more.

When I told Roy we were airborne, he opened his eyes and smiled broadly. He said his SUDS level was still about fifteen. The No Smoking sign went out just as we began to swallow and yawn to equalize the pressure in our ears. At this point, we reclined our seats once again, in order to assume more comfortable positions, ones conducive to diaphragmatic breathing. Roy started another relaxation exercise.

Relaxation is essential aboard a plane. White-knuckled fliers not only lock important chest muscles, making their thoracic breathing difficult; they also practically weld themselves to the chassis of the airplane. When tense muscles grasp the arms of the seat, they transmit every slight shock or vibration (signals of "danger") to the scanning centers of the brain. How much better it is to relax the large muscles, so that they act as soft shock absorbers, adding to the cushioning effect of the seat. It is well to remember the Oriental proverb in which the straight, stiff oak falls in a high wind, while the delicate but flexible reed bends with the wind and survives. In a plane, it is more comfortable to be a reed than an oak.

Soon we were at cruise altitude. The pitch of the engines lowered, and we passed through a momentary "suspended-in-air" sensation, which elicited no reaction from Roy. At low tension levels one does not tend to overreact to differences in sensation. Even though the Seat Belt sign was extinguished, we followed the captain's advice, keeping our belts loosely fastened across our reclined seats. Roy was now at his lowest SUDS level, about ten. He needed no prompting to congratulate himself for having brought this number down from the forty-five he had experienced in the boarding lounge.

"What a difference," he told me, "when you get all the systems working for you. I never would have believed fear can be controlled by what you eat and how you breathe, as well as what you think."

It was a good time to talk about looking out the window. You don't have to be a fearful flier to feel uncomfortable or apprehensive about peering downward from heights. Years ago, one of the first wide-screen films featured a scene from the nose bubble of a plane that was skimming across the desert, just a few feet off the ground. Suddenly, and without warning, the camera passed over the lip of a crevice, revealing the Grand Canyon stretching thousands of feet below. The camerawork was breathtaking, and, for some, stress-producing. This contrast in points of view — first skimming a few feet from the ground and then being suspended several miles in the air — demonstrates why many people feel drawn downward into a scene they observe from a height.

At close range — when we are skimming along the ground or sitting in the cabin of a jet plane, for example — our eyes must converge in order to focus. The eyeballs rotate inward, toward one another. When the viewpoint changes to a more distant range — for instance, the Grand Canyon or a scene seven miles below the window of a plane — the eyeballs must suddenly rotate outward, in order to allow the eyes to focus to infinity. It is the subtle muscular action of this outward rolling that creates the sensation of pitching forward.

An experiment will prove the point. Stand erect, with your arms extended in front of you, fingertips touching. Focus on your fingers. Now sweep your arms out to your sides, and you will feel that you are pitching forward.

After some practice at a simple physical maneuver, anyone can enjoy the panorama of flight. From delicate fleecelike clouds over rich farmlands to majestic bodies of water and sunset-washed skyscrapers, the view from a plane is beautiful, memorable, and ever-changing. First, look upward instead of downward. Tilt your head and gaze at a point about forty-five degrees above the horizon. Next, look slowly down at the horizon. Look up once more, and then back down at the horizon. Then lower your gaze to a point about forty-five degrees below the horizon. Look back up at the horizon. Bring your view down forty-five degrees again, and then look back at the horizon. By this time, you should have oriented your senses to looking downward without feeling that you are being pulled into the scene below. (This technique is very effective for those who fear heights and the edges of porches.)

I suggest, however, that the graduate take an aisle seat and save most of the skyscape-watching for his next flight. Remember, even though you are moving at about 600 miles per hour, from cruise altitude it appears that the plane is not moving. It will take some adjustment to accept this apparent incongruity.

On this short trip, there was no in-flight food service. At my suggestion, Roy had brought along some grapes, cheese, and crackers. While the flight attendant served the orange juice we had requested, there was time to look around and observe the nervous behavior of some of our fellow passengers.

Across the aisle, a young junior executive was using the flight time to down a scotch and soda (at 10:30 in the morning!), while making an intense appeal for a higher advertising budget. The man to whom he was talking was an older gentleman who looked like a senior officer of the company. He appeared uncomfortable and unimpressed.

A middle-aged woman sat with elbows jammed against the arm rests and hands tightly clenched. She was being completely ignored by her husband, who was heatedly discussing the Boston Bruins hockey team with the man next to him.

In the midst of her serving duties, the flight attendant was busy fending off advances from a heavily mustached young man in a three-piece business suit. Trying to be polite, she listened to his provocative questions while pushing the beverage cart and preparing drinks for other passengers. Another would-be Romeo held forth in the galley, occupying the time of a second flight attendant.

Finishing his protein- and fructose-rich snack, Roy released his seat belt, rose, and walked down the aisle toward the lavatory. There is a method of walking in a plane during a flight that will prevent you from becoming disoriented or losing your balance. Grasp the seat backs on either side as you move along. There is no need to establish a tight grip; a light touch will do. This gives a point of reference, balance, and stability to your walk. (Incidentally, it is unsafe and inconsiderate to walk down the aisle with a lit cigarette.)

Whether you have to use it or not, it's a good idea to become familiar with the "blue room" during your graduation flight. If you are smoking, be sure to extinguish your cigarette before entering. Slide the latch that positions the "occupied" sign on the door. Sit on the toilet, with the lid down if you are not going to use it, and do a relaxation exercise. Many people stonewall their fear of walking back to the bathroom because they don't want to let all the other passengers know they have to go. Others fear confinement in a small space. A few moments' exercise during your graduation flight can free you from these anxieties. If enclosed spaces bother you, enter the room with the door open. Then reenter the room, closing the door slightly. Next reenter the room and close the door without throwing the latch. Then throw the latch with the door open, examining how it works. Finally, enter, close the door, and throw the latch. (In some planes the lights in the room will get brighter when you throw the latch.) Remain in the room for a moment, then open the door. In this manner you can grow progressively more comfortable by spending increasingly long periods of time in the lavatory. This exercise can be performed on the plane before takeoff, if you wish. Every discomfort contributes to the pressure that propels people toward panic. Air travel is often accompanied by nervousness and excitement, which cause bladder pressure and the urge to urinate. Denying this body necessity in order to accommodate unreasonable fears can contribute to a conditioned flight anxiety.

On his return from the tail section of the plane, Roy said, "There's a woman in back who's not feeling well. Maybe you could help her."

I investigated and found an attractive young woman in her late twenties who was about six months pregnant. Her chest was heaving and she was gasping for breath as she pushed away an airsick bag the flight attendant was trying to place over her nose and mouth. I suggested that we have her sit in the attendant's jump seat, with a pillow placed at the middle of her back. After this was done, we held half a glass of club soda under her nose, and I instructed her in diaphragmatic breathing. Since we were at cruise altitude, the carbonation bubbling out of the soda was dense. Soon, the carbon-dioxide balance was restored in her system. She was breathing normally but feeling embarrassed.

"I have claustrophobia," she said. "I'm fine as long as I can get an aisle seat. This flight was full, and they put me between two fat ladies. I just felt closed in until I couldn't breathe." The pregnancy also contributed to her breathing problem. With less space in her abdomen, she was forced to breathe with her upper chest.

On a plane, the pressurization drives carbon dioxide out of a carbonated drink at such a rate that a glass of soda is perfect first aid for hyperventilation.

The captain had announced our descent into the Portland area. At the lower altitude, he cautioned, we might encounter some turbulence. As we had planned, Roy went into his two-step routine for coping with turbulence. First, he went through a forty-five-second jamming exercise. Then he took out his flight log, which contained SUDS levels and chop-chart sheets, and began charting the turbulence in the manner described at the end of chapter 9.

"Look at this," he said. "The bumps up here don't move the pen half as much as the bumps we hit in the car on the way to the airport."

Charting the chop puts airplane movement in perspective. We should encounter chop in a mood of relaxed observation. First, make sure your muscles are relaxed and not tense. Remember, if you are glued to your seat by white knuckles and tight muscles, the chop will shudder throughout your body and cause mental havoc. But if you are relaxed (after a jamming exercise) and breathing diaphragmatically, you, like the reed, can loosely bend and flex with the plane's motion. Casual observation, recorded on your chart, will give you an objective mental attitude.

Now we were yawning again to "open" our ears, while the plane was banking to the left. Roy chose this time to complete a full relaxation exercise and failed to notice the sound of the flaps being extended. He opened his eyes just as the landing gear went down and the No Smoking sign lit up for our final approach.

At treetop level, Roy began a relaxation exercise to prepare himself for the landing. The plane tilted slightly from side to side, accelerating and decelerating as the pilot lined up with the runway, while Roy once again tensed his buttock muscles and released them. Out of the window, I could see a blur of hangars and parked private planes. Roy hunched his shoulders. The wheels touched in a perfect landing as his shoulders dropped in relaxation. Roy took a deep diaphragmatic breath and . . . let it out as the engine exhaust roared against the reverse-thrust buckets. He immediately used the forty-five-second jamming procedure to counteract the pressure of deceleration. Pulling his feet back, he pressed himself into the seat as the slowing plane urged his body forward.

Roy opened his eyes and turned to me. "I made it and I'm

free to fly," he said. "Doctor, I think you know this has changed my life."

I reminded him that for the next five to ten flights he would have to repeat the procedure he had just used. The best way to master fear is through overlearning. Gradually he would be able to do condensed versions of the exercises, until, at some time in the future, his control would be exercised unconsciously.

Postgraduate Travel Tips

Of necessity, the graduation flight described here was short. We tailored the information to fit a round trip of less than an hour each way. The next step for most formerly fearful fliers is to increase the distance and the amount of time in the air. Below is a potpourri of hints to help you get the most pleasure per air mile on longer flights.

1. Plan to arrive at the airport early. Airlines usually sell more tickets to a flight than there are seats. This is done in order to make up for "no shows" (passengers who reserve seats but never buy tickets or show up for the flight). Once in a great while everyone shows up, and there are more passengers than seats. In this event, seats are given out in the order in which passengers arrive at the boarding-area desk. One airline estimates that only about two passengers in ten thousand are actually denied boarding, but arriving early is a good hedge against getting "bumped."

2. Pack a day in advance. Rushing around on the day of a flight is a stressful experience. Lock and strap your bags. Remove pull straps from luggage with wheels to prevent tearing. Many people place their address-identification tags inside-out on their suitcases, feeling that their absence from a home with silverware, television sets, jewelry, and personal property should not become a matter of public knowledge.

3. Your carry-on luggage should contain a change of underwear, stockings, essential toilet items, and medication. When you're prepared with these, you will not have to rush around buying things in a strange city if you should become separated

from the luggage you have checked aboard the plane. If at all possible, pack light and carry your luggage onto the plane in a hanging bag. This will save time. Some luggage companies make an over-the-shoulder carry-on bag that will hold two suits.

4. Dress comfortably. Long-distance fliers should wear casual, loose clothing. Even in the summer, carry a sweater or jacket with you, because a pressurized, air-conditioned cabin can become cool. Avoid fashionable shoes with high heels. If possible carry slippers and put them on after you take your seat. In the cloudless environment of air travel, the sun will be bright, so carry sunglasses to diminish the glare.*

5. Airlines usually provide nutritionally balanced food. You should plan on eating something every two and a half hours, however. The cabin atmosphere tends to be dry, and you will find that inhaling the steam from a cup of hot water helps. Sometimes a damp cloth over the nose is of value. Fruits such as grapes and plums can moisten your mouth and provide you with the necessary fructose. Other snacks will supply you with protein: unsalted nuts, small cubes of cheese with squares of whole wheat bread, and natural peanut butter. Orange juice and apple juice are usually available, and cabin galleys contain at least one brand of decaffeinated coffee. You can bring your own herbal tea and ask for hot water. Airlines carry artificial sweeteners, or you may wish to bring your own granulated fructose.

6. Alcohol is not recommended for fliers because of its effects on the brain and body when consumed under conditions of pressurization. You can achieve total relaxation by using diaphragmatic breathing, muscle relaxation, and passive mental imagery. Recent research shows that alcohol makes the effects of jet lag even worse by disturbing sleep cycles. After flying, allow your body a couple of days to readjust before you drink alcohol. The older you are the more you will be affected by jet lag.

---

* Research now in progress on causes of muscle weakness suggests it is also a good idea to avoid wearing metal-bridged glasses, neck chains, and metallic belts.

7. Carry a flight log for recording your SUDS level and charting your chop. This can also serve as a diary to help you remember the details of a pleasant vacation. Use it to write down captions for your pictures and record the names of restaurants and hotels. It will also be useful to keep in your log a running total of miles traveled.

8. If you see a passenger suffering from hyperventilation or air-travel anxiety, offer to help. Remember that inhaling carbonated beverages and breathing diaphragmatically, with a pillow placed in the small of the back, is good first aid for hyperventilation. Airlines give flight attendants excellent general first-aid training but scant instruction in the field of psychology.

9. Consider making a cross-country flight in two segments, with a night's rest in between. Crossing time zones creates the condition called jet lag. Your biological rhythms continue to operate according to the old time zone. Fatigue results. Even the three-hour time change between New York to Los Angeles is noticeable. A stop along the way helps your system adjust to the change, allowing you to be more refreshed and less susceptible to stress during travel. (You may also want to read "What Can We Do About Jet Lag," by Vicki Goldberg, *Psychology Today*, August, 1977. Information about reprints is available from *Psychology Today*, Consumer Products Division, 595 Broadway, New York, NY 10012.)

10. Jet lag is even more pronounced in foreign travel. We generally advise former fearful fliers to avoid the rush of high-pressure packaged and chartered tours. Some travelers indulge in experiential gluttony. I know one who visited a city a day for ten days. No matter how stimulating, new sights, sounds, and surroundings are stressful. To make a vacation a vacation instead of an exhausting experience, practice pacing and moderation. My rule is to plan to take in one or two events at a relaxed pace each day, knowing that I can return at a future date and enjoy the place even more fully. Planning ahead will help make the travel experience more enjoyable. Buy foreign currency at your bank or at the airport, and invest in a pocket dictionary to help with foreign words and phrases. When you reach your destination, remember to rest and eat properly. Above all, pace

yourself. Many travelers, in their eagerness to get every dollar's worth out of a vacation, jam so much stimulation into a short period of time that they wind up failing to fully enjoy their travel experiences.

To Your Health

Our time has been called "The Age of Anxiety." Today, more people exist under more daily pressures than at any period in the history of mankind. Squadron upon squadron of stressors bombard our senses from morning to evening. We are attacked by high-pressure electronic news-gathering, noise, air pollution, and a host of preposterous but real hazards to our mental well-being.*

The authors of this book believe that stress is more than an abstract environmental problem. We are convinced that it is a personal health challenge — one that can be met and overcome on an individual basis. To that end, we have presented a systematic pattern of behavior modification designed to make air travel a comfortable and stress-free experience. In so doing, we believe we have also provided you with the basic ingredients of a program for immunization to the other stressors in your life. Graduates of our classes have successfully applied the techniques of stress-resistant nutrition, diaphragmatic breathing, deep muscle relaxation, and passive mental imagery to family problems, the fear of heights, elevators, and crowds, and even the vague anxiety caused by undefined stressors.

We leave you with the hope that our method of Active Stress Coping becomes a mental-health habit that helps you achieve an orderly, meaningful, and optimistic life.†

---

* Loss of muscle strength has been found to result from a number of unexpected factors, many of which have been mentioned throughout this book. Most recent findings have added fluorescent lights to this list. Imagine the cumulative effect of fluorescent lights combined with metal-bridged glasses, neck chains, metallic belts, high-heeled shoes, steel-backed chairs, coffee, sugar, and thoracic breathing.

† The Institute for Psychology of Air Travel is interested in gathering data on your response to the program outlined in this book. Information about your graduation flight will be appreciated.

APPENDIX FOR PROFESSIONALS

REFERENCES

Appendix for Professionals

In *Modern Psychopathology*, Theodore Millon classifies theories of behavior along a dimension running from concrete to abstract. Here is a visual rendering of his concepts.

abstract	PHENOMENOLOGICAL (Existential, Gestalt)
	DYNAMIC (Intrapsychic, Social)
↑	BEHAVIORAL (Behavior Therapy)
concrete	BIOPHYSICAL (Constitutional, Physiochemical)

In addition to classifying theories of behavior along this dimension, we can understand the holistic treatment of fear of air travel (as well as any other psychological problem) by an analysis of all the factors that come into play at these different levels. For an individual, at any given time, is subject to the influence of factors present at all these levels of internal reality. Human behavior is a function of these factors interacting with external reality as it is perceived by the individual. Instead of treating the fear of flying by using only one therapeutic system at only one of these four theoretical levels, our practice is to approach fear either from all levels simultaneously or else in an ordered sequence of levels. Let us briefly examine some of the factors at each level of abstraction that affect an individual in the air-travel situation. As we do, we should consider the possibility that the more concrete the factors are, the more powerful their reinforcing effect is on the more abstract factors. The concrete factors may serve as an unconscious substratum for the more abstract, setting limits within which the abstract factors can vary.

For example, alienation from self may be reinforced by disorientation resulting from low blood sugar, vestibular problems, and reduced proprioceptive feedback from a clenched maladjusted dentition (as well as reduced interoception from high anxiety levels). This is not to say that these factors necessarily interact in only one direction. What is important is that they do interact. Of course, without the more abstract perceptual readiness conditioned by earlier life experience, disruptions in the physiological substratum may not precipitate anxiety attacks or reinforce the expectation of panic. However, should these physiological disruptions occur in a context of stress or during a life crisis, the theme of loss of control will be reinforced.

Listed below are some of the factors that may affect air-travel phobia. These factors are classified according to Millon's system of abstract to concrete.

Phenomenological Factors

Alienation — From Ground, Others, Self
Excitement vs. Anxiety
Growth vs. Fixation
Hypervigilance — A Protective Device: Floods with Excessive Stimuli; Distracts from Relevant Experience
Feeling of Being Overwhelmed

Insecurity
Personal Insignificance
Significance of Life
Vulnerability
Reflection on Death
Powerlessness — Environmental and Emotional
Harsh Self-Judgment Retroflected Anger

Dynamic (Social) Factors

Mistrust
Rigid Norms of New Environment
Social Rejection Potential
Pressure to Conform

Forced Dependence
Forced Group Participation
Forced Interaction with Attendants

DYNAMIC (Intrapsychic) FACTORS

Surrender of Control
Regression (Being Carried)
Repressed Hostility Triggered by
Power Symbols
Sexual Feelings Elicited by Being
Aloft
Conflicts Associated with Flight
from Responsibility
Conflicts Over Obligatory Flights

Elicitation of Paranoid Feelings
Projection of Self-Inadequacy
onto Airline Crew
Symbolic Departure from Earth
Generalization from Other Fears
Guilt and Need for Punishment
Failure of Traditional Defense
Mechanisms (Crisis of Adult
Life)

BEHAVIORAL FACTORS (Pavlovian)

Defense Reactions Elicited by
High-Frequency Sounds
Social or Other Fears Associated
with Travel
Generalization from Other
Trauma
Re-elicitation of Previous Trauma
Fear Elicited by Negative
Expectancies

Fear Elicited by Lower Oxygen
Pressure
Arousal Elicited by Self-Criticism
Spontaneous Recovery of Fear
Novelty Anxiety
Startle Responses

BEHAVIORAL FACTORS (Thorndike, Skinner)

Avoidance of Flying Reinforces
Sense of Control
Avoidance Prevents Practice of
Appropriate Behavior
Negative Image → Anxiety →
Assertion Not to Fly → Relief
→ Control
Absence of Control Reinforced
by Forcing Self or Being Forced
Negative Statements Reinforced
by Avoidance Behavior
Negative Expectancies
Reinforced by Seeking Horror
Stories, Watching Movies and
TV, and the like.
Pleading Behavior Reinforced by
Attention

Freedom Restricted and
Claustrophobia Reinforced by
Tensed Muscular Posture
Negative Expectancy Increased
by Jokes and Cynical
Comments
Overstimulation from
Hypervigilance
Anxiety Demands Fight or Flight
(Blocks New Learning)
Avoidance of Information-
Seeking Reinforces Powerless
Image
Anxiety Control Prevents
Learning
Absence of Stimulus Controls of
Familiar Environments

BIOPHYSICAL (Structural, Disease, Nutritional)

Thoracic Breathing	Physiological Response to
Posture	Reduced Air Pressure
Tooth/Jaw Problems	Thyroid Problems
Vestibular Organ Dysfunction	Disrupted Carcadian Rhythms
Sensitivity to Noise	Infections, Colds, Virus, etc.
Low Blood Sugar	Physiology Altered by Chemicals
Refined Sugar	Cardiovascular Problems
Fatigue	

After a patient has been taught to master the air-travel situation, he or she can spontaneously apply the techniques to other areas of life. The model presented in this book is a beginning — an attempt to sensitize the patient and the therapist to the fact that psychotherapy must recognize the role the body plays in thought and emotion. This is in agreement with Lang (1971):

> We will need to confine ourselves to measurable behaviors in all systems, and discover the laws that determine their interaction. The data suggest that we must deal with each behavior system in its own terms. Thus, a patient who reports anxiety, fails to cope or perform effectively under stress, and evidences autonomic activity that varies widely from the practical energy demands of the situation, needs to receive treatment for all these disorders. He should be administered a treatment directed simultaneously at shaping verbal sets (so as to reduce reported stress over the variety of situations in which it appears), assisted in building effective coping behaviors and practicing them in appropriate contexts, and finally, administering a program for attenuating autonomic arousal and excessive muscle tonus, with the goal of reducing the distraction and interference of peripheral physiological feedback. In short, psychotherapy should be a vigorous multisystem training program tailored to the unique behavioral topography presented by the patient. [p. 109]

Insight therapies aimed at central process, or behavior therapies aimed at relief of aversive feedback from the autonomic system, may lead to changes in the presenting complaint. However, the reinforcement of appropriate levels of functioning in all three divisions of the nervous system *and* the establishment of proper nutrition and physical function may well be necessary to ensure durability for the psychological change.

Once a phobic pattern is formed, attempts to alleviate the problem on a verbal or cognitive level do not necessarily solve it on the behavioral or biophysical level. For example, a person suffering from anxiety may understand the sources of anxiety and the associated symbolism of the air-travel situation (thereby deriving some sense of control) but at the same time may continue to breathe thoracically and load his system with coffee, doughnuts, candy, and alcohol. Insight therapy alone does not provide the client with a large enough variety of active coping skills to meet and quickly control emotions in times of crisis. Conversely, changing one's eating and breathing habits alone may result in lower anxiety, but a negative self-image and symbolically self-punitive expectancies associated with guilt may continue to trigger anxiety. In short, verbal therapy assumes that central process has an automatic superordinate influence over the other body systems — in other words, that all systems act in concert. The problem most phobics encounter is that cognitive processes do not coordinate with their feelings and tensions. The arousal level appears to perpetuate the neurotic cognitive pattern of avoidance of feelings as the sole method of control. Phobics may actually state that their feelings are stupid or alien. Once anxiety is reduced, however, appropriate learning — that is, the learning of patterns of coordinated thoughts and feelings based upon external reality — may occur quickly.

It is important to emphasize that most anxious fliers and phobics can find sufficient relief from their problems through the use of self-control. The approach is intended to get the phobic started on the road to self-mastery and to desensitize him to what psychologists do, so that he may, if necessary, seek out professional help more readily. It is our belief that not all problems require intensive behavior therapy or in-depth analysis. On the other hand, we acknowledge that not all anxieties and phobias can be treated simply and by self-control. The patient's attempts at self-control constitute a valuable screening technique. As their education in coping skills increases, those less seriously afflicted will care for themselves. The mental health professional is then free to devote his or her attention to the more severe problems that afflict the population.

Each patient who undergoes private therapy must be assessed to determine which theoretical level will benefit him most in the initial treatment of the problem. Then, an ordered treatment plan should be presented to the patient. For some, the behavioral and nutritional approach (usually for specific fear of air travel) is best. For those whose fear of air travel is only one of a number of fears, a combination of all the theoretical approaches may be necessary.

Group treatment as a matter of course should include components of all theoretical levels. It is necessary that a psychologist (or psychiatrist) screen and continuously observe all individuals involved in large group treatments. Otherwise, group pressure and pressure from the group leader may push certain individuals beyond their state of readiness. Of the approximately 500 people treated in courses at the Institute for Psychology of Air Travel, only one suffered an anxiety attack during a flight. The low incidence of attack is the result of careful screening and observation prior to flight. Large groups of forty to eighty cannot be properly attended to by one leader. The ratio in our groups is one staff member to eight students. For example, in a class of thirty students, one psychologist, two flight attendants, and one graduate or intern are present at each session.

For the therapist or interested reader a bibliography is included at the end of this appendix. The published papers and books listed there will provide the background needed for the study of various approaches to air-travel phobia. Some of the books are of historical importance and present various theoretical aspects of the problem. Should the reader wish to examine our plan of group treatment, it is outlined in chapter 12 of *Fear: Learning to Cope* (Forgione, Surwit, and Page, 1978). The group format we have employed over the years remains unchanged: there are twenty hours of group training, two hours per meeting; one meeting is held every week for ten weeks, at an airport room overlooking the airstrip. Our course outline is presented below.

CLASS 1
Introductions (Staff, Graduates, Class Members)
Fill out FFS
Lecture: How Fear Affects Body
Dynamics of Fear
How to Counteract Fear (the Exercise)

CLASS 2
Effects of Nutrition
Suggested Diet
Dynamics of Breathing
SUDS Level
Exercise Practice
SUDS Level

CLASS 3
Exercise (SUDS Readings)
Film (Travel)
Air Controllers
Group Exercises
Lecture: Traffic Control Supervisor
Individual Coaching Exercises

CLASS 4
Exercises
Lecture, Flight Attendants
Exercises
Pilot Lecture
Exercises
Oxygen Demonstration

CLASS 5
Exercises
Sounds of Airline
Demo. with GSR to Show Control by Exercises
Lecture: Thought Stopping
Mock Airline Seating

CLASS 6
Exercise — Assertion Training
Mock Seating
Film of Previous Graduation Flight and Exercises

View of Aisle — Jamming Exercise
Small Group Discussions of Progress

CLASS 7
Mock Seating
Aircraft Sounds with Oxygen Demo., as in Real Flight
Tour of Loading Area: Relax in It

CLASS 8
Elevator Practice
Trip to Tower and GCA Room

CLASS 9
In Plane on Ground
Relaxation Exercises and Orientation

CLASS 10
Loading Area
Plane on Ground, Door Closed
Flight Sounds
Reminder about Nutrition
Relaxation

GRADUATION FLIGHT
25–40 Minute Flight
Graduation Party: Awarding of Diplomas and Wings
FFS and Inventory

For the professional, paraprofessional, or flight attendant wishing to train air-travel phobics, an orientation procedure developed by Ron Jones should prove valuable. A description of the general methodology of this procedure is found in a case study published by the Flight Fear Orientation Clinic (Jones, 1978).

An adult 35-year-old female, commenting to her psychologist that she was extremely apprehensive during air travel, was referred to the Clinic. She agreed to meet with us for a general discussion and diagnostic consultation.

Anticipatory anxiety was high seven to ten days prior to flights. She could not eat during this period of time and during the few flights to which she had been exposed. Her hypervigilance during flights was explained to us as being unable to relinquish control of her well-being to the pilot who was a total stranger. The most internalized personal feeling expressed was: "I guess I don't have enough faith." Takeoff and landing bothered her most. She was an intelligent, active individual from an upper socioeconomic class.

METHODOLOGY

She was directed to schedule a flight to a destination that was not more than one hour flying time away. She notified me by telephone when this was accomplished. Every day until the date of our meeting I forwarded to her by mail, pamphlets produced by the FAA and airline organizations which described facts and explanations about passenger flight. None were critical or degrading to the individual being afraid to fly. Selection of pamphlets was based on general information factors.

Before I picked her up at her home on the day of our scheduled meeting, I canceled her planned flight with the airline. She was aware of this action. During the 20-minute trip to the airport a tape was played describing the analogy of driving an automobile and the flight of an aircraft. The tone of voice was conversational, instructional, and relaxing. Upon arrival at the airport a brief tour was made of the landing and takeoff areas at the perimeter of the airport.

I had previously scheduled a tour of an aircraft between flights with the local airline authorities. For approximately 15 minutes she was left alone in the empty aircraft. Her instructions were to envision the passenger compartment crowded with the normal array of passengers, and then, the compartment empty. Alternately, this transfer from one setting to another provided a controlled situational atmosphere and at the same time established a behavior pattern of relaxation for her actual flight. Before we left the passenger compartment a general discussion and familiarization of the aircraft was held and her questions answered.

A pilot preparing for the next flight on the aircraft gave her a tour of the cockpit area. Her primary interest was in the instruments and their function.

A senior pilot from a national airline joined us for lunch in the restaurant overlooking the aircraft departure area. For the first few minutes she was not interested in eating; however, after some conversation she stated she was hungry and we all had lunch.

A tour of the air traffic facilities completed the four-hour session.

A follow-up session in six months revealed she had flown for four-and five-hour durations. One flight was with her two children. She felt she had a modeling effect on them. Although her anxiety had not been totally eradicated, she stated she felt more comfortable while flying. Confidence in the flight crew was high. During the occurrence of different or strange noises and abrupt movements of the aircraft she would mentally review the information from our sessions. Rather than an immediate anxiety response, this led to a lessened degree of apprehension.

A generalization to any portion of the population cannot be made from this one case.

No intensive relaxation exercises were given this client during our initial session. Frequent telephone contact was maintained for two years. Later, the client was introduced to a psychologist who had developed a desensitization relaxation procedure specifically designed for flight fear. After three sessions the client experienced a breakthrough to a decreased level of anxiety that seemed to be a major step in finalizing total desensitization to flight.

Later in his book, Jones describes a more recent example of the effectiveness of the orientation process, discussing a client who had never flown.

Over a period of ten weeks the entire process was administered. The client experienced her first flight with some degree of anxiety. However, she has plans to fly "anywhere, anytime." The combination of *in vivo* training at the airport and in an aircraft, information sessions, air traffic control familiarization, discussion sessions, and a final phase with the psychologist provided the necessary ingredients for successful familiarization and desensitization. The entire orientation was accomplished on a one-to-one, client-to-counselor basis.

The general procedure of orientation therapy with flight fear involves (1) diagnosing the specific part of the "flight process" in which the fear is manifested, followed by (2) physical exposure to similar conditions in a controlled setting with (3) frequent contact with the therapist or personnel professionally trained in aviation.

It is absolutely essential that the therapist administering the *in vivo* training coordinate the field activities of desensitization with the psychologist.

Regarding a phobic reaction, information alone is not the most appropriate resolution to the problem. The sequence in which it is received, the assistance provided by another person, the environment, and the administering of the subject matter in controlled presentations, all have a direct bearing on the resultant positive influence on the phobic.

Providing a controlled effort, even somewhat protective as with orientation therapy, the client could maintain an atmosphere of hope under the umbrella of personal assistance.

In the near future, airlines will become more psychologically oriented. As commercial competition increases, emphasis will shift from media advertising to point-of-sale and point-of-contact efforts. The economics of fear, by sheer weight, will force the issue. Approximately 21.3 million air trips per year are avoided because of fear (according to information provided to the Institute for Psychology of Air Travel by the Boeing Company).

One step the airlines can take to alleviate novelty anxiety and apprehension in many fliers is to invite them onto the plane prior to the general boarding. In a short period of time, flight attendants and captain could orient new fliers and answer questions openly. Another desirable step would be to have relaxation tapes and flight-orientation tapes available on one of the entertainment channels. Lufthansa already offers an isometric program, based on NASA's training program for astronauts, on one of its music channels. In addition, instructions on how to cope with travel disrhythmia (jet lag) would be most valuable in minimizing another source of unconscious stress (Goldberg, 1977).

For general information about fear of air travel, and about programs available nationally, contact

Institute for Psychology of Air Travel, Inc.
Suite 300
At the Massachusetts Psychological Center
25 Huntington Avenue
Boston, MA 02116
Tel: 617-~~261-8121~~ 437-1811

The purpose of this institute is to distribute information and foster interdisciplinary professional communication.*

* Centers of treatment not listed in this book may wish to file information with the Institute for Psychology of Air Travel.

General information for air travelers is available from:

Air Transport Association of America
1709 New York Avenue, N.W.
Washington, DC 20006
  Brochure: "How to Fly." Send stamped, self-addressed envelope.

Aviation Consumer Action Project
P.O. Box 19029
Washington, DC 20036
Tel: 202–223–4498
  Brochure: "Facts and Advice for Airline Passengers." Send
  stamped, self-addressed envelope.

Sources of individual and group treatment:

Air Canada, Public Relations
1 Place Ville Marie
Montreal, P.Q. Canada H3B 3P7

Flight Fear Orientation Clinic
Attn.: Ron Jones
258 Midvale Drive, N.E.
Atlanta, GA 30342
Tel: 404–394–8810

Joyce Failing (S.A.F.E.)
1 Hummingbird Lane
Rolling Hills, CA 90274
Tel: 213–547–3493

Free to Fly
Attn.: Sheri Barthelmess
P.O. Box 1625
Arlington, VA 22210
Tel: 703–522–4000

Dr. Anne Blanchard-Remond
2 Rue Jules Breton
75013 Paris, France

Maurice Yaffe
Senior Clinical Psychiatrist

Guy's Hospital
London, England
  Hospital has set up a simulated passenger cabin for teaching and
  treatment of air-travel phobics.

Herb Gross
Fly Without Fear
310 Madison Avenue
New York, NY 10017

Doreen Powell
Director of Programs
Phobia Clinic
White Plains Hospital Medical Center
David Avenue
White Plains, NY 10601

Dr. Carol Lindemann
Director
New York Phobic Center
530 East 72nd Street
New York, NY 10021

Elaine Spears
Fear of Flying Program
Elizabeth General Hospital
Community Mental Health Center
925 E. Jersey Street
Elizabeth, NJ 07102

Dr. Martin Seif
Co-Director
Phobia Resource Center
263 West End Avenue
New York, NY 10023

Jay Beau-Seigner
Fearful Flyers
PAN AM Building
Room 4523
New York, NY 10017

British Airways
Victoria Terminal
Buckingham Palace Rd.
London SW8, England

In addition, state psychological and psychiatric associations will provide names of local specialists in the field.

References

NOTES

page

5   Dean, R. D., and Whitaker, K. M. "Fear of Flying: Impact on the U.S. Air Travel Industry." Boeing Computer Services Company, Document # BCS-00009-RD/DM, 1980.

32   Lande, N. *Mindstyles, Lifestyles.* Los Angeles: Price, Storm, Sloan, 1976.

34   Jacobson, E. *Progressive Relaxation.* Chicago: University of Chicago Press, 1938.

34   Wolpe, J. *Psychotherapy by Reciprocal Inhibition.* Stanford: Stanford University Press, 1958.

41   Cheraskin, E., Ringsdorf, W. M., and Brecher, A. *Psychodietetics.* New York: Bantam, 1976

41   Dufty, W. *Sugar Blues.* New York: Warner, 1975.

42   Newbold, H. L. *Mega-Nutrients for Your Nerves.* New York: Berkley Medallion, 1978.

53   Solberg, S. J. "A Comparison of Alternative Desensitization Procedures for Treatment of Flight Phobia." Ann Arbor: University Microfilms International, 75-2152, 1975.

54   Wolpe, J., and Lazarus, A. *Behavior Therapy Techniques: A Guide to the Treatment of Neuroses.* New York: Pergamon Press, 1966.

56   Malmo, R. B. "Activation: A Neuropsychological Dimension." In *The Cognitive Processes: Readings,* edited by R. Harper, E. Anderson, C. Christensen, and S. Hunka. Englewood Cliffs, N.J.: Prentice-Hall, 1964.

86   Kare, M. R., Schechter, P. J., Grossman, S. P., and Roth, L. J. "Direct Pathway to the Brain." *Science* 163: 952–953, 1969.

96   Burgess, M. "Alcohol: America's Most Widely Misused Drug." *Journal of Drug Education* 1: 25–31, 1971.

97   "Alcohol and Society." A report by the AMA Committee on Alcoholism and Drug Dependency, *Journal of the American Medical Association* 216 (6): 1011–1013, 1971.

110   Scholander, T., and Simmons, R. "A Conditioning Procedure to Increase the Influence of the Respiratory Cycle upon Electrodermal Activity." *Journal of Psychosomatic Research* 7: 295–300, 1964.

114   Dietz, J. "Jet Travel: Is Your Heart In It?" *Boston Sunday Globe*, May 20, 1979.

114   Galton, L. "Breathe but Don't Overdo It." *Parade*, April 16, 1978, pp. 6–7.

134   Forgione, A., Surwit, R., and Page, D. *Fear: Learning to Cope*. New York: Van Nostrand, Reinhold, 1978.

149   Coué, E. *Better and Better Every Day*. New York: Barnes & Noble, 1961.

152   Benson, H. *The Relaxation Response*. New York: Avon, 1975.

163   Fensterheim, H., and Baer, J. *Don't Say Yes When You Want to Say No*. New York: David McKay, 1975.

165   Morris, D. *Manwatching*. New York: Harry N. Abrams, 1977.

224   Mander, J., Dippel, G., and Gossage, H. *The Great International Paper Airplane Book*. New York: Simon & Schuster, 1967.

229   Varley, H. *The Air Traveler's Handbook*. New York: Simon & Schuster, 1978.

244   Schuele, J. "Autonomic Self-Reported and Observed Behavior Associated with Self-Evaluative Thoughts and Imagery." Doctoral dissertation submitted to the Graduate School of Rutgers University, January, 1980.

259   Millon, T. *Modern Psychopathology*. Philadelphia: W. B. Saunders, 1969.

262   Lang, P. "The Application of Psychophysiological Methods to the Study of Psychotherapy and Behavior Modification." In *Handbook of Psychotherapy and Behavior Change*, edited by A. E. Bergin and S. L. Garfield. New York: John Wiley & Sons, 1971.

266   Jones, R. *About Passenger Flight-Fear* (1978). Order Direct: $4.50 ppd. Flight Fear Orientation Clinic, 258 Midvale Dr. N.E., Atlanta, GA 30342

269 Goldberg, V. "What Can We Do About Jet Lag? *Psychology Today*
11: 69–72, 1977.

SUPPLEMENTAL READINGS

Aitken, R. C., Daley, R. J., Lister, J. A., and O'Connor, P. J. "Treatment of Flying Phobia in Aircrew." *American Journal of Psychotherapy* 25: 530–542, 1971.

Aronson, J. L. *How to Overcome Your Fear of Flying*. New York: Warner, 1973.

Bond, D. C. *The Love and Fear of Flying*. New York: International Universities Press, 1950.

Bucore, A. D., and Maioreilles, R. P. "Symptoms Without Illness: Fear of Flying Among Fighter Pilots." *Psychiatric Quarterly* 44: 125–142, 1970.

Denholtz, M. S., and Mann, E. T. "An Automated Audiovisual Treatment of Phobias Administered by Non-Professionals." [Flight Phobia]. *Journal of Behavior Therapy and Experimental Psychiatry* 6: 111–115, 1975.

Ellis, A. *How to Master Your Fear of Flying*. New York: Curtis, 1972.

Eversaul, G. A. *Dental Kinesiology*. Box 19476, Las Vegas, NE 89119.

Forgione, A. G. "Group Treatment of Flying Fear." Paper delivered at the annual meeting of the Association for Advancement of Behavior Therapy, San Francisco, CA, December, 1975.

Forgione, A. G. "Dental Medicine and Psychostomatology." Paper delivered at the 9th European Congress of Behavior Therapy, Paris, France, September, 1979.

Gelb, H. *Clinical Management of Head, Neck and TMJ Dysfunction*. Philadelphia: W. B. Saunders, 1977.

Gibbs-Smith, C. H. *Flight Through the Ages*. New York: Thomas Y. Crowell Co., 1974.

Goodheart, G. *Research Manuals*. 542 Michigan Building, Detroit, MI 48226.

Gross, S. M., and Vacchiano, R. B. "Personality Correlates of Patients with Temporomandibular Joint Dysfunction." *Journal of Prosthetic Dentistry* 30: 326–329, 1973.

Hurdle, F. *Low Blood Sugar: A Doctor's Guide to Its Effective Control*. New York: Parker, 1977.

Jacobson, E. *Anxiety and Tension Control: A Physiologic Approach.* Philadelphia: Lippincott, 1964.

Karoly, D. "Multicomponent Behavioral Treatment of Fear of Flying." *Behavior Therapy* 5: 265–270, 1974.

Kendall, H. O. *Muscles, Testing and Functions,* 2d ed. Baltimore: Williams and Wilkins, 1971.

Kent, F. *Nothing to Fear.* New York: Barnes & Noble, 1977.

Martin, C. G. *Low Blood Sugar: The Hidden Menace of Hypoglycemia.* New York: ARC, 1971.

Meldman, M., and Hatch, B. "*In vivo* Desensitization of an Airplane Phobia with Penthranization." *Behavior Research and Therapy* 7: 213–215, 1969.

Mondey, D. *The International Encyclopedia of Aviation.* New York: Crown Publishers, 1977.

Reeves, J. L., and Mealiea, W. "Biofeedback-Assisted Cue-Controlled Relaxation for the Treatment of Flight Phobias." *Journal of Behavior Therapy and Experimental Psychiatry* 6: 105–109, 1975.

Schwartz, R. A., Greene, C. S., and Laskin, D. M. "Personality Characteristics of Patients with Myofascial Pain Dysfunction (MPD) Syndrome Unresponsive to Conventional Therapy." *Journal of Dental Research* 58: 1435–1440, 1979.

Sheinkin, D., Schachter, M., and Hutton, R. *The Food Connection.* Indianapolis: Bobbs-Merrill, 1979.

Smith, S. D. "Muscular Strength Correlated to Jaw Posture and the Temporomandibular Joint." *New York State Dental Journal,* August 1978, pp. 278–283.

Smith-Sims, N. *The Air Passenger's Best Friend.* Order Direct. Mason-Croft Productions, P.O. Box 3585, Scottsdale, AZ 85257.

Solyom, L., Shugar, R., Bryntwick, S., and Solyom, C. "Treatment of Fear of Flying." *American Journal of Psychiatry* 130: 423–427, 1973.

Yemm, R. "Variations in Electrical Activity of the Human Masseter Muscle Occurring in Association with Emotional Stress." *Archives of Oral Biology* 14: 873, 1969.